D0671335

ST MARTIN'S
TRUE CRIME
CLASSICS

St. Martin's Paperbacks Titles
by Clifford L. Linedecker

The Man Who Killed Boys

Night Stalker

Killer Kids

Massacre at Waco, Texas

Deadly White Female

Poisoned Vows

Death of a Model

Smooth Operator

The Vampire Killers

Babyface Killers

Blood in the Sand

NIGHT STALKER

A Shocking Story of Satanism, Sex and
Serial Murders

CLIFFORD L. LINEDECKER

St. Martin's Paperbacks

NIGHT STALKER

Copyright © 1991 by Clifford L. Linedecker.
"2004 Update: After the Trial" copyright © 2004 by Clifford L. Linedecker.

Photo by Lennox McLendon/AP/Wide World Photos.
Photo enhancement by Rick Nemo.

All rights reserved. No part of this book may be used or reproduced in any manner whatsoever without written permission except in the case of brief quotations embodied in critical articles or reviews. For information address St. Martin's Press, 175 Fifth Avenue, New York, NY 10010.

ISBN: 0-312-92505-0

Printed in the United States of America

St. Martin's Paperbacks edition / April 1991

10 9 8 7 6 5 4

To
Bob Abborino and Maureen Sikorsky
for being there
when I needed them

Acknowledgments

AS IS ALWAYS THE CASE, SCORES OF PEOPLE play a part in putting together a manuscript for a book. I consider myself singularly fortunate to have the family, friends, and professional colleagues who cheerfully banded together to help me tell the story of the Night Stalker.

Some, of course, played bigger roles in the project than others, but the help of each individual was important. Sometimes, it was critical to the accurate reporting of the atrocities that occurred in Southern California during the period in 1984 and 1985 when the Night Stalker was carrying out his killing spree.

I wish to single out Sgt. Frank Salerno of the Los Angeles County Sheriff's Department and head of its Night Stalker task force, particularly for his patience and helpful information. The assistance of other law enforcement officers and all individuals associated with the Los Angeles criminal justice system who sacrificed the time from their busy schedules to help is also greatly appreciated.

Thanks as well to my longtime friend, Vanessa, for sharing her unique knowledge of modern-day Satanism and Satanists and for helping to sort out the charlatans, the serious, the dilettantes, and the crazies.

The residents of the East Los Angeles neighborhood where Richard Ramirez was finally brought to bay were friendly and eager to tell the stories of the roles they played in the capture—or merely to recount the bizarre chase that they witnessed on that crazy, blistering-hot day in August when the Night Stalker made his desperate, and doomed, dash for freedom.

At home in Florida, professional colleagues assisted with careful readings of the manuscript as it was being put together and contributed positive criticism to make the copy more grammatical and the story more accurate.

My agent, Adele Leone, and my editor, Charles Spicer, at St. Martin's Press, are due thanks for their faith in me.

And, finally, my appreciation to my lifemate, Junko, for putting up with my moods as I worked against yet another pressing deadline, grumbling with each chapter I completed that it should have been done yesterday.

Contents

Introduction

NIGHT STALKER RICHARD RAMIREZ HAS ALL the horror in his soul of a Stephen King or a Clive Barker fright novel—and more.

The dark horror that Ramirez allowed himself to become—in fact, invited into himself—is not the stuff of novels. It is as real as Jack the Ripper, Bluebeard, and Vlad the Impaler.

Ramirez prowled the quiet suburban streets of a dozen communities outside Los Angeles like a demon from Hell, spreading fear, agony, and violence wherever he walked.

In many respects, except for the victims he chose, he is a classic serial killer. Most serial killers, although not all, prey on the weakest, most vulnerable members of society: prostitutes, lonely homosexuals, alcoholics, drug addicts, hitchhikers, children, old women who live alone, and unwary young women in their teens or early twenties.

Ramirez was one of those who selected other types of victims. He didn't seek out society's rejects or the weak and helpless as victims. He targeted upscale suburbanites, professionals, or yuppies, law-abiding, churchgoing citizens who felt so safe in their cozy homes a few miles from the crime and violence of the city that they often left their doors unlocked or their windows open at night. The Night Stalker didn't have to break into the homes he entered. He merely walked in, or slipped through an unlocked window.

Suddenly, the people living in the comfortable suburbs outside Los Angeles were faced with a chilling reality. There was nowhere to escape. They couldn't move away from the violence and the fear. The terror followed them. They were no longer even safe in their own homes. They were being stalked by an equal-opportunity madman.

Recent statistics show that at any one time in the United States there are more than 35,000 murderers locked up in America's prisons, including approximately 1,500 on the death rows of the thirty-six states that carry provisions for the death penalty in their criminal codes.

Criminologists believe that there are many more men —and women—still walking the streets who have already committed murder. Criminologists, including experts from the FBI, also believe that many of those murderers are serial killers—perhaps as many as thirty-five or forty butchering victims at any given time. The FBI reported nearly a decade ago that serial killers were slaughtering about 5,000 Americans each year.

And serial killings are among those homicides that are the most difficult to prevent and to solve. Unlike Ramirez, most serial killers move around in broad geographical areas, sometimes spreading their devastation throughout a dozen states or more. Sometimes they carry their atrocities across national borders. Military men, civilian sailors, and truckers especially have opportunities to make their killing orgies international affairs.

Serial killers who move around are sometimes gone from an area before anyone knows that a crime has been committed. Prostitutes and the down-and-out do not always have family or friends who miss them when they suddenly disappear from the streets or highways.

Keeping on the move and selecting victims from a wide area can make it difficult for law enforcement agencies to recognize serial killings for what they are, to distinguish patterns and similarities in victims, the method of murder, and the manner in which bodies are disposed of. One police agency in Nevada may be investigating the killing of an alcoholic woman, while another in Texas may be probing the mysterious slaying of a barfly there. Unless some extraordinary event occurs to make the link between the two killings obvious, there is no reason for investigators to suspect they may be looking for the same killer.

For some reason, however, it appears that an inordinate number of serial killers in California, especially the Greater Los Angeles Southland, choose to select their victims from the same general geographical area. Some, of course, are cross-country killers, but many elect to return to the same hunting grounds over and over again. They troll for teen prostitutes on the Sunset Strip, slaughter winos on Los Angeles's skid row, or, like a pair of accused killers in Calavaras County, north of San Francisco, prey on their neighbors. Police accused that pair, one already a suicide and the other now in a Canadian prison and fighting extradition, of murdering husbands, boyfriends, and babies, then keeping the women as sex slaves until they tired of them and, at last, disposing of their victims like so much used toilet tissue.

Los Angeles isn't my town. The city itself is spread out and the accessibility to the suburbs is obscured by a bewildering maze of super highways that I find nearly impossible to figure out and negotiate. I get lost there, and have been in the city only a half-dozen times—always when I've had a book to research about brutal, sordid crime.

The Los Angeles area for me isn't the Dodgers, the Raiders, Disneyland, or Mann's Chinese Theater and the Star Walk. For me, it is the Skid Row Slasher, the Hillside Strangler, the Trashbag Murders, organized gangs of child molesters—and the Night Stalker. I go to Los Angeles and the surrounding countryside to look at the city's ugly underbelly. I don't go there expecting a pleasant time.

When I was researching an ill-fated book about a pioneer of Texas swing who brutally murdered his wife, I ventured into the desert and my car broke down at midnight near Tehachapi.

Another time I headed for the boondocks again and swung by the Spahn ranch while exchanging book talk with Lynette Alice "Squeaky" Fromme, the Manson groupie doing time in federal prison for trying to kill a president. The car held up that time, but the book project fell through.

I had better luck with my publisher after I journeyed to Watts to photograph and record the mutterings of a psychic while he stood on the site where the spoiled wacko revolutionaries who called themselves the Symbionese Liberation Army were incinerated during a firefight with police. The psychic was attempting to pick up vibrations from the surroundings to help us locate the still-missing heiress Patty Hearst, who had been identified as a kidnap victim of the SLA.

Yet another time I headed for Sunset Boulevard and talked to boys and girls who had been trapped into selling themselves to perverts attracted to Hollywood's notorious Meat Rack in their search for young flesh. I walked the same streets when I was writing about Douglas Daniel Clark, the sex-driven necrophile who called himself the King of the One-Night Stands, and who murdered and mutilated young girls, then sexually violated their remains.

Again, Hollywood and Glendale were my destinations while researching the terrible duo of first cousins whose sex-and-torture murders of young women earned them a shared nickname—the Hillside Strangler.

The last time I was in Los Angeles, it was to attend a few days of a trial and to talk with some of the courageous people who lived in an East Side barrio. They had run down and captured one of the most vicious and frightening serial killers of all. They had caught the Night Stalker.

In telling the story of the atrocious crimes he committed and of the people whose lives he touched, I have created no composite characters, made up no quotes, nor allowed myself the luxury of educated guesses or suppositions. Quotes are from statements made in court, transcript press conferences, and interviews.

I have, however, departed from my usual reluctance to use pseudonyms, and identified some of the individuals whose experiences or stories appear in the book by names that are not their own. Primarily, this was done to protect the identity of women who were sexually or otherwise emotionally abused by the madman who became known as the Night Stalker. When a woman victim of sexual abuse survived her husband's death, his name, too, has been changed. Pseudonyms are designated in the copy by italics.

Although the attacks were no fault of theirs, their ordeals were painful and humiliating, and there is no reason to add to their torment by needlessly identifying them publicly once again.

Here, then, is the Night Stalker. This is his story.

—Cliff Linedecker
Lantana, FL
July 1990

CHAPTER 1

Ice Cream

THE RINGING OF THE DOOR BUZZER WAS IN-sistent. No matter how determined the drowsy suburban-ite was in his sleepy attempt to burrow under the pillow and blankets to shut out the unwelcome intrusion, the shrill trill of the bell persisted.

Finally, accepting the sad fact that the ringing wouldn't stop and that his equally drowsy wife, who slept beside him, wasn't about to get up to answer the persis-tent summons, he slid to the edge of the bed and wriggled his toes around in the dark, feeling for his slippers. Find-ing them at last, he slipped his feet inside, stood up, and padded through a darkened hallway. As he shuffled into the living room and headed for the front door, he rubbed at his eyes and grumbled to himself about the kind of people who would ring someone's doorbell at this un-godly hour of the morning. It was nearly three A.M.

There was no reply to his hoarse demand to know who was there when he called out. But the ringing stopped. And, at first glance, when he opened the door a crack and cautiously peered into the darkness outside, there was no one to be seen. There was, instead, a crush of hot, moist air rushing from the pre-dawn darkness of the early Au-gust night in the San Gabriel Valley, and the quietness of the deserted suburban streets. He almost missed the diminutive pajama-clad figure standing at his feet until the child spoke:

"Ice cream?"

It was the neighbor's three-year-old, and, regardless of how quiet, free of traffic, and safe the comfortable valley community of Diamond Bar, some thirty miles east of Los Angeles, might be at three A.M., on Aug. 8, 1985 it was no time for the youngster to be wandering around looking for ice cream.

It seemed that the child had awakened and, as his parents slumbered peacefully, set out to find himself a latenight treat of ice cream. There was nothing to do but return him to his home, so the adult took the little boy by the hand and led him back to his house.

The man and the child walked into a scene of horror!

The child's mother was slumped bloody, bruised and naked, hanging by her wrists from a bedroom door. The frail East Asian woman had been handcuffed to the doorknob, and her slender body was covered with a mass of ugly gray welts and bruises. Rivulets of blood trickled from her nose and mouth, and her tear-streaked eyes were swollen. The horrified neighbor telephoned police.

Los Angeles County Sheriff's Deputy John Knight, a strapping six-foot-six veteran of the department, was the first police officer to arrive. Still handcuffed to the door and moaning with pain and fear, the woman begged him to check on her husband. She gasped that he was in the next room and needed help.

The body of thirty-five-year-old *Ahmed Zia* was stretched out on his bed in the master bedroom. There was a spot of blood on his left temple, and small flecks of blood speckled the pillow and the other bedclothing. Knight felt for a pulse. There were no signs of respiration, and it appeared obvious—although it would be up to a medical examiner to make an official pronouncement —that *Zia* was dead.

There was nothing Knight could do for the husband, so he returned to the wife, *Suu Kyi Zia*. Although he carried handcuffs of his own, the key wouldn't fit into the cuffs used on the woman. So the brawny peace officer lifted one leg and kicked the knob off the door.

Within minutes after the woman was freed, other uniformed officers, detectives, and evidence technicians began streaming into the house. The young Asian woman was taken by ambulance to a hospital for treatment. But it would be much later before her husband's body was removed from the house and taken to the county morgue to await an autopsy.

In statements at the scene, and later, the woman told investigators a chilling story of violence and perversion that was almost unbelievably savage and gruesome.

She said that a few hours after the family had retired for the night, she was awakened by a popping sound. She barely had time to open her eyes before someone began beating her with his fists, and demanding to know where she kept her money and jewelry.

Dazed and terrified, she told him, "I swear upon God, I don't know."

"Swear upon Satan," he demanded.

Moments later, the intruder was beating her again. Roughly, he dragged her from her silent husband's side and threw her onto the floor, ripping off her pajamas. The tiny woman was dazed and unable to defend herself as he kicked her with the hard pointed toes of his boots, and slammed her head and frail body into the floor and bed.

Finally, he rolled her over onto her stomach and handcuffed her hands behind her back. Then, grabbing her by the hair, he dragged her, bleeding from her nose and mouth, into a guest bedroom, where he flung her onto the bed and raped her. Howling that she was a bitch and heaping upon her a string of other curses and obscenities, he ordered her to swear upon Satan that she would not scream for help. He threatened to kill her little boy if she disobeyed. She was half-conscious and her mouth was half-filled with blood, but somehow she mumbled the words—swearing in Satan's name not to scream.

The boy was awake and crying, and the slender, curly-haired intruder angrily rolled off of the bed and turned his attention to the youngster. He tied up the boy and began ransacking the house, furiously ripping open dresser drawers and rummaging through closets looking for money and other valuables.

Then he returned to the woman, roughly threw her onto her stomach, and attempted to sodomize her. When he was unsuccessful at doing that, he raped her again. She was only half-conscious, in shock, and dazed as the nightmarish ordeal continued. Amid the pain and fear, there were glimpses of a scraggly, bony body, a cadaverous face with rotting and missing teeth, and unruly spikes of hair. And a constant, angry stream of curses and filth.

When the degenerate, vile assault ended at last and the savage intruder was ready to leave, he pulled his victim from the bed and handcuffed her to the door.

Despite the terrible battering and abuse she had suffered, she was still moaning about her husband. She was frantic for his safety. Her attacker told her moments before leaving that her husband was all right, that he had merely been knocked unconscious. She was still unaware that the "popping noise" that had roused her awake had apparently been the sound of the gunshot that ended her husband's life while he slept.

Somehow, after the intruder left, she managed to untie her son's feet and sent him into the master bedroom to look after his father. The child returned after a few minutes and told her, "Mama, he's not waking up."

That's when she began screaming.

But screaming didn't bring help. She finally told the child to go to the neighbor's home. The boy was afraid to go outside in the dark.

It would be safe, she assured him. And, if he did as he was told, she said, he could have some ice cream.

CHAPTER 2

A Serial Killer

AHMED ZIA'S BRUTAL SLAYING, AND THE AC-companying sexual assault on his wife, made more than sensational headlines in Los Angeles–area newspapers. They also brought Los Angeles County Sheriff Sherman Block face to face with two grim facts: one, as he had suspected for some time, he had a vicious serial killer on his hands; and two, it was time to alert the public that a monster was loose among them.

Evidence had been accumulating for several months that a depraved killer-rapist was prowling the Los Angeles suburbs. The *Zia* murder-rape now confirmed the veteran lawman's growing fear and suspicion. There were too many similarities among the *Zia* crimes and other murder-rapes that had been taking place in the area during the past five months. Since March 17, 1985 there had been at least ten similar rape-murders in valley homes outside the city.

The serial rapist-killer's modus operandi—method of operation, or MO—was beginning to emerge quite clearly as Block and his deputies tediously pieced together the growing mountain of evidence.

The killer appeared to focus on single-story homes in

middle-class suburban neighborhoods of the San Gabriel and San Fernando valleys. The homes were almost always located near freeway ramps, and for some inexplicable reason, the intruder seemed to prefer houses painted in light, pastel colors, usually yellow or beige.

And his method of entry was always the same. Late at night or during the early morning hours when occupants could be expected to be asleep in bed, he would slip quietly into the homes through an unlocked door or window.

Robbery was an obvious motive. But it was not the only one, nor, apparently, was it the most important. The intruder appeared to revel in his ability to instill fear, pain, and agony. His greatest thrills seemed to come with the savage murder, rape, and terrorizing of his victims.

Typical night burglars make every effort to avoid waking the occupants when they slip into homes, or they wait for opportunities when families are away. They are most successful when they can slip inside, quietly relieve owners of their money and other valuables, and slip away unseen and undisturbed.

But this burglar was different. It seemed that he deliberately sought out houses where the occupants were home. Typically, he murdered any males he found inside as quickly as possible. Then, with the husband or boyfriend out of the way, he was free to satisfy his perverted appetite for cruelty and sadistic sex on the helpless women and children. His attacks on the women were the most savage. They were threatened, beaten, raped, sodomized, and cursed. Sometimes male children were also attacked, and viciously sodomized. But other times the children would be left unmolested.

Investigators also found unsettling evidence of a Satanic connection with the vicious assaults. Pentagrams and other occult symbols commonly associated with Satanism had been found scrawled on the bodies of some victims and on the walls of the homes where they were killed.

One of the difficulties facing investigators was tied to the wide area prowled by the killer.

Los Angeles County is, in reality, one huge city that sprawls over 4,083 square miles. The county is bigger than the states of Rhode Island and Delaware combined. The City of Los Angeles itself sits in the center of the county, accounting for only 464 square miles of the total. Surrounding the city are eighty-two towns and cities, plus thousands of acres of unincorporated scrubland. More than a dozen super highways and freeways traverse the county, like bridges over a sea of industrial, commercial, and residential areas.

As an economic entity, greater Los Angeles is world class. If the area were an independent country, it would have a gross national product greater than that of Mexico or Australia. The motion-picture and television business is only the tip of L.A.'s huge service industry, which employs 900,000 people.

There is also a gritty and high-tech side as well. Manufacturing employs 875,000 workers, with a third of them in aerospace and other clean, high-tech industries. Some parts of the city could pass for Chicago's South Side. On the waterfront in Long Beach sit stacks of orange-and-blue cargo containers. In Lynwood, railroad tracks run past auto salvagers, truck-winch manufacturers, and scrap-metal piles.

If the sheer geographical and economical diversities were not enough, the polyglot of races and ethnic groups was a nightmare for social and governmental authorities whose job it was to make a community with such cultural diversity work. In 1985, Los Angeles County was undergoing an ethnic and racial metamorphosis not duplicated in America since the late 1800s and early 1900s in New York City.

In the fifteen-year period between 1970 and 1985, the

county's Mexican population climbed from 822,300 to 2,100,000; Iranians from 20,000 to 200,000; Salvadorans from 500 to 200,000; Japanese from 104,000 to 175,000; Armenians from 75,000 to 175,000; Chinese from 41,000 to 153,000; Koreans from 8,900 to 150,000; Filipinos from 33,500 to 150,000; Arab Americans from 45,000 to 130,000; Israelis from 10,000 to 90,000; Samoans from 22,000 to 60,000; Guatemalans from 1,000 to 50,000; and Vietnamese from 800 to 40,000.

To add to the problem, these ethnic and racial groups tended to settle in clumped groups: The Japanese, Koreans, and Chinese favored Cerritos, east of the city; Palos Verdes Estates, west of the city; Culver City, north, and Monterey Park, northeast of the city. The Thais, Filipinos, Salvadorans, and Guatemalans preferred the Hollywood Hills north of Los Angeles. The Mexicans, for the most part, stayed in the city and in East Los Angeles. The Vietnamese were grouped along the Los Angeles–Orange County border.

The real nightmare Los Angeles law enforcement had to deal with, though, was the fact that nearly eighty percent of almost 3,000,000 newcomers either could not speak, read, or write English, or they did so very poorly.

In many of these "colonies," police were viewed with suspicion and avoided.

It was against a background of this huge geographical area, with ethnic and language differences, that law enforcement officers faced the chilling prospect of ferreting out a strange, depraved killer who seemed to pick his victims at random. A serial killer who claimed affiliation with supernatural forces was bad enough; a random serial killer with demonic pretensions was a lawman's nightmare. Under the circumstances, tracking one down was like seeking a poisonous needle in a human haystack.

An official acknowledgment that such a killer was preying on the community had to be made. It wasn't that the information would come as any major shock. The string of recent killings, with their obvious similarities, was already beginning to attract public notice, thanks to alert newspapers and television reporters.

Police knew from past experience that public awareness of a cold-blooded random serial killer could lead to panic and at times result in dangerous vigilantism. On the other hand, if law enforcement agencies continued to deny what was becoming all too evident, circulation-hungry newspapers and the ratings-conscious electronic media might blow the facts out of proportion, causing even greater fear and panic—an overblown reaction based on ignorance and speculation.

So there really wasn't much choice. The Los Angeles area had a vicious serial killer on its hands—a cold-blooded monster who would kill and continue killing until Block and his deputies ran him to ground. The people of the area had to be alerted that a serial killer was at work, so that they could protect themselves.

On the other hand, the lawmen also knew they had to play their cards close to their vests. Killers read newspapers, too, particularly the headline-seekers who take relish in their gory crimes and the horror they spread. Police didn't want this killer to know everything that they knew.

Consequently, Block settled on a single terse announcement at a press conference, called within hours after the discovery of *Ahmed Zia's* body: "We have a serial killer in Los Angeles County," he told assembled journalists. In response to questions, Block provided some additional general information, but as police do, he held back certain details about exactly how the crimes were committed, and about evidence found near the bodies. Police have various reasons for withholding such information from the press during active investigations. But one of the most obvious uses of information withheld from the press is in screening out false confessions and pinning down legitimate suspects with facts known only to police.

The first murder in the bloody string, as far as law officers were able to determine at the time, occurred March 17, 1985, in the affluent, middle-class town of Rosemead, a few miles northeast of the Los Angeles boundary.

Pretty *Angela Barrios* was returning home at approximately eleven-thirty P.M. to the brown condominium about a quarter-mile from the Pomona freeway, which she shared with her roommate, Dayle Okazaki, when she was attacked.

Stopping her car outside the building, the twenty-year-old woman pressed a remote-control device, opening the automatic garage door. Then she drove slowly inside.

Angela was tired after a long day's work at her office, and she was looking forward to a quiet evening when she turned off the ignition and slid out of her car. As she walked to the door connecting the garage to her condo, her mind was on dinner and rest, when she was suddenly startled by a sound from behind her.

As she turned she glimpsed the ominous figure of a man slipping swiftly from the shadows behind her. He was dressed in black, and wore a dark blue baseball cap, and was holding a gun.

Angela tried not to show her fear. She stood perfectly still, perfectly quiet. Only her eyes moved, shifting to focus on the man's face, then darting away, desperately seeking some avenue of escape, but there was nowhere to go.

The intruder pointed the pistol at her, almost touching her nose with the barrel. He was going to kill her, she was going to die. There seemed to be no question about it. Instinctively, she raised a hand. "No. Please don't. Stop!" she begged.

But there was no mercy in the assailant's hard, dark eyes, or in his heart. She heard the roar of a gun firing and instantaneously felt a fiery, stabbing pain in her hand. *Angela* fell to the garage floor, rolled over on her side, and played dead. She would learn later that the car keys she was gripping in her upraised hand had deflected the bullet, and saved her life.

As she lay there, blood dripping from the injured hand, the gunman stepped over her body, then brutally kicked it aside as he pulled open the door leading into the condominium. Trembling, biting her lips against the pain, *Angela* forced herself to remain quiet and lie still on the hard, concrete floor until she felt certain her attacker had gone.

Finally, she crawled shakily to her feet, opened the garage door, and ran through an alley to the front of the building. As she slipped from the garage, she heard a loud, booming noise behind her. Her heart lurched painfully. She brought her wounded hand to her face. The blood was sticky, and she smeared some of it in her mouth. It tasted salty.

Then *Angela* stopped running. Astonishingly, she was face to face again with the gunman. He had emerged from the door of her apartment and almost ran into her. It was unbelievable. Too horrible to be true. Her legs felt like rubber, and she was afraid she would faint. Instead, she wheeled and stumbled away from the devilish apparition. She tried to scurry behind a car. But he had seen her, and he was right behind her.

She was dimly aware that her voice was a pitiful, embarrassing whine as she frantically pleaded, "Please don't shoot me again!"

It seemed as if an eternity elapsed. She was milliseconds from death. Then, without a word, the intruder inexplicably shoved the gun into his belt, turned, and melted into the darkness.

It seemed unbelievable! The gunman had let her live. Once again she had escaped. But the shaken young woman did not question her good fortune. She simply muttered, over and over, "Thank you, God, thank you. Thank you, God, thank you . . ."

Nor did *Angela* press her luck again. This time she remained where she was for a long time, until there was no doubt that the mysterious gunman was gone for good. Finally, she ventured cautiously away from the car and stumbled inside the condominium.

There, crumpled face down on the kitchen floor in a glistening pool of dark red blood, was her thirty-four-year-old roommate and friend, Dayle Okazaki. The Hawaiian-born traffic manager had been shot through the forehead. Blood was everywhere. It was splattered on the walls, on the furniture, and soaked the victim's clothes.

Angela was terrified, but she dropped to her knees beside the body of her friend to check for signs of life. The older woman was not breathing, and *Angela* could not detect a pulse. She lurched to the telephone, picked it up, and dialed 911. Then, sobbing quietly, oblivious to the blood still streaming from her injured hand, she waited for sheriff's deputies to arrive.

Deputies found the assailant's baseball cap on the garage floor. They not only had their first survivor, but had also recovered another important clue to the killer's identity.

Incredibly, within an hour, the killer struck again.

Thirty-year-old Tsai-Lian Yu, a native Taiwanese, lived in Monterey Park. A law student who hoped to become a top criminal defense attorney, she was known to her American-born friends as Victoria. She had spent the afternoon and evening enjoying a visit at the home of a friend, Jean Wang, in Arcadia. They talked about their childhood and shared some jokes. It was the last time Tsai would laugh with anyone.

Shortly before midnight, Officer Ron Endo was dispatched to North Alhambra Avenue in Monterey Park. As he arrived on the scene with the vari-colored lights on his cruiser flashing, the patrolman saw a yellow Chevrolet with its headlights and radio on. The engine was still running, and the gear shift was in Reverse. The automobile was prevented from moving backward, however, by a car parked behind it.

The crumpled body of a young woman was lying next to the Chevrolet. The officer ran to her side, crouched down, and felt for a pulse. She was still alive, but her breathing was shallow and labored. There was a rattle in her throat. At first glance she did not appear to be bleeding, but there was a noticeable bruise on her left leg, and her nylon stockings were ripped. A torn piece of a twenty-dollar bill and a gray-metal medallion were lying nearby.

Endo hurried back to his car and radioed for help. As he spoke, he cautiously kept his hand on the butt of his pistol. The assailant could still be lurking nearby.

When the dispatcher advised him that an ambulance was on the way, Endo returned to the comatose woman and attempted to question her. In response, her eyes rolled back in their sockets, showing white. The rattle from deep in her chest sounded like pieces of kindling snapping, as she drew a last, desperate breath. Endo didn't have to check. She was dead.

When homicide detectives arrived, they found the woman's purse and one of her blue shoes in the car. Another shoe lay near her body. She had been shot several times.

Los Angeles detectives were becoming apprehensive. Two murders within an hour and a short distance of each other. Was this the beginning of another "killing season"?

"It's too damned early. This is only spring," one detective said.

His partner sniffed the air. "The smog's bad already. It's the goddamned smog. It does things to people's minds. I can always tell when it's bad. First, my wife starts to bitch a lot. Then the sickos come out of the woodwork—like this turd who killed those two broads last night. It's the goddamned smog. It softens the brain."

Although it is particularly virulent in the summer, the smog hovers over Los Angeles like an evil curse all year long, even in the spring. And that spring was no exception. Its poisonous gases saturate everything from the San Fernando Valley in the west, to Pomona, the "armpit of Los Angeles," in the east. A mixture of fog, industrial smoke, and gasoline fumes trapped by the valley's unique geological formation, the smog has been blamed for a variety of physical and psychological ailments, ranging from respiratory failure and heart problems to shortened tempers and freeway shootings.

Police still chuckle when they recount the tale of a jogger confronted by two gun-toting muggers in Highland Park. The jogger, a young man in good physical condition, broke into a dead run.

The muggers, sallow-faced from too many cigarettes, too much alcohol, and too many drugs, took off in pursuit. They kept up for a few dozen yards, but it was quickly obvious that it was no contest. After a couple of minutes, their poor physical condition, combined with the deadly smog, took their inevitable toll.

As one would-be robber collapsed, breathing like an asthmatic old man, he gasped, "Buddy, what the hell's wrong with you? Give us a break!"

Ten days passed after the Monterey Park shooting. Greater Los Angeles residents were deluged with sensational stories—made even more frightening by circulation-seeking headlines and hysterical-voiced newscasters —about the serial killer and rapist who was running amok in their midst. Spurred by the growing hysteria, grim-faced law officers doubled their efforts to take the madman off the streets.

They checked out strange cars and faces, leaned on street informants, put out their own undercover men, sifted through any and all information that promised even the most tenuous connection to recent killings, and repeatedly questioned witnesses. They wanted to catch the serial killer before he could strike again.

But they knew, from past experience, that their desperate efforts were probably futile. They simply did not have enough information. They could only hope that their all-out assault might somehow frighten the killer into laying low for a time, leaving the area, or make a mistake.

Then the killer struck again, in what would possibly be his most savage and grisly attack of all. Vincent and Maxine Zazzara, who lived in a single story white ranch house about one-half mile from the San Gabriel River freeway, were the victims.

Vincent Zazzara was the sixty-four-year-old owner of a pizzeria in the Los Angeles suburb of Whittier. He was a robust man, in good shape, who loved his wife and family.

A former investment counselor, Zazzara had retired from that profession to follow his lifelong dream of operating his own restaurant. It wasn't a big place, but it was popular, and Zazzara enjoyed serving his customers with the "best pizza and pepperoni" in town.

Maxine Zazzara, who had just celebrated her forty-fourth birthday, was a lawyer with a thriving practice. She and her husband had labored hard to enjoy the good life, and their efforts had paid off.

Peter Zazzara went to his parents' house on a routine visit the morning of March 27, 1985, and rang the doorbell. Despite his repeated ringing, nobody answered. Since his parents' car was in the garage and they were supposed to be at home, he used his key to let himself into the house. A horrifyingly gruesome tableau greeted him.

Somehow, he dialed the police and gasped that there had been a murder. The victims were his parents.

Even hardened investigators felt the taste of sour bile when they inspected the phantom killer's gory handiwork. They would never forget the sight of Maxine Zazzara's mutilated face. Her eyes were gouged out, and the empty sockets were ringed with blackened gobs of blood and tissue.

The killer had plunged a knife through her left breast, leaving a large, ragged T-shaped wound. There were other cruel injuries to her neck, face, abdomen, and around the pubic area. She had been butchered, cruelly and with cold-blooded deliberation.

A coroner's autopsy disclosed a bullet wound in her head sufficient to have killed her instantly. The cutting, the gouging of the eyes, and the ripping knife wounds had apparently been afterthoughts—acts of perverse pleasure in which the killer had indulged himself. If there had been doubts before, investigators now knew they were dealing with a sick and evil mind that could be whipped into a sadistic frenzy by the sight and smell of blood.

Mrs. Zazzara's nude body was stretched on its back in her bed. The body of her husband was on a sofa in the den. He was fully clothed and had been shot through the left temple. Death had apparently been instantaneous.

The home had been ransacked. Police found a .45-caliber automatic pistol on the floor next to the woman's body. A bullet was recovered from the flooring beneath the bed.

Investigators gave the house a thorough going-over. They located footprints that appeared to be those of an adult male in a service-porch area, and in flowerbeds outside. The officers surmised that the killer had forced his way into the house through a bedroom window.

Initially there was some talk that the murders might have resulted from a drug deal gone bad, but after investigators took a hard look at the evidence, they decided it was more likely that the couple had been murdered by the same vicious serial killer they were already seeking.

The eye-gouging was especially appalling, even to veteran officers who had witnessed outrageous examples of human butchery before. One shaken law enforcement officer who examined the body later recalled, "The eyes were missing. There were . . . little indentations . . . and scratch marks around the eyes. It was very bloody, a lot of blood and disfigurement. I hope I never live to see anything like it again."

But there was more to come, much more, and, if possible, much worse.

The public, even the police, can understand a crime of passion, perhaps sympathize with the killer, even if they don't approve. A husband comes home early from work, finds his wife in bed with his best friend, and, in a rage, murders one or both of the lovers. People can relate to, if not excuse, the passion that produced the motive.

But this bloody rampage was different. It was the sadistic, systematic slaughter of innocent people. Someone with a vampire's taste for human blood was creeping into houses in middle-class neighborhoods after dark to work nightmarish evil. And the ghoulish intruder was not satisfied simply to kill his victims; he added torture, rape, and mutilation. He dehumanized his victims. It was villainy beyond ordinary comprehension; evil that truly chilled the soul.

In the early morning hours of May 14, the killer-rapist struck again—once more in Monterey Park. The victims were Mr. and Mrs. *Harold Wu*. They lived in a one-story beige stucco home about two-and-one-half miles from the San Bernardino freeway.

The sixty-six-year-old *Wu* and his sixty-three-year-old wife, *Jean*, were sound asleep when a prowler entered their home by forcing open a window. The intruder crept inside, and padded quietly to the bedroom. As the couple slept, unaware of the swiftly approaching horror, the killer leaned over the bed, placed a gun next to *Wu's* head, and squeezed the trigger.

A hand over *Mrs. Wu's* mouth suppressed her scream as the sound of the gunshot that killed her husband jarred her suddenly awake. A moment later someone was punching her viciously with his fists, slamming her body around as easily as if she were a rag doll. Then he was demanding to know where the couple kept their money and jewelry. Between sobs, while desperately trying to shake her dead husband back to life, the terrified woman told him where to look. Moments later her arms were roughly jerked behind her back and her hands fastened with a pair of painful thumb cuffs.

Left alone in the bedroom with the corpse of her husband, the woman could hear the intruder stomping through the house, pulling out desk and bureau drawers, spilling papers, clothes, and other personal effects all over. Then, cursing wildly, he returned to the bedroom, pulled her to the edge of the bed, and raped her. Finally, he left.

Harold Wu, however, was not dead, and slowly regained consciousness. Then, leaving his wife moaning in the bedroom, he stumbled and crawled to the den. Knocking the phone off its cradle, he managed to dial 911.

It was about five A.M. when Darlene Boese, a dispatcher for the Monterey Park Police Department, took the call on the 911 emergency line.

"Police. Can I help you?" she asked briskly.

A male voice was on the line. He seemed to be struggling for breath.

"I asked if he needed an ambulance, but he couldn't do anything except choke or gurgle," the dispatcher later recalled. "Then he finally said, 'Help!'"

She dispatched a police cruiser and an ambulance to the *Wu* residence. When the first officers rolled to a stop at the home on shady, tree-lined Trumbower Street, the only sound was that of a dog barking a few houses down the block. A pale, waning moon shone through the trees as the two officers walked up to the door and rang the bell. When there was no answer, they forced the door open.

They found *Harold Wu* sprawled on a blood-soaked sofa in the den. He was semiconscious and near death, Monterey Park policeman Michael Gorajewski told reporters. *Jean Wu* was standing in a hallway, her eyes staring unseeing and straight ahead, in shock. She "was in her nightgown. She had a pair of thumb cuffs on her left thumb . . . her face was swollen and there was bluing around her mouth and chin area. She wasn't speaking," Gorajewski said.

Paramedics immediately began treating her for shock. Police tried to question her, but at first she seemed unable to understand them. At last, she began to reply to their questions, in shaky, uncertain croaks. Slowly and patiently the paramedics drew the story from her.

She described the killer as a male Caucasian; thirty to forty years old; about five feet, ten inches tall; one hundred sixty pounds; with dark brown hair.

She said that she and her husband had no enemies they knew of. The crime seemed to be senseless, without a motive, other than burglary. Like the other houses, the *Wu* residence had been ransacked.

Harold Wu was taken by ambulance to Garfield Hospital in Monterey Park. He died a few hours after he was admitted.

Police responding to reporters' questions called the crime shocking, brutal, and senseless. The killer was an animal who had no feelings for his victims, a beast who could cold-bloodedly murder a man, then brutally rape his wife, one detective said through clenched teeth.

On the clear moonlit night of May 30, *Ruth Wilson,* an attractive forty-one-year-old Burbank woman, was making sure her twelve-year-old son was safely in bed before retiring to her own bedroom. Then she put on a filmy pink nightgown, turned out the lights, and climbed into bed.

Sometime during the night, the intruder forced his way into the home. The woman was in a deep sleep when a flashlight shining in her eyes awoke her. She struggled to sit upright, then froze. A gun was pointed at her head.

"Where is it?" demanded a voice from the darkness. The bright beam of the flashlight blinded her.

Still groggy, paralyzed by fear, she could not answer.

"Get out of bed," the voice ordered.

Terrified, she did as she was told. The figure pushed her in front of him, forcing her down the hall to her son's room. The intruder climbed on the bed and placed a gun against the boy's head.

"Don't make a sound or do anything," he warned as he fumbled in his pockets and pulled out a pair of handcuffs. He cuffed the frightened boy's hands behind his back.

"Mama," the boy whimpered.

The woman choked back a sob. Her eyes darted helplessly about until they locked on her son's.

"Don't say anything," the intruder hissed again. "I warn you!"

He pushed the boy into a closet and slammed the door shut.

Turning to the mother, he growled, "Don't look at me. If you look at me again, I'll shoot you."

"What do you want?" the woman pleaded. Before he answered, she said, "I have only one thing of value. If I give it to you, will you please leave?"

"Sure," he replied, shrugging his bony shoulders.

A faint hope surged through her as she led him to a dresser drawer and took out a gold-and-diamond necklace. After examining the jewelry, he ordered her to put her hands behind her back. His voice was edged with contempt.

"But you promised . . ."

"Quiet, bitch! I told you to put your hands behind your back."

He tied her hands tightly with a pair of pantyhose. Then he pushed her to the bed and forced her onto her back. She stared at him, wide-eyed, watching in disbelief as he unzipped his pants. Then, smirking cruelly, he tore the pink nightgown from her body. She was naked and helpless.

"Please don't do this," she begged.

"Shut up," the stranger warned. "If you make another noise, I'll kill you."

She turned her head to avoid his foul, laboring breath, and bit her lip against the tearing pain as he raped her. Then, still unsatisfied, he unceremoniously turned her over and cruelly sodomized her.

When he was through, she struggled to sit up, and, speaking softly through her pain and tears, she said, "You must have had a very unhappy life to have done this to me."

He looked at her strangely. "You look pretty good for your age," he said. "I don't know why I'm letting you live. I've killed people before. You don't believe me, but I have."

He continued to stare at her. Then he turned and stalked from the room. She could hear him as he rampaged through the apartment, ransacking dresser drawers, looking for cash and other valuables. After a few minutes, he returned to the bedroom. The woman complained that the pantyhose hurt her wrists. He loosened the knot. He even brought her a robe to cover herself so she would not be naked when he brought her son out from the closet. Then, he handcuffed her next to the boy, and left.

A short while later, the boy managed to reach a telephone and awkwardly dial 911. When the police arrived, they obtained an important eyewitness description of the man who was terrorizing suburban Los Angeles. There were slight differences in the descriptions police had been compiling. But that of the rape victim and most of the others agreed on three important features:

The man was thin, Hispanic, with long dark hair. . . .

CHAPTER 3

Rampage

PIECE BY PIECE, POLICE WERE COMPILING A dossier on the killer. Slowly his description and method of operation were coming into clearer focus.

What's more, three of the survivors, *Wilson, Wu,* and *Barrios* felt sure they could pick him out of a lineup.

Sheriff Block was pleased with the growing file on the killer, but the case was a long way from being solved. The description was pretty general. It could fit 10,000 men, maybe even more, among Los Angeles County's teeming millions.

Many more would die before the serial killer would be brought to account for his evil rampage.

Police continued to press their investigation in the murder of Tsai-Lian Yu, the thirty-year-old woman who was forced from her car and left to die on a sidewalk on North Alhambra Avenue in Monterey Park. And their persistence paid off when detectives found a witness, twenty-two-year-old Jorge Gallegos, who had seen the crime being committed.

Talking through an interpreter, the Spanish-speaking Gallegos told the officers he was sitting in a parked truck with his girlfriend when he heard two cars squeal to a

stop behind him. He turned and saw one of the drivers—
a tall, skinny man—trying to force the other driver, a
young woman, out of her car.

Gallegos told police he didn't pay much attention, fig-
uring it was probably just a lovers' quarrel. But the alter-
cation continued and the man suddenly jumped into his
car and drove away at a high speed. Then Gallegos heard
the woman crying feebly, "Help me . . . please, somebody help me." She was crawling on all fours. Gallegos
had seen enough. He telephoned police.

Officers found another witness to the shooting as well.
Joseph Duenas was in his apartment when he heard a
woman's shrill screams. He ran to a balcony, peered
down, and saw a man and a woman on the sidewalk. He
told police it looked as if the man were trying to walk
away from the woman. The man even told her to get
away, Duenas recalled. Then he heard the woman sobbing, "Help me, help me!"

Duenas said that as the man stalked toward his car, the
woman collapsed. She crawled after him in the grass and
tried to hold onto the man as he pulled away from her.
Duenas described the man to police: He was slim, with
an unruly shock of dark, curly hair.

The next homicide to be eventually attributed to the
mysterious killer especially piqued the curiosity of investigators because it reinforced a suspicion Sheriff Block
and his deputies had considered earlier—that some sort
of Devil worship or Satanism was involved!

The two seemingly unlikely victims were eighty-three-
year-old *Malvia Keller* and her invalid sister, seventy-
nine-year-old *Blanche Wolfe.*

They lived in a modest two-bedroom house painted
beige with brown trim in a quiet neighborhood about two
miles from the 210 freeway. *Malvia* had lived in the
house for twenty-five years. A retired teacher, she had
taken *Blanche,* an invalid, in to live with her, rather than
allow her to be institutionalized. Friends and neighbors

remembered her as a "gutsy, independent old lady." She had twelve grandchildren and had helped put two of them through college.

On the morning of May 29, Carlos Venezuela, a seventy-eight-year-old gardener who often did work around the house for the women, went to the sisters' home to carry out some routine chores. When he realized after a time that he hadn't seen any sign of activity in the house, he decided to look in on them, and let himself inside.

He found *Malvia* barely conscious, lying in a pool of drying blood on the floor of her bedroom. Her head was covered with deep cuts and bruises. She was moaning.

Blanche was a short distance away in another bedroom. She was lying on her bed, wrists bound behind her back with the cord from an electric clock. Black electrical tape was wound around her ankles. There was a puncture wound over one ear. A bloodstained hammer with a cracked handle lay on a nearby dresser.

The house had been thoroughly ransacked. Papers, clothing, and various odds and ends, such as pictures and vases, were scattered over the floors. A half-eaten banana was still laying on the dining room table. A television set was missing.

Investigators guessed that the women had lain helplessly in their home for two days before the worried gardener found them.

Police found a pentagram—an encircled five-pointed star often linked to Satanic worship—drawn in lipstick on *Malvia Keller's* thigh. Another pentagram had been crudely scrawled in lipstick on the bedroom wall where *Blanche Wolfe* lay in a comatose state. The tip of the pentagram was inverted, pointing down, an indication of evil. Of Satan!

Even seasoned detectives found the viciousness of the attacks difficult to comprehend. A small table had been overturned on *Malvia Keller's* chest. Both old women had been viciously beaten, apparently with the hammer, and slashed. They had been tortured, and there were signs that the attacker had tried to rape the older woman.

Malvia Keller died from her injuries about six weeks later. Her sister survived.

On June 27, pretty thirty-two-year-old Patty Elaine Higgins was found dead in her yellow one story frame duplex in Arcadia about two miles from the 210 freeway. Her throat was cut from ear to ear. The brutal murder fit the pattern of the other senseless sex killings.

A police captain on the scene said, "This is the work of the Valley Intruder." The press, exercising its penchant for catchy, dramatic labels, had come up with the "Valley Intruder" nickname as well as others, including the "Midnight Stalker." It would be changed eventually to one that even better described the madman's dreadful deeds. He was a monster who made Freddie Krueger, the fictional archvillain of *Nightmare On Elm Street,* seem almost like a character from a Disney movie.

There were other crimes that authorities suspected were the handiwork of the same serial killer.

A nine-year-old boy was kidnapped from his home in Monterey Park, sodomized and left bleeding in the town of Elysian Field near Silver Lake. An Eagle Rock girl was kidnapped at gunpoint and raped by a man who broke into her residence at night while her parents slept. A teenaged babysitter fell asleep at a neighbor's home and an intruder entered through an open window and raped her. They were the lucky ones. They were allowed to live.

On July 2, seventy-five-year-old Mary Louise Cannon was found dead in her one-story beige house about one-half mile from the 210 freeway in Arcadia. She had been brutally beaten, and her throat slashed with a knife. The house had been ransacked.

Three days later, sixteen-year-old *Deidre Palmer* was attacked in her home in Arcadia about two miles from the 210 freeway by a crazed intruder who viciously beat her about the head with a tire iron. The teenager survived.

On July 7, police found the dead body of sixty-one-year-old Mrs. Joyce Lucille Nelson in her beige single-story stucco house in Monterey Park, about two miles from the Pomona freeway. The assembly line production worker and grandmother had been bludgeoned to death.

But even more horror had been visited on Monterey Park—apparently on the same night that Mrs. Nelson was murdered. A sixty-three-year-old registered nurse, *Linda Fortuna,* was also brutalized in her own home.

A grandmother, Mrs. *Fortuna* was sleeping when she was awakened at about three-thirty A.M., by someone placing a hand over her mouth. As her eyes flicked open in terror, she saw a tall, bony man dressed in black, looming over her. He pointed a gun at her head and hissed, "Make a sound and I'll kill you."

As the woman sat up trembling, the intruder roughly pulled her hands behind her back and handcuffed them. Then he pointed to the bathroom and ordered her inside, telling her to sit down. He warned her not to make any noise and not to look at him. Struggling to control her fear, and forbidden to speak, she nodded her head in mute agreement.

Quickly, the stranger ransacked the home for valuables. Then he returned and gruffly ordered the nurse back into the bedroom. Inside, he ordered her to lie down on the bed, and stuffed a glove in her mouth.

"Bite down on this so you won't scream," he demanded, speaking with the voice of death. She did as he commanded. The glove kept her teeth from chattering. When he shoved a pillow over her face, she thought he meant to suffocate her. Instead, he unzipped his trousers and attempted to rape her. But he couldn't get an erection. Cursing, he ordered her to turn over on her stomach, and tried to sodomize her. He failed in that attempt as well.

The nurse's terror increased with each of his sexual failures. It seemed that her attacker, embarrassed at his inability to perform, might kill her to salvage his sick pride. Instead, after cursing her, the intruder gathered together all the valuables he could carry and left. Astonished and thankful that she had escaped with her life, she telephoned police. Her detailed description of the intruder matched information police had already compiled about the savage marauder who was terrorizing the valley communities outside Los Angeles.

Still, law officers were no closer to identifying the brutal sex killer, much less making an arrest. And while law enforcement officers endured humiliating frustration at their inability to put a stop to the horror, the public's panic began to approach epidemic levels. But just as the summer heat became more oppressive, the situation was to become much worse.

On July 20, the maniacal killer struck in an unequalled paroxysm of savagery, carrying his orgy of rape and murder to two homes in Glendale and Sun Valley.

It was shortly after midnight when a dark-clad man broke into a house on Stanley Avenue, near Zerr Court in Glendale. It was one of the older neighborhoods in Los Angeles County, a quiet, neat area where generations of quite ordinary people lived quite ordinary lives. In some cases, three generations of the same family lived within blocks of one another.

The sinister stranger unlatched the side gate at the white, one-story Spanish-style home where Maxson and Lela Kneiding had lived for twenty-eight years, and entered through the unlocked french doors. The house was located about three-quarters of a mile from the Ventura freeway.

As was his custom, the skulker passed quietly and unobserved through the house, moving with Ninja stealth until he came to the bedroom where sixty-six-year-old

Maxson was sleeping alongside his sixty-four-year-old wife, Lela.

Maxson, a gentle man who owned three Shell service stations with his son, Rob, had heart problems and was considering retirement. He was a man who was content with his life. He had a loving wife, a son who would have made any father proud, a fine daughter, and grandchildren. He was a deacon in the nearby Seventh-Day Adventist Church.

He also had a habit of collecting change. At any one time, he might have as many as ten peanut-butter jars filled with pennies. It was a habit that his wife, children, and grandchildren constantly teased him about.

Lela, a sweet-tempered, silver-haired woman, had a back ailment. Sometimes it made physical movement difficult, but that did not stop her from babysitting for her grandchildren whenever she was asked. On weekends and during the summer there were always some of them around the house.

This was a particularly happy summer for her. Not only was there a constant coming and going of youngsters, some in their teens, but it was a wonderful year for her beloved Dodgers, who were ruling the roost in the Western Division of professional baseball's National League. Sometimes, it seemed that Lela lived and died with the rise and fall of the Dodgers' fortunes.

In many ways, Maxson and Lela lived their lives much as their fathers and mothers had: traditional, safe from the disturbing world beyond their neighborhood and family circle—until the intruder peered into their bedroom. . . .

It's quite likely that the Kneidings died without knowing what had happened to them. The intruder shot and savagely butchered both of them in a killing frenzy. Lela's body was lashed with gaping slash wounds, exposing bone and vital organs. Maxson's throat was so severely cut that he was nearly decapitated.

The pitifully mutilated bodies were found Sunday morning by their daughter, thirty-six-year-old Judy. She had become worried when they failed to meet her and her husband, Bill, at a nearby restaurant where they often ate breakfast together after church services.

Monterey Park Police Chief Jon Elder and his officers appeared helpless in their efforts to deal with the homicidal madman's reign of terror. Elder told reporters grimly and matter-of-factly, "That son-of-a-bitch has scared the hell out of this city." Then the police chief appealed to the public to "be our eyes and ears . . . tell us what you see and help us catch him."

The deviate had been operating in a wide geographic area, but had limited his killings and rapes to communities ringing Los Angeles. That would soon be altered.

Outraged over the killer's audacity, police were even more disgusted with his cowardly behavior. If men were present in a house, the intruder quickly killed them, then raped their helpless wives or girlfriends.

One officer asked reporters, "If that isn't a coward, what is?"

The kill-crazed butcher used exactly that cowardly technique to brutalize an innocent family a few miles away from Monterey Park, in the neighboring community of Sun Valley. He had chosen July 20 to commit chilling back-to-back outrages.

Thirty-two-year-old *Chitat Assawahem* was a professional man who appeared to have a bright future with his company. His petite, attractive twenty-nine-year-old wife, *Sakima,* was working on her Master's degree in medical technology. With their two well-behaved children, aged two and eight, they appeared to be living the American dream. But during the early pre-dawn hours of the morning of July 20, their idyllic existence took a nightmarish turn.

Sakima Assawahem was sound asleep in her yellow single-story tract home about a mile from the Hollywood

freeway when she was awakened with a start by a popping sound. The noise sounded like a car backfiring. But
it was no car backfire. Her husband had just been shot in
the head and killed, execution style, as he slept peacefully
in his bed beside her.

Despite the darkened bedroom, the woman could see
the gory hole in her husband's shattered head. She was
crying when she looked up at the shadowed figure of a
strange man, dressed in black, hovering over her with a
gun in his hand. He laughed, as if her husband's terrible
injury and her shocked reaction was funny.

"Don't worry, bitch, I just knocked him out," the man
said with a smirk. "I hit him over the head."

The intruder pulled a sheet over the dead man's face.
Then he took off one of his gloves and began beating the
helpless woman with his fist. After pulling her from the
bed and throwing her to the floor, he began to punch and
kick her. The punches and kicks were delivered with such
savage ferocity that the tiny-framed, fragile-appearing
woman almost fainted from the pain.

Finally, weary of beating her, the gunman handcuffed
her hands behind her back and dragged her by the hair
into another bedroom. Bleeding from her mouth and
nose, she was hurled brutally onto the bed. As she lay
there, helpless, he deluged her with a string of vile names,
names she had never heard before and barely understood:
"bitch, whore, . . ."

"Swear," he commanded, "swear upon Satan that you
won't scream for help!"

Gasping with pain, she swore.

He ripped off her nightgown and, at gunpoint, dragged
her naked through the house. They stopped in her bedroom, where he told her coldly, "This is your husband.
He's already dead." Warning her that she either cooperate or he would kill her children, too, he raped her. Then
he forced her to perform oral copulation on him. He
dragged her behind him by her long hair as he searched

the house for cash and other valuables, demanding in a raspy voice that she tell him where they were hidden. She told him where to find some jewelry, but he wasn't satisfied. In the kitchen, he stopped to drink some apple juice from the refrigerator. Then he dragged his helpless captive back to her bedroom and raped her again, this time on the floor.

Then the intruder committed an atrocity that was so monstrous that *Mrs. Assawahem* could barely recount the details to the police. He tied her up in the bedroom and took a bottle of baby oil into her eight-year-old son's room. She was forced to listen helplessly to the boy's piercing screams, and several slapping sounds. Finally, the screams and sobs subsided to pathetic whimpers.

"It was a very painful cry," the sobbing mother later told police. "I couldn't do anything to help him."

Returning to the woman, the intruder threw the valuables into a suitcase and pillowcase, stuffed a sock in her mouth, and left—with jewelry and cash worth an estimated $30,000.

After a brief effort she managed to free herself and ran into her son's bedroom. The boy was whimpering in pain, and bleeding from the rectum. She picked him up and carried him out of the house in her arms, while she screamed for help.

Satisfied that she had attracted the attention of neighbors, *Mrs. Assawahem* ran back into the house and pulled the sheet from her husband's head. Her attacker had told her the truth. Her husband was dead. Police found her collapsed over his body.

Much later the tormented widow asked authorities, "Why, why, why? I gave him everything he wanted! Why did he murder my husband?"

They had no answers for her.

Virginia Petersen, a postal employee, and her husband, Christopher, a truck driver, who lived in a brown one-story house about five miles from the Simi Valley freeway, were the next victims.

It was the middle of a steamy-hot summer night in the valley on August 5, 1985, when Virginia sensed the presence of a stranger in her darkened bedroom. She sat bolt upright in bed and demanded, "Who are you? What do you want?"

The intruder simply laughed. Her husband, still half-asleep, suspected that it might be one of her brothers acting out a bad joke. That was when the shadowy intruder pointed a gun at Virginia and pulled the trigger. She felt her face literally explode. The bullet tore through her cheek next to her left eye, passed through her palate, and exited through the back of her head.

As she fell back against the pillow, her husband sprang up, realizing this was no prank. The gunman fired again. The bullet ripped through his temple and passed through the side of his head, lodging finally at the base of his brain, in the back of his neck.

In the next room, the couple's young daughter screamed, "Mommy, what's going on?"

Virginia didn't know what had happened. Strangely, she felt no pain. She asked her husband if they had been shot with a stun gun.

He gasped, blood streaming from his head wound. Her face was gone.

The intruder just laughed.

Christopher Petersen, a big, powerful man, his body fine-tuned by hard work, had put up with enough. He was not about to lie there, listening to this monster giggle, waiting to be finished off like some helpless sheep in a slaughterhouse. If he was going to die, he would die like a man.

Growling, Petersen leaped from his bed and began chasing the armed man around the room. The intruder backed up, taken by surprise and startled by the brave, unexpected act. Then he turned and ran, firing two wild shots, while he screamed at the enraged husband to stay away.

Christopher Petersen was fighting for his own life and for his family's also. The animal growl that started low in his stomach grew louder. He was all that stood between the gunman and his young daughter, crying in the next room.

The intruder, so arrogant while he had the upper hand, suddenly knew confusion and fear. Although he still had the pistol, he scrambled panic-stricken from the house, chased by an unarmed man with a bullet embedded at the base of his brain.

Christopher Petersen had proven, if there was any doubt, what the investigators had always maintained: that the so-called Valley Intruder, faced by a real man, was a mere punk, a two-bit coward. There was bone-satisfying pleasure in knowing that.

The couple survived. Christopher lost part of his memory and much of his strength, but he and his wife lived. They were among the few to escape with their lives after a direct confrontation with one of the most deadly and prolific killers in Southern California's bloody history.

Two nights later in Diamond Bar came the attack on *Ahmed* and *Suu Kyi Zia.*

Rape, oral copulation, sodomy, mutilation, murder. The stalker's appetite for butchery and sexual perversions seemed to grow with each attack. Frustration and anger on the part of the sheriff's department and police officers grew in proportion to the public's fear.

His scorecard was enough to strike terror in the bravest soul:

• March 17—Dayle Okazaki, thirty-four, of Rosemead; shot to death; her roommate, *Angela Barrios,* shot and wounded.

- March 17—Tsai-Lian Yu, thirty, of Monterey Park; dragged from her car and shot to death.
- March 27—Vincent Zazzara, sixty-four, and his wife, Maxine, forty-four, of Whittier; both stabbed to death, and bodies mutilated.
- May 14—*Harold Wu,* sixty-six, of Monterey Park; shot to death in his home; his sixty-three-year-old wife, *Jean* was brutally beaten and raped.
- May 30—*Ruth Wilson,* forty-one, of Burbank; rape, sodomy, oral copulation, burglary.
- June 1—*Malvia Keller,* eighty-three, and her sister, *Blanche Wolfe,* seventy-nine, of Monrovia; *Keller* was bludgeoned to death; *Wolfe* was beaten but survived; Satanic symbols marked on *Keller* and on walls with lipstick.
- June 27—Patty Elaine Higgins, thirty-two, of Arcadia; found dead in her duplex, her throat slashed.
- July 2—Mary Louise Cannon, seventy-five, of Arcadia; found dead in her home, beaten, with throat slashed.
- July 5—*Deidre Palmer,* sixteen, of Arcadia; survived beating with tire iron in her home.
- July 7—Joyce Lucille Nelson, sixty-one, of Monterey Park; beaten to death; house ransacked.
- July 7—*Linda Fortuna,* sixty-three, of Monterey Park; raped and sodomized in her home.
- July 20—Maxson Kneiding, sixty-six, and his wife, Lela, sixty-four, of Glendale; both shot to death; home burglarized.
- July 20—*Chitat Assawahem,* thirty-two, of Sun Valley; shot to death while sleeping; his twenty-nine-year-old wife was raped and forced to perform oral copulation; their eight-year-old son was sodomized; approximately $30,000 in cash and jewelry was taken.
- August 6—Christopher Petersen, thirty-eight, and his wife, Virginia, twenty-seven, of Northridge; both survived bullet wounds in the head; although seriously

wounded, Petersen chased the Night Stalker from the house.

- August 8—*Ahmed Zia,* thirty-five, of Diamond Bar; he was shot to death while asleep; his twenty-eight-year-old wife was raped, sodomized, and forced to perform fellatio.

Lawmen carried a mental image of the skulking murderer around with them while they patrolled the neighborhoods of suburban Los Angeles. They thought about him in their sleep—his pockmarked face, the sinister smile, the broken and rotted teeth with the gap, the sallow complexion, the high, pronounced cheekbones, the shock of curly dark hair. They knew what he looked like, but they still couldn't find him. And while they searched, the killer hid in the night shadows, waiting to strike again.

Detectives recalled other serial slayings, and ritual killers who had terrorized Los Angeles. This killer was different from most, though. The closest parallel was Charles Manson and his homicidal hippie "Family," who for a time terrorized the affluent communities and citizens along the shore.

The scruffy, unwashed losers hid out in the high desert on the Spahn movie ranch near Los Angeles, killing and robbing because "Charlie said so." The Family members had fried their brains with LSD, peyote, belladonna, and other drugs before they could carry out Manson's deadly orders.

Susan Atkins, Tex Watkins, and other members of the Family had practiced their "creepy crawlies," getting into the homes of well-to-do strangers just for the thrill of doing it. They dressed in dark clothing, put on gloves, and slipped stealthily inside, as quiet as shadows. Sometimes they would take something; more often than not they simply left after gaining entrance. The bloodletting would come later.

Now someone equally as dangerous as Manson and his Family was using the "creepy crawlies."

There was an eight-year-old girl in Eagle Rock who had been sexually molested, plus a six-year-old girl in Arcadia, and an eight-year-old boy in Sun Valley. Thousands of parents throughout Los Angeles had the same deadly thought: If they caught the killer-rapist before the police did, there would be no need for a trial.

Yet, despite the rage being focused on him, the loyal servant of the Prince of Darkness continued to have his way.

CHAPTER 4

The Night Stalker

WHILE LAW ENFORCEMENT OFFICIALS WERE having problems coming up with a clear psychological profile of the man whose bloodlust seemed to increase with each murder, the media was experiencing a crisis of its own.

Police viewed the serial killer as a frustrating challenge to their professional skills. The public feared him because, at any time and in almost any place, any one of them might become his next victim. And the media saw him as a commodity—something that would sell newspapers or attract viewers.

What the media needed was a "hook," an attention-grabbing name. Newspaper readers and television viewers like labels—catchy titles or nicknames—especially for serial killers. The name has to be short, so it will fit easily into headlines; colorful and attention-grabbing, so readers or television viewers won't be bored. And the name must do a good job of describing the killer and his actions.

Over the decades, American journalists have developed a highly effective formula for dealing with sensational crime stories, particularly those involving bloody murders, lurid sexual perversions, and mysterious killers.

Although constrained by factual evidence, or at least its bare bones, journalists have couched their stories in the trappings of fiction. A good fiction mystery story, for instance, should have a protagonist—a good guy; and an antagonist—a bad guy. The good guy usually is the police, hopefully a particular policeman. And the bad guy is . . . the bad guy.

But just any bad guy won't do it. No matter how evil his deeds, no matter how vile his crimes, the bad guy must have something about him with which the reader can identify. Some of America's most infamous criminals have been romanticized by the press, ranging from Revolutionary War traitor Benedict Arnold to Wild West desperadoes Jesse James and Billy the Kid to Depression era gangsters John Dillinger and Al Capone.

During the Vietnam War, the press romanticized a mixed bag of radicals and terrorists, including the Symbionese Liberation Army (SLA), the Black Guerrilla Army, the Weathermen, and other groups. Members of these groups murdered police and other figures of authority, kidnapped diplomats and the wealthy, and robbed banks, but, somehow, in their accounts, the press managed to drape them in mantles of heroism—spoiled brats, social psychopaths, and common criminals had become "heroes of the people," according to some media accounts.

A very common technique by which journalists transform the dregs of society into romantic figures is to interview psychiatrists, psychologists, sociologists, and other so-called experts and allow them to speculate on what might have motivated the bad guy "to turn bad." Did his mother deny him love? Was he raised in a ghetto environment where his emotional development and social conscience were stunted? Did the poor guy get off to a bad start because his early, formative years were spent in foster homes, reformatories, and prisons?

The key to this journalistic selling of an inhuman killer, including the bestial intruder who terrorized Los Angeles County during the torrid summer of 1985, was a provocative, commercial name for the murderer. And this time, normally imaginative newsmen were having problems coming up with the right one.

This was an especially unusual problem for the Los Angeles media, which, in the past, had shown a remarkable talent for devising highly marketable names for the state's seemingly endless string of serial killers. Some of their most highly acclaimed successes include the "Hillside Strangler," the "Trailside Slayer," the "Freeway Killer," and the "Skid Row Slasher."

A Hispanic male. A bony six-feet to six-feet-two inches tall. Probably twenty-five to thirty years old. Long, dark curly hair. Badly stained, wide-gapped teeth. Putrid breath. Black eyes that stared a sinister hole through his victims. An insatiable sexual appetite that covered the gamut of sexual perversions. Satanic overtones. Savage mutilations. A shadowy figure of mystery seemingly capable of appearing anywhere, anytime.

All wonderful characteristics for a monster of classic proportions—all that was needed was just the right name to capture his evil essence.

The media's first attempt to name the black-clad killer was the "Valley Invader." That didn't quite hit the mark, so they tried the "Walk-In Killer." When that failed to fire the public's imagination, someone came up with the "Valley Intruder." Close, but no cigar. It still didn't quite create the lurid image needed. Above all else, a serial killer's nickname must be lurid—".45-Caliber Killer," the "Hillside Strangler," the "Lady Killer," the "Vancouver Butcher," the "Killer Clown," or history's most infamous serial killer, "Jack the Ripper."

Appropriately enough, the *Los Angeles Herald-Exam-*

iner, one of the last surviving members of a once impressive string of sensationalistic daily newspapers, spawned by the father of American tabloid journalism, William Randolph Hearst, came up with the "Night Stalker." Bingo! Reporters and editors both knew immediately that the name was perfect for this particular serial killer. So, apparently, did the public.

The Night Stalker! The name shocked and thrilled at the same time. It was sinister. It spoke of evil committed in the dead of the night. It hinted of gore and other unspeakable things. And yet, somehow, it also possessed that mantle of romanticism with which Americans like to clothe their monsters, real or fictional—Dracula or the Godfather, for example. It spread across the country and immediately took hold.

The coup bolstered the sagging pride of the *Herald-Examiner.* Once again, it had proven itself the master of lurid journalism, a tribute to its founder, Hearst, even though it was a dying dinosaur, and would finally go out of business five years later.

Though admired by journalists, the "Night Stalker" appellation drew fire from both critics of the press and from police. Both complained that the press was trying to "romanticize" a cold-blooded killer. The press critics harped like nagging old women that the lurid name and press coverage, especially that of the *Herald-Examiner,* was in the worse tradition of American journalism. Police complained that press sensationalism was beginning to throw the public into panic, making their job more difficult.

But police problems running the Night Stalker to ground had little to do with the way the press covered the case, or with the rising panic and dissatisfaction of the public.

Multiple killers are an American phenomenon. An estimated 6,000 people die each year at the bloody hands of serial killers. The victims range from prostitutes, drifters, and the homeless to children, nuns, the elderly, housewives, and traveling salesmen.

There were only a handful of known serial killers in the United States in the 1950s. Charles Starkweather, a Lincoln, Neb. garbageman and mean-tempered runt was the best known. He captured the public imagination when he killed ten people and a dog in Nebraska and Wyoming during a bloody spree in Dec. 1957 and Jan. 1958. But, by the mid-1980s, one new serial killer was being uncovered every forty-five days. Now experts say the U.S. is producing one serial killer per month. Los Angeles, capital of serial killers, seemed to spawn them as effortlessly as garbage draws maggots.

Among the most infamous—and bizarre—of these were the Hillside Strangler, the Skid Row Slashers, Douglas Daniel Clark, and Lawrence Bittaker and Roy Norris.

"Hillside Strangler" was a misnomer, because the Strangler was actually two people—cousins Kenneth Bianchi and Angelo Buono. In the brief period of two months—October through December—the pair abducted, raped, and murdered ten women, many of them prostitutes.

Their favorite method of slaying victims was as monstrous as their minds. While one cousin raped the victim, the other slipped a plastic bag over her head and sealed it with a cord. The strangler gained as much satisfaction as the rapist, watching the victim struggle for air, the bag billowing less and less, until finally it was still.

The cousins were arrested in 1979. Buono was sentenced to nine terms of life in prison without parole. Bianchi received two similar sentences in Washington state, where he had been arrested for the rape and murder of two women in Bellingham after separating from Buono a few months earlier.

There were also two Skid Row Slashers, one succeeding the other. The first was Vaughn Owen Greenwood; the second was Bobby Joe Maxwell. Both men were black and their killing sprees appeared to have had some Satanic or occult connection.

Greenwood apparently began his killings in 1964, when he murdered two derelicts on successive days. His victims were ritually posed after death, with salt sprinkled around their bodies and cups of blood left standing nearby. Their wounds were surrounded by markings of unknown significance. He apparently did not kill again until December 1974, when he murdered three homeless men during the month.

Two more transients were chopped to death in January before the Slasher switched to more affluent victims in the Hollywood area. He was apprehended after dropping a letter addressed to himself in the driveway of Burt Reynolds's home. Police learned that Greenwood cut his victims' jugulars and, while they were still alive, hearts pumping blood through the slashed flesh, he would drink from the wound.

In December 1976, he was convicted on nine counts of first-degree murder, and sentenced to life in prison. The judge recommended that he never be released because "his presence in any community would constitute a menace."

Bobby Joe Maxwell picked up where Greenwood left off. He was convicted of killing two skid-row derelicts after police caught him standing over a victim, clutching a ten-inch dagger. Like Greenwood, Maxwell followed a ritual, scrawling "Satan" on a piece of cardboard and leaving it alongside some victims. But, unlike Greenwood, who was also dubbed the Vampire Killer, Maxwell was an admitted devil worshipper.

He also left messages for police. One such message was "My name is Luther. I kill winos." Others said, simply, "Satan." "Luther" was Maxwell's familiar name for Satan. His reign of terror caused panic among the skid-row denizens, who, at one point, formed a vigilante group in an effort to run him down. Many simply left the city for safer environs. Maxwell received two life sentences in 1979. While in prison, he told a cell mate that he had killed the derelicts to "recruit their souls for Satan."

Douglas Clark called himself "King of the One-Night Stands," dispensing sexual favors to frowzy matrons, and participating in kinky liaisons with underaged girls and young women. Although he nourished dark fantasies of rape and murder, mutilation and necrophilia, he did not embark on his monstrous "career" until he met Carol Bundy, an overweight, diabetic, thirty-seven-year-old mother of two.

At the time they met, Bundy had just been kicked out of her apartment by her married lover, who was manager of the building. Heartbroken, she took up with Clark, who, unleashing all his considerable skills as a lover, turned her into a virtual slave. She was so smitten with him that when he started bringing home younger women for sex, she did not object. She even consented to snap pictures of Clark making love to an eleven-year-old he had picked up at a skating rink.

When police found the bodies of a fifteen-year-old and a sixteen-year-old, Clark confessed to Bundy that he'd killed the two girls. He told her he'd forced them to fellate him, shooting each in the head at the moment she brought him to a climax. It turned out to be a standard ritual for several murders that followed.

Once, Clark surprised Bundy by plucking a woman's head from the refrigerator. Placing it on the kitchen counter, he ordered Bundy to make up the twisted face with cosmetics. She later recalled, "We had a lot of fun with her. I made her look like a Barbie [doll]." Clark then took the head to the bathroom for a shower and used it for necrophilic sex.

Despite Bundy's hot romance with Clark, she could not stay away from her ex-lover. Unable to hold her liquor very well, she blurted out some hints about her newest lover's criminal actions. He suggested she go to the police. Suddenly realizing what she had done, and fearful of what her ex-lover would tell Clark, or worse, the police, she lured him to his van, where she killed him. He was discovered several days later, stabbed nine times and slashed across the buttocks. His head was missing and was never found.

A few days later, she broke down and told a fellow worker, who tipped off police. Clark was arrested. Police found the panties belonging to several of the murdered women, the snapshots Bundy had taken of him with his eleven-year-old playmate, and the gun he had used in several of the murders.

He was sentenced to death in February 1983. Bundy was given twenty-five years to life.

When Lawrence Bittaker and Roy Norris met in prison, they discovered they were kindred spirits. They laid plans to kill at least one girl for each teen year—thirteen through nineteen—after they were released. They embarked on their murderous spree in 1979, using a silver van that Bittaker dubbed "Murder Mack."

Over the next five months, they embarked on a grisly murder spree, littering the area around Los Angeles with the raped and mutilated bodies of forty to fifty teen-aged victims—they killed so often that they themselves didn't know how many people they had dispatched.

The two were arrested on charges stemming from an assault in Hermosa Beach. Their victim, who had been sprayed with Mace, abducted, and raped in Murder Mack before escaping, described Bittaker and Norris, as well as their van, to police. Later, the girl was unable to give a positive identification, but police held the pair for parole violation after they found drugs in their possession.

Norris cracked under the strain of being back in custody and, at a preliminary hearing, told police of his and

Bittaker's bloody spree. Police found more than 500 pictures of victims, and a tape recording of one girl's final moments alive. Norris, after leading police to shallow graves in San Dimas Canyon and the San Gabriel mountains, struck a deal with police and turned on Bittaker.

In return for turning state's evidence against Bittaker, Norris received a sentence of forty-five years, with parole possible in thirty years. Bittaker was sentenced to the gas chamber, and to make certain he stayed behind bars, the judge imposed an alternate sentence of 199 years plus 4 months to take effect in the event that the death sentence was ever commuted to life imprisonment.

These were among the most infamous of California's recent serial killers to precede The Night Stalker. Serial killers are difficult to catch. Often they are extremely intelligent, with "street smarts." Rarely do they have a prior link to their victims. They move around, strike, move, and hit again. Faced with even these handicaps, police manage to painstakingly put together some standard patterns, or MO. Some, for instance, favor knives. Or they kill only prostitutes.

The Night Stalker, however, did not seem to be following any readily discernible pattern. What similarities did exist applied only to a portion of his attacks.

He played no favorites in his random savagery, choosing victims of various ages, race, and both sexes, and in a maddening, inconsistent pattern that confounded and confused police. He had preyed on at least eleven different suburbs as far as forty miles apart.

He was an equal-opportunity monster, raping and sodomizing women and children, young and old, and killing with guns and knives or by simple bludgeoning.

He defied the pattern of the typical serial killer, criminologists said, both in his choice of weapons and in his chilling readiness to kill almost anyone.

"Most serial killers will kill with an axe or knife, rather

than a gun, in order to achieve intimacy with the victim," observed Richard Rappaport of Northwestern University's School of Medicine in Chicago.

Rappaport, an expert witness in the trial of John Wayne Gacy, Jr., who was convicted in 1980 and sentenced to death after the murders of thirty-three young men in the Chicago area, also confirmed that the Night Stalker's unusual choice of victims was especially baffling.

The Stalker's victims covered a much broader spectrum than those of most serial killers. They were young, middle-aged, and elderly. Some lived alone; others were married, or lived with a friend, relative, or companion. They were usually middle class, and, if they weren't exactly affluent, they were at least without serious financial concerns. And most owned their own homes or condominiums.

There were no known down-and-outers among his victims—no prostitutes, no runaways, no derelicts. While victims of the run-of-the-mill serial killers were likely to be people no one would miss, unless a body turned up somewhere, the Stalker's victims were high profile. Their deaths were discovered within hours. Their survivors were respectable, tax-paying citizens who could put pressure on police and demand justice.

The killer also appeared to have a racial bias. His victims were either Caucasian or Asian. There were no blacks and no Hispanics among those killed. In fact, police noted, there appeared to be a disproportionate number of Asians and East Indians among his victims. They included Dayle Okazaki, Tsai-Lian Yu, *Harold Wu, Chitat Assawahem* and *Ahmed Zia*. Early in the case, when three of the first four victims were Asian, investigators began to wonder if the killer had not especially targeted them because of their race or ethnicity.

One investigator observed that the Stalker's victims were more likely to appeal to a burglar than a killer-rapist, and the Stalker, for the most part, seemed at least as interested in jewelry and money as he did in murder and rape. He was not exactly a penny-ante thief, either. He'd stolen close to $30,000 in jewelry and cash from the home of *Chitat Assawahem*, after murdering him and sexually assaulting his wife and son. The fact that he stole jewelry, even demanded it, further suggested that he was a professional burglar. Jewelry must be fenced, and a burglar is more likely to have a fence than a killer and rapist.

Burglar or not, the investigator's partner observed, the Stalker was still a ruthless sex-killer. Sex and murder were important aspects of his MO. Curiously, the lives of women were sometimes spared, but, whenever a man was present, the Stalker shot him before attempting anything else. In fact, whether he stole something or not, he still either killed or raped, or both.

One of his victims, *Patty Elaine Higgins*, was a thirty-two-year-old special-education teacher who lived alone with her cocker spaniel. Her partially clad body was found in her bathroom, her throat slashed.

Another was a thirty-five-year-old unmarried female psychologist whom the Stalker raped vaginally, orally, and anally several times over a three-hour period. When the woman, fearing she would be killed after her ravisher had finished with her, tried to engage him in conversation to gain his empathy, she was surprised that he spent the next hour talking to her calmly, then left quietly, after tying her up.

Sometimes, after raping or otherwise sexually assaulting one of his female victims, he would stop to have a snack, or make her cook him a meal.

The Night Stalker was also believed to have been the stranger who snatched at least three children off the streets during the murder-and-rape orgy, sexually assaulted them, then let them go.

At least one nationally known pop psychologist, commenting about the case, reasoned that the shadowy marauder was symbolically looking for the family he never had.

Dr. Martin Blinder, a San Francisco forensic psychiatrist, and an expert psychiatric witness at the celebrated murder trial of Dan White, the San Francisco politician who gunned down San Francisco Mayor George Moscone and fellow Supervisor Harvey Milk in 1978, observed about the killer, "He enters homes under the cover of night and strikes while his victims are asleep. The murders, which have been by beating, throat slashing, and shooting, display a gratuitous violence that indicates that the Stalker delights in the victims' suffering.

"This kind of serial killer selects people who have a sense of vulnerability. They take on people who are particularly helpless. They don't take on John Wayne."

Blinder, author of *Lovers, Killers, Husbands, Wives,* a study of murderers, pointed out that almost all serial killers are relatively young men, seldom over the age of thirty, and must kill over and over again to relieve their tension.

"Compulsivity is a major ingredient in the psychopath. Their first killing makes them feel good, but the euphoria eventually wears off, and they must kill again. The murders get closer and closer together. The killer is like a heroin addict—he needs more and more," Blinder explained to reporters.

He said the serial killer often gets his thrills by taunting police, thereby overcoming feelings of powerlessness and hostility when he gets away with his crimes.

"They get off on the Sherlock Holmes-Professor Moriarty aspect of it," he added. "The serial killer moves around and is rarely apprehended on the basis of good detective work because he is not the standard criminal type."

Blinder also speculated that the Stalker might be a "Rambo gone awry."

"He may well be a Vietnam veteran with a grudge, and

Vietnam may be where he broke down initially and learned to kill," Blinder told reporters.

He pointed out that four of the Night Stalker's first seven murder victims were Asian, a proportion that seemed too high to be random.

It was just the kind of psychological and sociological jargon in which investigative reporters delighted, and they dished out what they were told to the reading and listening public by the trowelful.

Police investigators, on the other hand, were in no mood for "voodoo" psychology. They didn't want to sympathize with their prey, they wanted to catch and convict him. And they didn't want to be told by ivory-tower theorists that their dogged detective work would not pay off.

They didn't want to hear about a disadvantaged childhood or any search the Stalker might be making to find "the family he never had." They were dealing with a fiend, a killer, a rapist, a butcher, and no amount of rationalizing would change that.

Los Angeles County Deputy Sheriff John Brossard told reporters that the police considered the Night Stalker "cold-blooded and extremely dangerous."

"If there is a husband or a male companion involved, the killer immediately tries to put him out of commission and attacks the wife," Brossard said. And there was nothing romantic or sympathetic in that, he added.

Police, however, did admit that this particular serial killer did not fit the norm. Other than his apparent penchant to strike white, yellow, or beige homes located close to freeway ramps, there were few consistencies in his reign of terror.

These inconsistencies were also breeding terror for millions of Los Angeles County residents. They fell asleep fearfully at night, cringing at the sound of barking dogs or rustling leaves, sweltering in a Southern California heat wave behind deadbolts and nailed-shut windows, in dread that they might become the Stalker's next random victims.

But, even their families lived in the same dread as everyone else, area law enforcement officials were pleased by the growing vigilance.

"Better to wake up in a pool of sweat than a pool of blood," one pragmatic police officer observed.

CHAPTER 5

The Terror Builds

TEARS OF RAGE, HUMILIATION, IMPOTENCY, and frustration . . . painful memories that sear the soul and mind . . . red-hot anger that can be cooled only by vengeance for the victim . . .

"I open the cover. I see a bullet hole in the side of his head. I know he's dead. Police and the neighbors pull me out of the house. But I don't want to go out. I am so afraid. . . .

"My son crying. Such a terrible sound. I can't do anything for him because this animal has me. He shot my husband. Why? I do everything he asks. Everything! I can't do anything more. . . .

"He hurt me. Slap me and hurt me and push me on the floor. He does things to me no man has ever done to me. Things I think only one animal would do to another. Things only the Devil does to evil souls in Hell. And the stink, the awful stink. . . .

"This man is Satan. Or maybe Satan has taken his soul. There is no other explanation. He is spawn of the Devil. . . .

"I know him. I know him well. I won't ever forget his face. Never!"

Investigators listened to the litany of agony pouring from the Night Stalker's victims, helpless to console them, except with vague, uncertain assurances that they would catch the intruder and make him pay. Police suffered their own rage and frustration, too. The killer would pay for that, as well, more than one law officer vowed silently.

The media succeeded almost too well in packaging the Night Stalker. Before he had been a shadowy figure who preyed on other people. Despite the headlines, the bloody succession of crimes, the warnings from police, he wasn't quite real. He was something that happened to others, in other places.

Now, there was a name to go with the chilling description. The beast was no longer a mythlike figure. His name made him frighteningly real. Although the odds of the Stalker's selecting any one person as a victim were millions to one—about the same chance as being struck by lightning—thousands of people were suddenly afraid they would be his next victim.

The result was raw panic. There was a run to buy guns, firearms of all types—from CO_2 air pistols to high-powered semiautomatic handguns, shotguns, and everything in between. Sporting-goods stores, pawnshops, and gun shops were deluged by the demand. If the worried valley residents couldn't get guns, they bought knives, Mace, and crowbars. There was a booming business in guard dogs and electronic security systems. Others signed up for karate and kung-fu classes, and joined health spas and gymnasiums to work out and build their muscles and sharpen their reflexes.

An elderly widow owned a big Dalmatian house pet. The dog was so gentle it even allowed neighborhood children to ride on its back. But as the fear built and turned into paranoia, the widow enrolled the animal at a guard-dog training school. When it graduated, the dog was no longer friendly to the kids and, unfortunately, neither was its fearful owner.

Some of the most timid called the police every time they noticed anything going on that looked the least bit suspicious, or whenever they saw an unfamiliar face in their neighborhood. Many people came home a little earlier. They checked the backseats of their cars, looked around carefully when they left a building to make sure they weren't being followed, traveled in pairs and groups, and were suspicious of all strangers.

While law enforcement agencies were forming new plans and employing every manhunting technique they could think of to track down the killer, citizens formed their own protection groups. Neighborhood Watches and informal bands of men and women worked together, checking up on one another with regular telephone calls, providing escorts for lone women and children when they left their homes—and, above all, keeping their collective eye out for strangers. They were scared, and determined to protect themselves and their neighbors. Whether or not it was his intention, the Stalker held a large portion of Los Angeles and Orange counties in a frozen grip of fear that was nearing panic proportions. Nerves were frayed and no one trusted anyone he or she didn't know well.

One young man was jogging along a street in West Los Angeles near seven one morning in mid-August, when he trotted up behind an elderly man and his wife. Suddenly the old man whirled, set his feet firmly in the jogger's path, and raised his arms with the edges of his palms held defensively in front of him in a classic karate stance. Trembling with fear, and angry beyond words, the elderly man eventually calmed down and accepted the jogger's stammered apologies.

Pointing a still-unsteady finger at the jogger, the older man commanded, "Don't you ever run up behind somebody again. This is Los Angeles. Haven't you heard of the Night Stalker?" The young man decided to give up jogging until things settled down.

Area residents no longer went out at night. In some homes, children slept in their parents' bedrooms. Even on the most humid nights, windows were shut and locked as residents without air conditioners substituted safety for comfort. Many residents installed floodlights outside their homes and kept them on all night.

A thirty-four-year-old housewife whose Pakistani neighbor had been murdered by the Stalker was so terrified that she begged her father to build a special door to keep intruders out of their second-floor bedroom. Using plywood, hinges, rope, and metal, he built a storm door that fit over an inside stairway leading to the bedrooms his daughter shared with her husband and children. He also installed a deadbolt so that if they pulled the door shut, they would be locked upstairs with their three children, safe from the Stalker.

One man borrowed a .38-caliber revolver from his father-in-law and took it to bed with him. One night he woke up, convinced the Night Stalker was in the house. He pushed open the door to his bedroom and, panic-stricken, fired a shot through the closet door. The closet was empty, of course. Nevertheless, the nervous homeowner called police, who conducted a fruitless room-to-room search.

Cynthia Roberts, a Northridge housewife, symbolized how heavy the hand of fear held residents in its grip. Northridge was the suburb where the Stalker attacked, then was routed by the Petersens.

"If you were in our house, you'd think we were crazy," Mrs. Roberts told a reporter. "We check our locks and double-check them. If there is a strange car in the neighborhood, my husband will write down the license plate number and call police. He'll even go up to the car and ask them what they're doing," she explained.

The woman added that she would not turn into her driveway if she saw a strange car in her cul-de-sac.

"No way am I going to show anyone where I live unless I know where they're from," she said.

North Hollywood community relations officer Dennis Atkinson told interviewers that he was often busy all day answering phone calls from frightened residents. In the evenings, he helped them conduct Neighborhood Watch meetings.

"We'd get calls like 'My God, I live in a yellow house and we're only four blocks from the freeway.' We were all scared. Even the cops were scared," he recalled.

North Hollywood officers conducted eight Neighborhood Watch meetings in July 1985, said Atkinson. A month later, in August, at the height of the Stalker's reign of terror, they conducted forty-six.

The Guardian Angels started a San Gabriel Valley chapter and quickly signed up forty new members. The group initiated a "house-sitting" program in which Guardian Angels would sit up all night watching over the homes of frightened people.

For the first time in anyone's memory, real terror descended over Temple City, a town of 30,000 in the San Gabriel Valley, thirteen miles northeast of Los Angeles. It was a quiet, peaceful, family-oriented community that could have been a model for a typical American town in the 1950s, a Norman Rockwell painting come to life. But in a matter of a few weeks, the Stalker changed all that.

"I never before kept lights on while I slept," one woman told reporters. "But you start to freak yourself out. You start to believe you're hearing noises."

In Temple City and similar communities, there was another emotion mixed with the fear. Anger over the threat stemmed not only from obvious disgust with the killings, but also strong resentment over the extent to which their previously serene lives had been altered.

"I hate him for creating this fear in me," a single

mother confessed to an inquiring journalist. "He has no right to do this to people. We have a right to live our lives in peace. He's a monster, a beast!"

Hillary Johnson, like a lot of Temple City residents, made a point of being home before dark. She kept her radio on, and went to bed in fear.

"Before this creep came along, I felt gutsy being alone. I thought I could do everything alone. I felt I was an independent woman," the forty-one-year-old secretary recalled. "It made me angry to know there was someone out there, affecting what I did."

To some, there were aspects of their fear that were worse than death at the hands of the Stalker.

A University of Southern California junior, after having read about some of the sexual torment the Stalker had forced women to endure during his attacks, swore, "He will have to kill me before I'd let him do *that* to me."

The father of a teen-aged daughter insisted on driving her to and from high school every day. She could date only inside her own home, or at daytime school functions on weekends. And her father or mother drove her to and from the date.

One husband handed his beautiful young wife a cyanide capsule and told her she should swallow it if the Stalker broke into their home, killed him, and tried to rape or force other sexual perversions on her.

There was an up side to the public's sudden, frenzied awareness of the prowling evil and danger among them, however. Overly suspicious residents were producing a record number of leads for law officers. The police received more than 1,000 tips and leads over one two-day period. Most turned into dead ends. But there was yet one other advantage.

Concern over the Night Stalker's atrocities, increased citizen awareness of crime, and the flurry of police activity were putting the pressure on the average nickel-and-dime criminals. Crime in Los Angeles County dropped by as much as a third in some communities as smart criminals stayed at home. Those foolish enough to venture out, especially burglars who specialized in suburban break-ins, were often apprehended before they could even finish jimmying a door or forcing open a window.

"People are armed and staying up late," one police officer told a reporter. "Burglars want this guy caught like everyone else. He's making it bad for their business."

The Los Angeles County Board of Supervisors tightened the screw a turn or two by offering a $10,000 reward for information leading to the capture and conviction of the Stalker. Other rewards were to follow: The Los Angeles City Council offered a $25,000 reward; the city of Arcadia put $5,000 into the kitty; San Francisco and California Governor George Deukmejian each threw in $10,000.

As might be expected, police officials were concerned about the large number of guns on the streets, in the hands of inexperienced, trigger-happy men and women. Sooner or later, they feared, someone was going to shoot someone else by mistake. It was a volatile situation.

One police captain said, "If something sets somebody off, we could have a massacre out there. Once one guy starts to shoot, everyone will start." Then, with a shrug and a sardonic grin, he added, "If that happens, maybe the Stalker will get caught in the crossfire."

Most police departments welcomed citizen involvement in the effort to collar the killer, even though they were distressed about the burgeoning citizen arsenal. As long as there were so many alert and suspicious people out there, it made good sense to put them to use. The police department in Monterey Park, scene of at least three of the Stalker's attacks, asked residents to keep their eyes and ears open, and to report what they saw.

"We can't do it alone," a high-ranking police officer said.

With extra investigators available, the sheriff was able

to follow a lead that had developed a month earlier. A business card found in a stolen Toyota used in a child-abduction case led detectives to a Los Angeles–area dentist. The dentist recognized the sketch they showed him and said he had a patient who matched the Stalker's description.

Unfortunately, the man had used a false name and paid in cash. The alias was one the Stalker had used before. Police took the man's dental charts and began checking other dentists in the area.

Police said that the Toyota used in the child abduction had been stopped for a routine traffic violation off the Glendale Freeway near Eagle Rock. The driver fled on foot from the car and escaped, despite a search by Los Angeles city police. The fugitive fit the Stalker's description. The incident occurred on July 19, the day before Maxson and Lela Kneiding were murdered in Glendale.

Despite the increase in manpower for the hunt, Neal Johnson, acting Arcadia police chief, said he doubted that an arrest would result from the investigative efforts, despite their unprecedented intensity. Instead, he conjectured, the break would occur when someone recognized the Stalker's haunting, scarecrow face, which was now burned into the public mind by composite sketches being published in newspapers and shown on television.

"The biggest thing this creep has going against him is that he is so frigging ugly someone is sure to spot him," said one police officer.

Arcadia, like other communities in the Los Angeles County area, was experiencing the same terror. Citizens were hypersensitive to anything and anyone unusual. At times both watchful residents and eager police officers became overzealous. Any tall, skinny male with bad teeth and shaggy hair could create panic merely by walking up to a bus stop or crossing a street.

"One poor guy was stopped five times," Johnson later recalled.

One night a rookie patrolman was making a routine traffic stop in San Marino, an affluent suburb of Los Angeles, when, suddenly, the young driver threw open the door of his car and raced away on foot.

Even as the officer grimly ran after the elusive suspect, he thought, *Oh, my God! He looks just like the Night Stalker!*

The fleet-footed youth disappeared into the sheltering darkness of a quiet residential street, but, within minutes, the patrolman's radio call for assistance had brought a dozen patrol cars. The streets were quickly blocked off. Helicopters were sent aloft. Minutes after the traffic stop, the peace of the neighborhood had been shattered by the shrill scream of police squad-car sirens, and the roar of helicopter engines and rotor blades. Searchlights from the helicopters hovering overhead like angry dragonflies turned night into day.

Sheriff's deputies, backed by dogs and armed with shotguns, began a door-to-door search. A deputy used a bullhorn to warn residents, "Stay inside! Lock your windows and doors!"

Dozens of heavily armed officers and dogs moved slowly and methodically, closing a ring on the fugitive they suspected might be the Night Stalker. In their homes, residents stood fretfully behind locked doors, or peered fearfully from behind window curtains. The helicopters sometimes swept so low over the houses that wooden shutters vibrated on windows and dishes rattled on shelves.

Then, police had their quarry. Dogs found him squatted down behind a row of bushes. He was a badly frightened seventeen-year-old who looked nothing like descriptions of the Night Stalker.

"Why the hell did you run?" an angry lieutenant demanded.

The teen-ager stammered that he thought he was wanted on a juvenile warrant. The disgusted officer turned him over to juvenile authorities, and the manhunt was called off.

Investigators had learned that the Stalker appeared to prefer small-caliber handguns as weapons, including a .22-caliber revolver. The small-caliber weapons explained why many of the Stalker's victims survived despite being shot at such close range.

Unfortunately, in California, almost anyone over the age of eighteen could buy a handgun at a pawnshop, sporting-goods store, or gun shop. The information about the guns helped police tie together killings, and once the killer was caught, the guns could help convict him.

The terror still seethed and bubbled on the streets, but police were growing more and more confident that a break was coming very soon. The evidence and potential evidence continued to mount. They would soon have either the key piece of evidence they sought, or some citizen would spot the killer. It was just a matter of time.

But Dr. Joseph Tupin, a professor of psychiatry at the University of California, Davis, warned that a high price might be extracted from citizens for the spring-tight tension that pervaded the area.

An expert on serial killings, he said the terror spawned by the Stalker's shocking murders and brutal sexual assaults could cause permanent damage to the self-image of stricken Southern California communities.

Dr. Tupin explained that although tension usually eases after the cause for terror is eliminated—in this case, when the Stalker would finally be caught—some communities take years to forget, and for things to return to normal. There was also a possibility that in some cases the residue of fear and terror may never leave.

CHAPTER 6

Task Force

THE FIRST MAN TO SUSPECT THAT SOUTHERN California might have another serial killer on its hands was Det. Sgt. Frank Salerno, one of the top homicide investigators in the Los Angeles County Sheriff's Department.

In June 1985, Salerno, a twenty-year veteran in the department and one of the lead investigators on the Hillside Strangler case almost ten years earlier, sent a memo and six homicide reports to Capt. Robert Grimm.

The reports dealt with five unsolved murder cases that had occurred in the county since March. The memo noted certain similarities Salerno had detected among the killings. The investigator had been keeping a wary eye on the cases for the past two months.

The memo not only suggested the slayings might be connected, but that it would be a good idea to check with the Los Angeles Police Department to find out if it had any similar unsolved murders during the past several months.

Later, Salerno said there were many aspects of the homicides that aroused his suspicions, despite some inconsistencies. Given the fact that California appears to spawn thrill killers, and that Los Angeles already had three known cases of serial killings under investigation at that time, Salerno's early detection of the Night Stalker probably had much to do with the veteran detective's experience. He had dealt before with serial killers, and his years as an investigator had equipped him with a finely tuned intuitive and deductive mind. He was a good cop, and a good detective.

Grimm recognized the wisdom in Salerno's suggestion to check with LAPD. No one wanted a situation similar to the Hillside Strangler case, when both the LAPD and the Los Angeles sheriff's deputies worked their investigations alone and independent of each other.

The result for the police agencies had been missed opportunities, confusion, and embarrassment. Investigators from both departments learned later that one of the killer duo, Kenneth Bianchi, had been named in at least five tips very early in the case. But, since the tips were spread between the two departments, and no one had compared information, Bianchi and his cousin, Angelo Buono, continued to kill with impunity until they were at last caught months later. Even then it wasn't Los Angeles area police who broke the case, but small town police in Bellingham, Washington, where Bianchi had moved and resumed his killing ways.

Grimm, however, anticipated a problem in contacting the LAPD. He agreed with Salerno that there were strong indications that a serial killer was out there, and that he had to be stopped. But if he started to communicate with other agencies, such as the LAPD, the press was certain to find out and might hinder the investigation with premature publicity.

There were good points and bad points in press coverage. Sometimes the media—both newspapers and television—handled stories about serial killers in ways that provoked public panic. On the other hand, if there really was a serial killer out there, police wanted people to be warned so they could take extra precautions. Many times, too, an alert public provided helpful extra eyes and ears for police.

Grimm looked over the unsolved homicide reports collected by Detective Salerno. The victims were Dayle Okazaki, Tsai-Lian Yu, Vincent and Maxine Zazzara, *Harold Wu,* and *Malvia Keller.*

The homicide captain noticed that fingerprints collected at some of the crime scenes matched, as did the small-caliber bullets recovered in the shooting cases. There were similarities in methods of entry of the burglarized homes—and in some instances bizarre occult symbols that are generally associated with Satan worship were left behind.

In each case in which there was a survivor, the killer was described as a tall, thin male with rotting teeth and curly hair. Most witnesses thought he was Hispanic.

Grimm was an experienced police officer and he was no stranger to homicide investigations. He knew that killers crushed skulls, cut flesh to the bone, and burned victims alive. Nevertheless, reviewing Salerno's collection of case files, he was appalled by the needless brutality that had accompanied the killings. These were not random burglaries. The usual burglar, who is trapped and kills from fear or what he perceives to be the necessity of the moment, doesn't terrorize, mangle, and sexually abuse victims with such obvious enjoyment. The burglar who committed these crimes was different. He was a special case. A homicidal monster.

Grimm called in Det. Russell Uloth, who had been the investigating officer in the Zazzara slayings. Uloth, a twenty-three-year veteran on the force, verbally recounted details of the bloodbath for his boss. Mrs. Zazzara had died from the bullet wound in her head, and there had been no need for her gross mutilation. And not only had the fiend gouged her eyes out, but he had apparently taken them with him, Uloth said.

The baseball cap and its AC/DC emblem also caught Grimm's attention. "What's this all about?" he asked Sergeant Salerno, who told him that AC/DC was a rock group popular with kids, and that one of its albums had Satanic imagery on the cover. He said he believed there was a Satanic connection in the hideous slayings.

Grimm also noted the inconsistencies, including the different methods used to kill and slaughter the victims, the wide variation of ages, and various ethnic groups involved. Nevertheless, he agreed with Salerno that another serial killer was apparently on the loose.

It was time to organize a task force of the best investigative talent that could be collected from the sheriff's department and other area law enforcement agencies. The obvious choice to head it up was the sharp-eyed, quick-witted homicide sergeant, Frank Salerno.

Salerno set up the Night Stalker task force in a homicide-division office. Initially he was given a computer and assigned a few detectives. He would eventually have as many as twenty-four detectives under his command. One was Det. Gil Carillo, who had investigated the Okazaki murder and had computer experience.

In a short while, the LAPD would organize its own task force and join with Salerno's group. With smaller cities in Los Angeles County joining in, the combined forces reached 200 investigators by the end of August. It became the largest task force ever assembled in the county, including the combined city-county team that investigated the infamous Hillside Strangler case in the 1970s.

Two months before County Sheriff Sherman Block made his announcement, in August, of a serial killer at work, Grimm made a preliminary announcement. Few reporters attended the first press conference.

Salerno scarcely had time to get his task force organized before the killer struck again. Thirty-two-year-old Patty Elaine Higgins was murdered in Arcadia. Her death was followed a few days later by that of seventy-five-year-old Mary Louise Cannon, another Arcadia resident. Three days later, sixty-one-year-old Joyce Lucille Nelson of Monterey Park was added. Finally, there was the terrible 24-hour period—July 20—when Maxson and Lela Kneiding, and *Chitat Assawahem* were murdered and *Assawahem's* wife was sexually abused.

It was then that Sheriff Block decided it was time for a full-scale public alert and, with Grimm, announced that Los Angeles County was once again being terrorized by a virulent serial killer-rapist. This time there were more reporters than policemen at the press conference.

Carillo's computer was operating eighteen hours a day. Investigators consulted a variety of national experts on serial killers, and even some who claimed expertise in Satanic-inspired killings.

Among the experts contacted were members of the Federal Bureau of Investigation's Behavioral Science Unit, the so-called "Mind Squad," or "Mind Hunters" stationed at the FBI Academy in Quantico, Virginia.

Among their jobs, the unit profiles serial killers and other murderers and high-profile criminals for state and local police departments. The profiling program was started in 1977 by veteran FBI Agent Howard Teten, who taught criminology at the academy. When former students began contacting him with questions involving dead-end investigations, Teten started a file on the cases. As the file grew, he began to notice intriguing patterns emerging.

The psychological profile team, dubbed the "Mind Hunters," has been so successful in determining characteristics and backgrounds of suspects that state and local police agencies have also begun to use them to track down a variety of other criminals, including rapists and child molesters.

The FBI service, which is free to agencies that call on it for help, reports that about seventy percent of the individuals convicted of profiled crimes match the information developed by the Mind Hunters.

At about the time Salerno first picked up the trail of the Night Stalker, FBI Special Agent Roger L. Depue told the *Washington Post,* "We believe that in most crime cases, the killer leaves his signature. If you're sensitive to what those things are, you can construct the profile of a killer."

A profile of a serial killer dubbed by the press as the Atlanta Child Killer put together by FBI psychologist John Douglas fit Wayne Williams, who was eventually arrested and convicted of two of the murders, almost to a T.

Douglas theorized:

"Your offender is familiar with the crime-scene areas he is in, or has resided in this area. In addition, his past or present occupation caused him to drive through these areas on different occasions . . . the sites of the deceased are not random or 'chance' disposal areas. He realizes these areas are remote and not frequently traveled by others."

Police found:

In doing free-lance work for a television station in 1978, Williams shot one assignment at Redwine Road and another at Interstate 285 and Washington Road, near Redwine Road. Two bodies were found on Redwine, and another nearby. Other burial sites of victims also proved to be locations where Williams had photography and videotaping assignments.

Douglas theorized:

"A frequent tactic [used to abduct streetwise kids without being seen] is offenders impersonating the law enforcement officer. He shows concern for the victim's safety, places him into his personal vehicle, and promises to take the victim home. He may conversely admonish the victim for walking the streets at night, and threaten to arrest the victim."

Police found:

Neighborhood youngsters thought Williams was a policeman because he drove "detective-looking" cars, carried a badge, and gave them orders.

Douglas theorized:

"In all probability your offender is black. Generally, offenders of this type are fixated on same-race victims."

Police found:

Williams was black. All the victims he was accused of killing were black. Witnesses testified that he had a deep disdain for lower-class blacks, whom he called derogatory names.

Douglas theorized:

"Your offender has, in all probability, a prior criminal history for aggressive and/or assaultive behavior. . . . He will always carry a weapon of some sort on his person and has threatened to use it on others in the past."

Police found:

Williams's only prior criminal record was for impersonating an officer, unauthorized use of emergency equipment, and filing a false stolen-auto report to police. At the time of his arrest on the first two charges, he had a twelve-gauge shotgun in his four-door Plymouth. Acquaintances, however, said he liked to "scuffle" with them, and one said Williams liked to spray him with Mace.

Douglas theorized:

"His favorite colors are black, dark blue, and brown. This can be observed particularly in the clothes he wears, and the car he drives."

Police found:

Williams favored drab browns. His cars were faded white, burgundy, light blue, silver gray, brown, yellowish brown, white, and blue.

Douglas theorized:

"This offender in all probability is single. He has always had difficulties relating to members of the opposite sex. As a youth, he was sexually abused. . . . The odds are high that he has spent time in juvenile detention homes, as well as other forms of incarceration."

Police found:

Williams was single, he was rarely seen with a woman. However, there was no evidence that he had ever been sexually abused, or that he had ever spent time in juvenile detention.

Douglas theorized:

"Your offender will generally fall between ages twenty-five and twenty-nine."

Police found:

Williams was twenty-three when he was arrested.

Douglas sat through Williams's nine week trial and concluded afterward that he was "very much like other serial killers researched and interviewed in the past by the FBI's Behavioral Sciences Unit."

Lt. John Decker, commander of a New York City police task force, said the FBI profiles helped tremendously in solving four sex crimes. "They've worked in many homicides as well," he added. "In one ritualistic murder of a female, our leads and our witnesses said it was done by two Hispanics. The FBI said it was a single killer, and he was white. It turned out the profile was right. We arrested and convicted him."

A few years ago the residents of Columbus, Georgia, were reeling from more than a half-dozen rape-murders of elderly white women. The murderer entered their homes during the night and sexually assaulted them before strangling them with their stockings. The local press quickly dubbed the killer as the Stocking Strangler.

The community's already shaky nerves were further rattled when the Columbus police and local news media began receiving letters and telephone calls from a person who identified himself as the spokesman for the "Forces of Evil." In one letter to the chief of police, the Forces of Evil identified itself as an organization of seven people.

The letter writer claimed to be holding a Columbus woman captive. He named her as Gail Jackson, and said she was black. The letter was printed in block letters on army stationery. It also claimed the group had information that the local coroner suspected the murderer of the white women was black.

The writer said that since the strangler was believed to be black, the group had decided to try to catch him themselves or put more pressure on authorities. At that point, Gail Jackson was still living, the writer claimed. But he vowed that if the strangler wasn't caught by 1 June, she would be murdered and her body dumped alongside a local road.

The writer threatened that more and more black women would be killed until the killer of the white women was caught.

A few weeks later, the body of Gail Jackson was found some one hundred yards from Fort Benning.

The Georgia Bureau of Investigation stepped in and asked the FBI profilers for help.

The Mind Hunters, after analyzing the letter and details of the crime scene, surmised that the Forces of Evil was not an organization but a single black male, twenty-five to thirty years old.

Although almost anyone who wanted to could easily obtain army stationery, the FBI decided that the letter was, in fact, probably written by someone in the army. He was most likely an enlisted man who was either a military policeman or an artillery man stationed at Fort Benning.

He had a schizoid personality, and may have been responsible not only for the murders of the black women, but of the white women as well.

The GBI began questioning soldiers at Fort Benning

and, two days later, Columbus police identified William Henry Hance as the man they wanted.

Twenty-six-year-old Hance matched the profile almost exactly. He was an enlisted man and was assigned to an artillery unit. Through comparison of handwriting, voice analysis, and other physical evidence, he was tied to the threats and to the murder of Jackson. He was not, however, tied to the murders of the white women. It was many months later before a local career criminal, Carlton Gary, was arrested and convicted of several of the murders.

The profiling technique seems simple. Members of the Quantico unit have analyzed hundreds of murder scenes from photographs and details supplied by police, and have matched the characteristics of the suspects who were subsequently caught and arrested.

In the Columbus, Georgia, murders of the white and black women, slip-ups by the killers, and careful investigative work were required before Hance, then Gary, was identified.

Hance initially managed to sew some confusion among police about his race, but the FBI profilers, reviewing the syntax of the letter, determined that, based on reviews of similar letters, the writer was probably black.

Using the same approach, the profilers decided that he was in the army, based on the terminology and the format of his letter, including such examples as writing a date as "1 June" instead of "June 1."

The Mind Hunters have supplemented crime scene information with information gathered from interviews with scores of criminals, including such high-profile lawbreakers as David R. Berkowitz (Son of Sam); Charles Manson and his follower, Lynette Alice "Squeaky" Fromme; Sirhan Sirhan, Robert Kennedy's assassin; and Sarah Jane Moore, who pulled a gun on then President Gerald Ford.

These interviews now number into the hundreds, and

are used to help pinpoint the types of individuals who commit similar crimes and the methods they use. They also enable the FBI to provide tips to police on what to look for at crime scenes.

"When we went to New York to talk to Berkowitz, he told us that on the nights when he couldn't find a victim to kill, he would go back to the scene of an old crime to relive that crime and to fantasize about it," explained Special Agent Robert K. Ressler: "Now, that's a heck of a piece of information to store somewhere, to see whether other serial killers do the same thing."

In analyzing crimes, the profilers look for patterns: A rape victim with a single slash across the throat indicates that the murderer has killed before. The more brutal a facial attack, the closer the relationship between victim and killer. A blitz style of assault indicates a youthful killer who feels threatened by his victims and believes that he must subdue them immediately. A slower, more sadistic murder points to a slightly older killer, possibly in his twenties or thirties. If the killer used whatever weapon was handy, such as a venetian-blind cord, for example, the act was probably impulsive and the murderer lived nearby and came on foot.

And some killers do return to the scene of their crimes or take souvenirs. As a result, the FBI has advised local police to watch cemeteries where victims are buried, sometimes even to place a microphone on the tombstone. A listening device in 1979 picked up a graveyard plea from a guilt-ridden killer for mercy and forgiveness from his victim. The killer even provided his name. Several murderers have been caught when they returned to put flowers on the graves of their victims.

According to the Mind Hunters, the typical serial killer is an eldest son, has average or above-average intelligence, and has a father who is generally an unskilled laborer, although steadily employed.

About seventy percent of the cases they have studied

show a history of alcohol abuse in the killers' families, and about thirty-three percent have a record of family involvement in drug abuse. Most of the serial killers were mistreated during childhood and had unhappy or unsatisfactory relationships with their fathers. About half reported cold or lukewarm relationships with their mothers.

Serial killers also appear to indulge themselves in violent or sadistic fantasies. Eighty-one percent of the serial killers studied by the FBI put pornography at the top of their reading list.

Female serial killers on the scale of the Hillside Strangler and the Night Stalker apparently are rare. Most females who commit multiple homicides are "black widow" slayers who murder a succession of lovers, husbands, or other family members, usually for insurance money or other types of monetary rewards. Or they are nurses or other medical personnel who become self-appointed "death angels" and murder ailing babies, the elderly, or the desperately ill, usually in misguided efforts to end their pain and suffering.

So far as is known, there have been no random female serial killers working alone without male companions, who indulge in gratuitous slaughter or needless brutalization of victims for thrills.

There are also several popular misconceptions about serial killers that sometimes throw investigators off the track, FBI profilers say. One is the idea that anyone who would perform a seemingly senseless, brutal murder must be insane. The truth is, very few brutal killers are insane.

Special Agent Ressler has concluded from interviews with such apparent human monsters as Manson and Berkowitz that many vicious killers can present themselves as likeable, intelligent people if they wish. "The image you have is of a person with fangs and drooling." But that's not necessarily true. Manson, for example, can be a fascinating conversationalist, he pointed out. And

Ted Bundy, who slaughtered more than twenty young women from Washington to Florida, was literate and charming. And he was intelligent. He frustrated the justice system for ten years before one of his death sentences was carried out and he was finally executed in Florida's electric chair, "Old Sparky," in January 1989.

The Mind Hunters say "pop" psychologists have gotten criminals used to the idea that they can invent psychological excuses for their action and avoid prosecution. Ressler said he makes it clear that he's not interested in psychological explanations when questioning a suspect. He told Berkowitz point-blank that he was not interested in, nor did he believe, any of the killer's fanciful baloney about a dog ordering him to murder six young women. Later, Berkowitz admitted he manufactured the story about the dog and used it as an excuse to justify his actions.

The investigators also consulted with other national experts, including Harvey Schlossberg, a forensic psychologist and former New York City police officer, who explained: "A serial killing is just like a sex crime. There's a buildup of tension, and killing is like a sex release for the killer."

Dr. Park Elliott, an associate professor of law and psychiatry at the University of Virginia, agreed with Schlossberg that sex and sadism are a part of a typical serial killer's mental makeup. "Almost without exception, serial killers are sexual sadists and psychopaths," he told a *Washington Post* reporter.

Psychopaths, often referred to as sociopaths, usually show delinquent conduct from childhood, and may suffer, in part, from a genetic disorder that deadens the nervous system's ability to feel fear. As a result, serial killers act boldly and often believe they cannot be caught.

Sadists who act out their violent sexual fantasies usually find that the pleasure was not as great as they had hoped, Elliott explained, so they try different victims or increasingly more violent acts in search of the expected thrill.

Other experts thought the Night Stalker deliberately sought and reveled in publicity about the attacks. Still others believed the killer received progressively less satisfaction from each murder and, like a drug addict, was compelled to kill more often to satisfy his desires.

Captain Grimm and Sergeant Salerno found some of the theories interesting but not practical enough for down-to-earth police work.

Profiles don't catch criminals, Salerno said later. It's careful investigative work, long hours, informants' tips, and a lot of luck—such as a slip-up on the part of the criminal, he said.

Wayne Williams was a case in point. Although he was correctly profiled by the Mind Hunters, he was not caught until after he tossed a body off a bridge where police were on a stakeout. (Both of those he was convicted of killing were young adults.)

No profile catches a criminal by itself. And, too often, the profile may be so broad that many people fit it. Even if the profile had provided the name of the Night Stalker, the police still would have to find him—and in an area as highly populated and spread out as Los Angeles County, that could prove a monumental task.

The Stalker's murderous toll was mounting in direct proportion to the frustration and anger of investigators. With "twenty-four of the best detectives in the country," as Salerno later described some key members of his task force, the investigators felt they were just a step away from solving the case.

The file of clues and evidence on the Night Stalker continued to grow as lawmen sifted carefully through every tip and every scrap of information, fed to them from thousands of telephone calls that came pouring in.

They had already pieced together certain helpful information from crime scenes and backbreaking legwork about the Night Stalker's methods.

But in late July, police added another important clue. When they searched an East Los Angeles area where they believed a Satanic cult met, they found tennis-shoe prints that matched prints left at some of the Night Stalker crime scenes.

The tennis-shoe prints and an unfortunate personal physical resemblance to descriptions of the Night Stalker made for some hairy moments for a twenty-three-year-old senior at California State University at San Bernadino.

Sheriff's deputies picked up *Jerry Nigel* as he stepped off a bus in San Bernadino and questioned him for several hours before he was able to convince them he was not the man they were looking for, and had no involvement with Satanic cults.

"He was so close to the composite drawing that we had to stop him and ask questions," explained San Bernadino County sheriff's deputy Jimmy Watkins.

When he was taken into custody, *Nigel* was also carrying a pair of size-eleven Reebok hightop sneakers, which added to police suspicions. When they showed *Nigel* a picture of the killer's footprint, the young man was shocked.

"After they showed me that, I was stunned. I looked at the bottom of my Reeboks and it was the same."

During the early part of the investigation, area newspapers and television stations constantly pressed lawmen for new leads and developments, while criticizing them because they had not brought the Night Stalker to justice. Finally, it was the turn of the police to use the newspapers.

One of the techniques suggested by FBI profilers for local police, when they feel a nameless killer is jumpy or under a great deal of stress, is to promote stories in the news media to indicate that investigators are closing in on the killer's identity. The stories don't have to be strictly true, but with luck they can flush a fugitive from hiding, or make him commit devastating mistakes.

There have been many cases when heavy publicity hinting that police were closing in on a killer made stress so unbearable for the murderer that he abruptly changed his behavior. When he does that, he can lose control of his evasive skills. Consequently, he is easier to catch.

Almost hourly, police tipped off reporters to new leads, some real and others not quite so legitimate. Finally, a police spokesman told newsmen with seeming great confidence that it was only a matter of time—probably hours —before an arrest would be made.

The Stalker apparently did feel the heat, and he began to look for new hunting grounds.

Fear of the killer's mobility increased. Police departments from across the state were keeping an eye on the Stalker killings. They requested information on what he looked like and how he operated. It was not unusual for a killer to seek safer environs when pressure became too great in one area, as it was in Los Angeles County.

Suddenly, the ominous shadow of the Night Stalker spread across all of California. Rumors in Sacramento suggested the governor was considering putting out a statewide alert for the killer.

Police stepped up their pressure. Leaflets and posters with the Stalker's composite sketch and description were put in grocery stores, gas stations, and any other place where they might be seen by the widest cross-section of people. By the end of August, the police fliers were in almost every public place from Orange County to San Francisco.

Hundreds of police officers poured into the streets, from Santa Ana to Sacramento, with mug shots of suspects whom Los Angeles lawmen had not yet located for questioning.

Detectives continued to probe. They started to work on the Satanic connection, and found an interesting song in the heavy-metal band AC/DC's album, *Highway to Hell.*

The song "Night Prowler", while not containing any Satanic references, seemed tailor-made for the Stalker. The lyrics talked of someone lying down, fearful of shadows and noises, terrified of shutting off the light. And they spoke of a midnight prowler slipping stealthily into the room, while the frightened victim lay waiting in dread, unable to move.

CHAPTER 7

Satan's Work

THE NIGHT STALKER HAD A THEME SONG—an anthem. The media loved it. With their usual thirst for sensationalism, and eye on circulation and rating build-ups, newspaper and television reporters latched on to the "Satan Connection" and played it for all it was worth.

"Did the Devil make him do it?" one newspaper asked in a headline.

"Rock and Roll Feeds Night Stalker's Satanic Cravings," another trumpeted.

Local television talk shows and news programs featured "experts" who explained how heavy-metal bands were promoting a "worldwide" Satanic movement bent on perverting Christian values.

And heavy-metal bands were Satan's missionaries! It was a beautiful combination, a tailor-made lure certain to attract conservatives—the John Wayne/Ronald Reagan/Barry Goldwater element—as readers and listeners.

The religious fundamentalists loved it, too. A wedding of Satan and the devilish heavy-metal rock bands, with the Night Stalker as its unholy offspring, was indeed an occasion to praise the Lord.

From leading evangelists to backwoods Bible-thumpers, the cry rang out: Rock and roll is Satan's music, and it is tempting our youth to the path of the Evil One!

They laid the blame for teen drug abuse, murder, suicide, depression, and rebellion against the "old-time" morality on rock and roll, and the Satanic plague it promoted.

Fundamental devotees in the chrome and plexiglass air-conditioned cathedrals of Orange County and the San Fernando Valley, as well as the virtue-white modest churches around Bakersfield, responded with a resounding "Amen. Praise Jesus!"

It was an hour of triumph for the righteous, for the prophets of the old-time religion. And fearful Southern Californians, especially the middle-aged and elderly, flocked to listen to them.

Confused by a world moving much too quickly, yearning for the simplicity and security of the Eisenhower years of the 1950s, they sought refuge, if only for a few hours, from an era that could spawn a Night Stalker. Fire and brimstone, good and evil—without the shades of gray in between: these they could understand.

Preachers warned the faithful to be vigilant in watching over their sons and daughters, their grandsons and granddaughters, lest they be seduced by the evil, because they are the prizes Satan seeks. As preachers thumped Bibles on their pulpits and looked out upon their flock, they saw faces that were drawn and wide-eyed with fright and concern at the darkness that had overtaken their community.

The churchgoers raised their voices in song, praising God with His own beloved music, doing their best to drown out the devilish din created by Satan's musicians, the rock-and-roll bands. Congregants stood shoulder-to-shoulder as they belted out such familiar, comforting hymns of their youth as "Rock of Ages," "Onward Christian Soldiers," and "The Old Rugged Cross."

Smalltown preachers with holes in the soles of their shoes and sophisticated evangelists in five-hundred-dollar suits sounded the same clarion call of warning: Satan spreads his message of evil in rock-and-roll music, they cautioned. Sometimes the evil is plain and clear, as in the Night Stalker's favorite, "Night Prowler." But at other times, they cautioned, one must be even more vigilant, because the messages are cunningly hidden. Records, tapes, and CDs must be played backwards and listened to carefully before lyrics praising Satan or encouraging drug abuse can be recognized by the vigilant.

The reputed messages were chillingly demonic. One rock band was accused of cutting a record with the admonition: "Satan, Satan, Satan. He is God! He is God!" A perverse message blamed on another rock band targeted by the preachers reputedly announces, "I will sing because I live with Satan."

But the fears of a demonic conspiracy and sinister assault on conventional religious and social mores were not confined to heavy metal or reputed Satanic rock bands. The fearful are convinced that the evil is much more pervasive.

"Rock stars want to subvert the minds of our young people, to destroy their morals, and lead them into drugs and sex," a famous television evangelist cautioned.

Television talk shows brought in international experts on Satanism. Michael Buschmann, a West German theologian, claimed top rock bands were being inspired by Satan, and that rock-and-roll songs are the hymns of Hell.

Buschmann said the Devil's words in rock songs take over the subconscious and make young people turn to drugs and join Devil cults.

The West German theologian claimed many of the top rock-group hits have hidden messages that can be heard only when the record is played in reverse.

Devil sects, he claimed, had increased at a frightening

rate over the last ten to fifteen years. In the U.S., there were at least four hundred Satanic churches.

There were many people, especially in Southern California's weird, flaky subculture, who literally believed the Night Stalker was the Devil's tool—if not the Devil himself. But not all the believers were part of the state's space-cadet corps.

Some vocal Pentecostals and other critics claim that the name of the Night Stalker's favorite heavy-metal group, AC/DC, was not inspired by the two types of electrical current, alternating and direct, nor by use of the letters in common slang as a term for bisexuality. They insist the letters are really an acronym for "Anti-Christ, Devil's Child," or "After Christ, the Devil Comes." These are claims which those in the music business scoff at as absurd.

Defenders of the band point out that heavy metal is played with loud electrical sound, so the true meaning of AC/DC as the group's name is obvious. It is used as an electrical term. The band's logo even includes an electrical volt.

Writing in the now-defunct *Los Angeles Herald Examiner,* music critic Mikal Gilmore declared of AC/DC, "The group has never hinted at any other possible interpretation of its name—not even the obvious bisexual reference that the initials also sometimes stand for."

And AC/DC bassist Cliff Williams told a reporter for an article in the *San Francisco Chronicle* during a telephone interview that attacks on the band were insulting, pointing out that the musicians themselves were "family men. We've got wives and children who are at home and unprotected," he asserted.

The Australian rock group, which was considered for a time by many heavy-metal fans as over the hill, appears to have acquired its troublesome reputation for deviltry in part because of its 1979 hit album title, *Highway to Hell,* and for the cover photo showing one of the band members wearing a pair of horns, while another bands-man sports a pentagram pendant.

Some detractors of heavy-metal, and especially critics of AC/DC, even attempted to draw a link between Satanism and the tragic death of Bon Scott, former lead singer for the band. Scott succumbed to heavy drinking in 1980, but he was no Satanist. The raspy-voiced lyrics sung by Scott treated sex, liquor and the rock-and-roll lifestyle with a cynical humor that angered many critics of the popular music style, nevertheless.

But growing fears of lurid Satanic practices in our society are being fueled by more than the revulsion of some people to heavy-metal rock bands and their music. The hideous Night Stalker killings were occurring while the country was awash in reports of ritualistic cattle mutilations, grave and church desecrations, mysterious disappearances of infants and other young children, widespread sacrifice of animals—and unconfirmed suspicions of ceremonial baby killings by blood-mad cultists. Many of these anomalies were being blamed on Satanists.

At the time of the Stalker murders, one man from Santa Rosa, California, became so upset over the use of Social Security numbers, which he believed were "the mark of the beast," that he refused to allow his daughter to apply for one.

The Book of Revelations, he contended, forbids the use of universal numbers to identify human beings because the numbers are the "mark of the beast" by which the Antichrist seeks to control humans.

Many fundamental Christians—spurred by the Night Stalker and other crimes attributed to Satanists—saw the fulfillment of Biblical prophecies dealing with the end of the world.

The last days leading to Armageddon, believers say will bring a living nightmare of wars, cataclysms, and persecutions. The scenario includes a series of futile peace efforts followed by wars, famine, and mass death.

Such things are now possible, they said, pointing to the hydrogen bombs, bacteriological warfare, changing weather patterns, and mass starvations already taking place in Africa and other parts of the world.

When things get to the point where they can no longer be tolerated, an Antichrist—a world leader of such compelling power, given to him by Satan—will appear to unite all nations under his rule. Once that is accomplished, he will demand everyone's worship, they believe.

To consolidate his power, the Antichrist will unleash a seven-year period of Great Tribulations, which will include war, famine, plague, and tyranny.

He will unmercifully hunt down Jews and Christians, the only ones who will be capable of seeing through his power.

Earthquakes, eclipses of the sun and moon, and other natural disasters and phenomena will signal God's impending vengeance on Satan, his tool, the Antichrist, and those who follow them, the doomsayers are convinced.

But Christ will return as an "avenging lion," to destroy the Antichrist and his assembled armies at the Plain of Armageddon. It is then that the "Millennium," a 1,000-year reign of righteousness in Jerusalem, will be established, the believers say. Jews will be restored to the Holy Land, and Christians will reign with Christ.

This is a traditional interpretation of Revelations, which many Christians, aside from some fundamentalists and "born-agains," have rejected. But there are many Biblical scholars who interpret Revelations in yet a more literal sense.

The "beast from the seas" in Revelations 13, for example, is seen as the government apparatus of the Antichrist. The European Common Market, with its ten member nations, seems to fit perfectly with the horns on the monster.

Current social trends, including breakdown of the family, the growing power of government, centralized data banks, electronic scanning of groceries, and computerized mail are all seen as signs that Armageddon is rapidly approaching, by these Biblical scholars.

Throughout history, there have been any number of accused Antichrists, including the Roman emperor Domitian, Mohammed, Napoleon, several popes, Hitler, Mussolini, Henry Kissinger, the Ayatollah Khomeini, and Anwar Sadat.

Using variations of numerology and other arcane systems, the number of the Beast of Revelations, 666, has been applied to the names of William Franklin Graham (Billy Graham), Ronald Wilson Reagan, and Jerry Falwell himself.

Some traditionalists, and new interpreters, agree that the birth of Israel in 1948 signaled at least the beginning of the prophetic countdown to the coming of the Antichrist and Armageddon. Nuclear winters, nuclear fallout, and radiation sickness are as bad, if not worse, than anything predicted in Revelations, some scholars point out.

Most Americans, however, including hard-nosed practical members of most law enforcement agencies, had little interest in the supernatural or the fulfillment of Biblical prophecies. If Satanic cults were indeed involved in these bizarre happenings, they had to be the work of "crazies." But, "crazies" or not, if there was a growing Satanic movement sweeping the country, there was reason to be concerned.

Except for religious fundamentalists, who saw Satan as the Biblical Devil, complete with horns, tail, and pitchfork, surrounded by gargoylish creatures, few average Californians had any clear notion as to who was a Satanist or what constituted a Satanic cult.

For most Americans, Satan was a concept of evil, rather than its personification. He was a name they gave to evil rather than to someone who caused it, or tempted others to cause it. And as for many people who considered themselves to be Satanists and members of Satanic cults, much of what they imagined came from sensational movies and books—depicting bands of deformed, slavering, subhuman psychopaths gathered around stone altars, perhaps with well-proportioned nude girls awaiting sacrifice or use in depraved rites.

Satanic symbols can include circles, triangles, squares, and pentagrams—five-pointed stars (the star must have its center point down to be Satanic). There are also significant colors: red, orange, green, yellow, blue, purple, black, and white. The rainbow and unicorn are claimed by some to have Satanic significance, as well. And there are certain numbers, too, including the infamous 666, which is considered to be Satan's personal identification number.

According to some experts, there are three types of Satanists:

- traditional Satanists—those who have been Satanists for generations and pass their faith from parent to child. These are secretive and avoid any publicity.
- "pop" Satanists—neo-Satanists, such as Anton Szandor LaVey's Church of Satan and its various offshoots.
- "solitary" or "maverick" Satanists—These usually belong to no cult and follow their own, made-up brand of Satanism, sometimes supported by books like LaVey's *The Satanic Bible* and *The Satanic Rituals.* They are usually socially alienated teen-agers and adult sociopaths. The group also contains a certain number of psychopaths, and it is these who most often prove dangerous.

There is a popular misconception, especially in Hollywood, that the nouns *Satanist* and *witch* are interchangeable. In the strictest sense, however, the two are quite different.

Witches consider themselves followers of a pre-Christian, pagan, fertility religion, and resent the label of "Satanist." Modern witchcraft is splintered into denominations, as is modern Christianity. And they are as quick to quarrel and form breakaway covens due to disagreements about matters of theology and personalities as any Christian or church would be. There are warrior witches who are generally male-dominated. And a few years ago witches locked horns in a divisive dispute over the right of homosexuals to join in witchly affairs. Witchcraft, after all, is a fertility religion. The horned god is an ancient symbol of fertility found in many pre-Christian religions. He is not Satan. Witches, in fact, do not believe in either Hell or the Devil. But, overall, witches get along fairly well, and most recognize a supreme force or godhead, as well as a Goddess personifying the female element, and the Horned God, personifying the male.

They claim their magic and spells are derived from the forces of nature and not from demons. Their rituals, they explain, allow them to tap into that natural source of power. What's more, most use their powers for good.

Satanism, on the other hand, is necessarily linked with Christianity, because Satan is the creation of Christianity. It is the dark flip side.

Before the seventh century A.D., in both the Hebrew and Christian religions, God was the source of both good and evil. In the Old Testament and other sacred Jewish writings, Satan was little more than a somewhat rebellious angel who disapproved of, and was jealous of, mankind. He tried to get man into trouble with God, as in the Biblical tale of Job.

Somehow, in its battle against pagan religions from the fifth century A.D., the Catholic Church managed to meld into one the innocent horned nature gods with the Biblical Satan. Satan was transformed from a cranky troublemaker to the "father of evil" and leader of the "hosts of Hell," which was invented at about the same time as the

Devil himself. The gods of older religions, forced to move aside, often become the devils of stronger new religions.

For the most part, our popular modern physical images of Hell and the Devil are derived from Dante's *Inferno* and Milton's *Paradise Lost*.

According to the Reverend J. Gordon Melton, director of the Institute for the Study of American Religion, and author of the *Encyclopedia Handbook of Cults in America*, traditional Satanists have been in existence for the last two centuries. They are generally believed to be descended from certain heretical Christian sects wiped out by the Roman Catholic Church between 1,000 and 1,300 A.D., including the Albigenses, the Cathari, Waldenses, and Knights Templar.

According to the Dominicans, who spearheaded the Inquisition, the Cathari's meetings were called *Synagoga Satanae*, and, along with the Albigenses, they practiced homosexuality and sodomy. The proceedings of the *Synagoga Satanae* were similar to what were later to become descriptions of the witches' Sabbats, complete with anti-Christian symbolism and wanton sexuality. Although these groups were thought to have been exterminated by the Church, many followers are believed to have escaped and gone underground.

The Knights Templar was a fraternal organization of Christian crusaders. Members of the group were accused by the Church of abominable practices, including worship of a deity called Baphomet, who was described as a bearded man's head with one or three faces, as a human skull, or as a monstrous figure with human hands and the facial features, body and hooves of a goat.

Initiates were reputedly required to spit and trample on the cross, renounce Christ as a false prophet, and perform homosexual acts. The last Grand Master of the Knights Templar, Jacques de Molay, was burned outside Paris in 1313.

Many secret societies today, both Satanic and non-Satanic, trace their own practices to the Knights. The Templar legend has also played an important role in Western magical tradition.

Factual information about traditional Satanists is sketchy. They are said to be highly secretive and, on the surface, can appear quite normal. In public, they live in traditional family units, but in private, sex is not restricted to one partner, and multi-partner orgies are believed to be common. Satan is not seen to be a god who condemns fleshly pleasures.

Some experts report that at the age of twelve, a virgin is deflowered by the group's leader. The girl then services other members of the group, both male and female, in a variety of normal and deviant acts. If the virgin becomes pregnant during her sexual initiation—which is quite common, since she might couple with as many as fifty men on her "wedding night"—the baby may become a human sacrifice to Satan.

Some of these groups have been blamed in recent years by parent groups and law enforcement officials for an epidemic of child molestations at day-care and pre-school centers.

They have alleged that children are sexually molested and forced to take part in vile rites by adult members of a secret nationwide Satanic cult who have worked their way into teaching and administrative positions to gain access to the children.

Testimony of the children, according to some experts, is too similar to have been made up. They have described scenes in which they were reputedly forced to participate in sexual acts with robed, chanting adults, to drink blood, eat feces, witness animal and human sacrifices, and consume the flesh of roasted babies.

One ten-year-old boy reportedly rescued from a Devil-worshipping cult claimed he'd been forced to take part in shocking rituals involving the sacrificing of babies, cremations, and sexual orgies.

A Los Angeles sheriff's deputy, a member of the department's child-abuse unit, said the young boy and several others of similar age provided too many details to have made up what they saw or took part in to have been lying. He said the boy even accurately described the taste of human flesh.

Some anti-Satanists claimed 60,000 human sacrifices a year were being performed by devil worshippers.

From Vancouver, Canada, to Miami, Florida, Satanists have been blamed for grave robberies, animal mutilations and sacrifices, human sacrifices, vandalism, and other bizarre happenings. Some of the blood rites, especially in south Florida and other areas with large Hispanic populations, are actually carried out however by followers of the religions of Santeria, Macumba, or the necrophilic Palo Mayombe—all of which have their origins in Africa, but are sometimes mistaken by the uninformed for evidence of Satanism.

Many "pop" Satanists trace the genesis of their interests in devil worship to the writings of Anton Szandor LaVey, a former lion tamer and police photographer, who shaved his head in the tradition of black magicians and medieval executioners, and, in 1966, announced the formation of the world's first Church of Satan. Most other "pop" Satanic churches are either splinters of the Church of Satan, or rely on LaVey's works, *The Satanic Bible* and *The Satanic Rituals.*

These groups appear surprisingly staid, however, renouncing violence and sacrifices, including those of animals. They actively seek members, some through newspaper and magazine ads. The Church of Satan and its breakaway offshoot, the Temple of Set, have telephone listings in the San Francisco telephone book.

Over the years, LaVey's church attracted mild to strong interest from a bevy of celebrities, including Hollywood sexpot Jayne Mansfield, and Sammy Davis, Jr.

Davis even became a recruiter for the cult among his Hollywood friends.

While LaVey's Church of Satan seems guilty of little more than some hucksterism, his two books, *The Satanic Bible* and *The Satanic Rituals,* are another matter. There is disturbing evidence that the books have become resource material for troubled young people dabbling in Satanism, and for "solitary" or "maverick" Satanists, many of whom have been responsible for murder and other crimes.

Solitary or maverick Satanists usually are, as the names imply, loners. They belong to no organized cult or Satanic grotto; or, if they do, the group is made up of only a few individuals. They are usually young people who have problems at home, at school, and in socializing with their peers. The rituals they perform are often aimed at goals like acquiring money, becoming popular, finding a loving girlfriend or boyfriend, or fulfilling other sexual fantasies.

Those in this category tend to be involved with drugs and often have a fanatical devotion to heavy-metal rock. Their Satanic rituals can involve getting drunk or high on drugs, lighting black candles, torturing animals, occasional drinking of blood, and reading from LaVey's books. Their interest in Satanism usually lasts until they realize the Dark Prince is not going to make their dreams come true.

But serious danger enters the picture when the would-be Satanist is an emotionally or mentally disturbed individual, or too strung out on drugs. Then the trappings of evil inherent in Satanic worship can become an excuse for violence.

One such case was that of seventeen-year-old Sean Sellers, a self-admitted Satanist who was sentenced to death after the 1986 murders of his mother, stepfather, and a convenience-store clerk in Oklahoma City.

Sellers, who was a good student in high school but

suffered secret and deep-seated feelings of rejection, became interested in the occult when he was twelve. After a breakup with his girlfriend in 1983, he began drinking, taking drugs, and studying and experimenting with Satanism. He read works on Satanism and, on an altar in his bedroom, held his own Satanic rituals.

In school, he developed a number of attention-seeking tricks, including allowing the fingernail on his left pinky to grow abnormally long and painting it black. He also drank vials of his own blood, obtained by slashing his fingers, in the school cafeteria. After a time, he formed his own Satanic grotto, but it did not last long.

When his mother and stepfather ordered him to get rid of a girlfriend they were opposed to, he killed them. Earlier, he murdered the convenience-store clerk as a human sacrifice to Satan, he claimed. Police later learned that he disliked the clerk because he'd refused to sell Sellers cigarettes.

Henry Lee Lucas presents possibly an even more frightening case study. He confessed to the murders of more than 600 people in a ten-year killing spree across the United States and Canada.

The one-eyed bisexual drifter told the FBI and other local police agencies that he belonged to an international Satanic cult called the Hands of Death. He claimed the cult had a training camp in Florida's Everglades. The Satanic rites supposedly included animal crucifixions, drinking of the urine and blood of decapitated victims, and cannibalism. The group's other activities supposedly included contract killings, child trafficking, and kiddie porn.

Neither the training camp nor other members of the cult was ever found. They apparently didn't exist. Red-faced police around the country who had been clearing homicide cases by the hundreds based on the confessions of Lucas and his sometime partner, Ottis Elwood Toole, reluctantly admitted they had been duped. Lucas said he told his tall tales because he enjoyed the notoriety and wanted to embarrass police. Although he eventually claimed he killed only one victim—his alcoholic prostitute mother—he was eventually convicted of three murders in Texas and is currently on death row.

In 1984, just before the Night Stalker claimed his first victim in California, another AC/DC addict, seventeen-year-old Rick Kasso of Riverhead, New York, stabbed a friend seventeen times. Kasso plucked out the victim's eyes before finishing him off. The similarity with the Zazzara murders and mutilations were not missed by Southern Californian lawmen.

Kasso, an admitted Satanist, and seventeen-year-old Gary Lauwers were involved with a group of teenagers called the Knights of the Black Circle. Several members of the group professed to be Satanists, and to be involved in drug use, blood-drinking, and animal sacrifice. They were also avid heavy-metal addicts and listened to such groups as AC/DC, Black Sabbath, and Judas Priest.

Kasso lured Lauwers into the woods and tortured him for hours. Then the victim was forced to proclaim his love for Satan before being stabbed to death. A few days after his arrest, Kasso hanged himself in his prison cell.

When nineteen-year-old Randy Duncan shot himself while listening to rock star Ozzy Osbourne in late October 1984, Duncan's father sued Osbourne and CBS Records in a Los Angeles Superior Court, claiming his son was driven to take his life as he listened to Osbourne's "Suicide Solution." The young man had been listening to Osbourne's music for hours and was still wearing headphones when his body was found.

Judge John Cole threw the lawsuit out, ruling that the song lyrics are protected by the First Amendment of the United States Constitution. In his decision, the judge pointed out that holding the rock musician and CBS

Records responsible for the teenager's self-inflicted shooting death would cast a chill over free-speech rights.

CBS Records and another popular British heavy-metal band, Judas Priest, were named in a somewhat similar suit filed after the self-inflicted shotgun shooting of a pair of hard-drinking, pot-smoking fans in Sparks, Nevada. It was two days before Christmas in 1985 when eighteen-year-old Raymond Belknap and his twenty-year-old buddy, Jay Vance, got together to blow some smoke, drink beer and listen to Judas Priest records.

Somewhere along the line they lapsed into a fit of violence and tore up Belknap's room. Then Belknap picked up a sawed-off shotgun, and both youths ran to a nearby churchyard. Belknap was the first to turn the weapon on himself. He blew most of his head away. Then Vance picked up the bloodied weapon, reloaded it and pulled the trigger. Miraculously, he survived, but his face was demolished. Plastic surgeons and other medical experts restored most of his features before he died of an overdose of methadone on Thanksgiving Day nearly three years later.

Relatives filed suit against the band and record company, claiming that hidden messages on the 1978 album *Stained Class,* which the two pals were listening to, drove them to the suicide pact. The song, "Better By You, Better Than Me," was especially singled out for allegedly including a subliminal message, "Do it."

The message was reputedly included through backmasking, which some critics of rock music believe involves a system of backward recording to hide the words from all but the most careful or obsessive listeners. The lawsuit was filed as a product liability case, claiming negligence and intentional misconduct on the part of the defendants.

Lawyers for Judas Priest and CBS Records argued that it was the troubled lives, including histories of drug and alcohol abuse and psychiatric disorders, that led the two young men to the violent acts. And they denied that the records contained any subliminal messages, or that Judas Priest promotes suicide or Satanism.

Judas Priest's lead singer, Rob Halford, provided a moment of drama when he testified during the trial that he had, indeed, put a backward message on one of the group's pieces, although it was not included in the album or piece cited by the plaintiffs.

But he strongly denied that there was any so-called "masking" of backward messages to influence behavior. In a later interview with an Associated Press reporter, Halford expanded on his courtroom remarks and explained that all that was going on were attempts to create specific sound effects. He pointed out that it was a simple task to record a cymbal, a guitar, or other instruments— even voices—backwards to create desired sounds.

"It's been going on for thirty or forty years," he told the reporter. But he stressed that there was no proven instance of anyone being able to interpret anything backwards—especially sounds or words that are below audible level.

In August 1990, Washoe County District Court Judge Jerry Carr Whitehead cleared the band and record company of the charges against them.

In a ninety-three-page decision, the judge stated that he could hear the subliminal command, "Do it," on the album, but that the words were no more than an inadvertent combination of the unintentional exhalation of breath by the singer on one track, and a "leslie" guitar on another track.

Judge Whitehead declared that the families of the two young men had failed to prove that subliminal messages were a precipitating factor in the tragedy.

But the judge ordered CBS to pay the families of the men forty thousand dollars in legal expenses for inadequate compliance with pre-trial procedures. And he stated that it was unknown what future technology and research might bring to the field.

The fact that the judge ruled that subliminal messages did indeed exist on some records left the door wide open for similar actions, however.

Barely six weeks after the conclusion of the trial in Reno, a pair of product liability suits were filed in Macon, Georgia, blaming Judas Priest's fellow British rocker, Ozzie Osbourne's music in the suicide deaths of yet two other young men in separate incidents. This time the victims were sixteen-year-old Michael Jeffrey Waller, and seventeen-year-old Harold Hamilton.

Waller had been drinking beer and listening to heavy metal late on the night of May 2, 1986, at a friend's house party in Fitzgerald, Georgia, when at about 2 A.M. on May 3 he scribbled a suicide note, picked up a gun and blew a hole through a refrigerator door. Then he turned the weapon on himself, firing a shot into his temple. According to the teenager's father, Thomas Waller, and to police, the last tape Jeffrey had listened to was Osbourne's *Blizzard of Oz* album. And one of the songs on the album was the recording "Suicide Solution."

The suit filed on behalf of the Hamilton boy claims that he killed himself after listening to the same song on Osbourne's earlier album, *Tribute.* Young Hamilton was found in rural Washington County, Georgia, at about 11 A.M. on March 20, 1988, with a gun in his hand, a bullet hole in his temple, and *Tribute* in the tape deck. He was still alive when found, but died seven hours later after being rushed to a nearby hospital. Like Waller, he had also written a suicide note.

The Georgia lawsuits, as well as other subliminal message and backward masking cases filed in New Jersey, Utah, Michigan, Oregon and Washington state against various heavy metal bands, are still in litigation as of this writing.

Not all subliminal message activities are considered

negative, and for years tapes and records have been marketed to help people feel better about themselves, improve their motivation, sharpen memory and accomplish other self-improvement goals. And although there is little indication that the burgeoning industry dealing with reputed subliminal messages is likely to subside, recent scientific studies have provided some rays of light for critics who consider the entire subject nothing more than pseudoscientific gobbledygook.

Dr. Anthony R. Pratkanis, a researcher from the University of California at Santa Cruz, and an expert witness who testified for the defense in the trial in Reno, is one of the leading scientific debunkers. Pratkanis and five fellow researchers revealed in Boston in August 1990 that they had conducted a series of sophisticated tests, including an acoustic analysis of four subliminal-message tapes with machines called spectrographs. Dr. Philip M. Merikle, professor of psychology at the University of Waterloo in Ontario, one of Pratkanis' colleagues in the project, told reporters that they had found no evidence that subliminal messages existed on any of the tapes.

Nevertheless, it seems a sure bet that the subject of subliminal messages and backward masking will continue to be a hard-fought point of debate as opponents continue to argue about the purported influence, or non-influence, of heavy-metal music on violence and Satanic activity in our society.

Many police departments across the country have established special task forces to investigate Satanic and occult-related crimes.

Religious leaders were not the only ones who found perceived evil in the lyrics of heavy-metal musicians. Parents' groups, backed by psychologists, sociologists, and psychiatrists, have fought rock and roll since the advent of Elvis Presley.

Presley's gyrating hips were said to be lewd and capable of turning teen-aged boys and girls into sex-crazed pawns of the devil. When he appeared on the "Ed Sullivan Show," cameras showed only the King's face and upper body, to escape the wrath of censors.

In recent years, a variety of local and national parent and citizen groups, headed by the prestigious National PTA, and the Parents' Music Resource Center, have objected to certain rock music groups, especially those espousing sex and violence.

Tipper Gore, president of the Parents' Music Research Center and wife of Tennessee Sen. Albert Gore, Jr., said in 1989 that American parents are concerned about the glorification of violence, particularly against women, graphic sex, and suicide in some rock music.

Gore's group and the National Parent-Teachers' Association were recently successful in getting the music industry to agree voluntarily to affix warning labels to certain rock and rap music albums and jackets, warning that contents of the records or tapes may be objectionable to some parents because of sex, violence, suicide, drug abuse, bigotry, or Satanic worship references.

Dr. Paul King, medical director of the Charter Lakeside Hospital in Memphis, Tennessee, revealed a few years ago that a study of 470 adolescents admitted to the hospital showed that there is a strong link between heavy-metal music, drug abuse, violent crime, irresponsible sexual behavior, and a fascination with Satanic themes.

Southern Californians began to wonder if there really could be a heavy-metal-Satanic link with the Night Stalker's gruesome crimes.

Judging from the horrific crimes committed by the Night Stalker and what the public read in the newspapers and heard on television, it did appear that the country, and especially Southern California, was gripped by a Satanic crime wave.

Satanists stood accused of serial killings, human sacrifices, kidnappings, sexual abuses, child pornography, and animal mutilations—to say nothing of their excessive love of heavy-metal rock.

And certainly the Night Stalker's demonic activities justified alarm over the spread of Satanism in California.

But there are murders, and then there are murders.

An armed robber shoots a 7-11 clerk. A mob hitman blows away a snitch. A husband kills his wife out of jealousy. A wife kills her wealthy husband so she can inherit his fortune and marry her lover. A son kills his father to save himself or someone in his family from abuse. A shot fired, the thrust of a knife, a drink laced with poison—then, death.

Such murders fill the pages of newspapers every day. For the most part, they are inspired by one of the seven deadly sins—most often greed. We disapprove, but we can understand, if not sympathize with, the motivation. We're appalled, but rarely sickened.

The Stalker's slayings, on the other hand, transcended ordinary human understanding. They seemed almost whimsical, random, like the work of nature. It seemed, in fact, that he did not know himself what he would do until he acted.

His abominations were beyond normal murder. He appeared to be performing some evil, incomprehensible ritual. Given their subhuman aspects—the senseless slaughter, his vile sexual perversions committed on women and children, and the overtones of Satanism—the killings smacked of insanity or demonic possession. Some experts claimed there was little or no difference between the two.

At the time police were not primarily concerned with his motivation, aside from the possibility that he might use insanity as a way to escape retribution, once he was run to ground. The initial concern of law enforcement agencies was capturing the Night Stalker and putting a stop to the slaughter and terror.

The Night Stalker was a murderer, pure and simple. They didn't want to hear any insanity cop-outs, or nonsense about the Devil. If the Night Stalker drew pentagrams on victims and on walls, or showed a preference for songs played by heavy-metal bands, they were merely peculiarities that could be useful in catching him.

And one thing was certain: They were determined to catch him and send him to death row.

CHAPTER 8

New Horizons

THE STALKER WAS BEGINNING TO FIND IT more difficult to stalk victims in the Los Angeles area. Quiet neighborhoods that once dozed peacefully under the shadow of night were suddenly alert, flooded by lights and watchful eyes. There were barking dogs in yards. Patrolling cars manned by volunteers, private security guards, and city police constantly cruised streets, even in the early morning hours.

It was no longer a simple matter of strolling up to a darkened house and finding an open window or door through which to enter. And if there was an easy way in, there was also a good chance that someone inside was waiting with a shotgun or a pistol.

There were also the ever-present composite sketches, becoming uncomfortably more accurate as each surviving victim added yet another detail or two, and the ominous statements by police, suggesting an arrest was imminent.

It was time for the Night Stalker to move his evil act elsewhere.

Sixty-six-year-old Peter Pan seemed an unlikely candidate for murder. The mild-mannered, semi-retired Asian accountant lived quietly with his sixty-four-year-old wife,

Barbara, in Lake Merced, an affluent suburb of San Francisco. But when Pan's forty-two-year-old son looked in on his parents' white two-story luxury home about two miles from Highway 80 on Sunday morning, he was horrified and shocked to find his father and mother lying in their blood-soaked bed, each shot in the head.

Pan, who was of Chinese descent, was pronounced dead at the scene. His wife was rushed to San Francisco General Hospital, where doctors quickly stabilized her condition and expressed cautious expectations that she would survive.

San Francisco police said the killer entered the Pan home through an open window, a hallmark of the Stalker. There were also Satanic messages and drawings, including an inverted pentagram, and the words "Jack the Knife," scrawled in lipstick on the walls of the bedroom. The couple had been shot, investigators said, sometime between ten P.M. Saturday Aug. 17 and ten A.M. Sunday Aug. 18. The house had been thoroughly ransacked.

Homicide Lieut. George Kowalski, who almost immediately recognized Pan's murder as the work of the Night Stalker, contacted the task force at the Los Angeles County sheriff's department. He said there was another piece of evidence, in addition to the small-caliber bullet and the Satanic symbols, that definitely tied the crimes to the Night Stalker. San Francisco police, however, would not reveal to reporters just what this evidence might be, except to say it was "hallmark."

Kowalski felt certain the murder was the work of the Night Stalker. There was even a pentagram drawn on a wall in the Pan residence. He said he was sending the bullet that had killed Pan to Los Angeles, as soon as it was removed from the victim, so that it could be compared with those from Stalker killings in the Los Angeles area.

A few hours later forensic experts and Stalker specialists from Los Angeles were on their way to San Francisco. They quickly determined that the bullet matched those taken from two Los Angeles killings attributed to the Stalker.

Los Angeles County sheriff's detectives learned a maroon or brown 1978 Pontiac Grand Prix with a damaged right fender had been seen near the scene of one of the Stalker's murders. The description of the car was dispatched to other departments in the state. The San Francisco police reported that the car might have been spotted in the Lake Merced area the day of the Pan murder.

When Sergeant Salerno learned the Stalker had extended his murder spree north, he shook his head. He told reporters that his experience in helping solve the Hillside Strangler murders in 1978 and 1979 had taught him one chilling fact about serial killers: "Most serial murderers don't stop. They might relocate. [But] they will kill again."

San Francisco police, however, were determined not to allow the Stalker to pick off its citizens with the same shocking impunity as he had exhibited in Los Angeles County. They launched an all-out manhunt for him, the biggest since the hate-crazed Zebra Killers had roamed the city spreading fear and violent death in the early 1970s.

During a dreadful six-month period—between October 1973 and April 1974—members of a fanatical Black Muslim splinter group who called themselves "Death Angels" held white residents of San Francisco in a grip of terror.

The group, comprised mostly of social misfits, ex-convicts, and psychopaths, was responsible for a series of random, racially motivated attacks on white men, women, and children that claimed at least fifteen lives, and left another eight victims emotionally scared for life after suffering horrible injuries or sexual abuse.

The Death Angels were apparently founded in California in late 1969 or early 1970. Members adhered to a ludicrous, science-fiction-like notion that whites were "evil beasts" and "grafted Devils" spawned by an ancient crazed genetic experiment.

The theory, as nonsensical as those espoused by some white-supremist groups, might have been laughable had it not produced such deadly results. Members of the cult attempted to put their beliefs into actions by actively striving to exterminate Caucasians. To achieve the rank of Death Angel, a recruit was required to kill a specified number of whites based on a point system: four white children; five women; or nine men; or a combination adding up to the desired point total.

Murders were verified for the organization by media reports, eyewitness accounts by fellow Angels, or Polaroid pictures of victims snapped by the killer.

Deaths and attacks occurred not only in San Francisco, but also in Oakland, Berkeley, Long Beach, Signal Hill, Santa Barbara, Palo Alto, Pacifica, Los Angeles, and San Diego. And some experts believe hundreds of people may have been killed during the orgy of violence, many of them never missed because they were flower children, skid-row alcoholics and other rootless transients.

Dubbed the "Zebra Murders," because of call letters on a police radio frequency, the first known attack took place in San Francisco on October 19, 1973, when Richard Hague was hacked about the head and face with a machete. Stunned and left for dead, Hague somehow survived. His wife, Quita, was not so fortunate. After raping her, the thugs chopped her head and neck with the machete, nearly decapitating her.

The second known victim was a young white woman who was raped twice and forced to perform oral sex. She, however, escaped by outsmarting her attacker, pretending to sympathize with his explanation that he was abusing her to make up for the oppression of blacks by white society.

Others were not so lucky. They were shot, stabbed, or hacked to death in their cars, at bus stops, walking on the streets, or in their homes. The psychopathic killers unleashed an especially murderous rampage on January 28, killing four victims within the space of two hours.

Infuriated and frustrated, and under intense political pressure to bring an end to the vicious attacks, police cracked down hard. And their desperate and sometimes heavy-handed actions brought accusations of civil rights violations. Police randomly stopped blacks on the streets and searched them for weapons. There were beatings and some blacks objected to what they labeled Nazi-like tactics. A flurry of suits charging civil rights violations hit the courts. But despite all the effort, all the anger, and all the fear, the killings continued. And racial tensions threatened to rip the city to pieces.

The case was broken in late April when an ex-convict, Anthony Cornelius Harris, contacted police and identified the kill-crazy cultists for a cash reward. He named eight suspects as Zebra killers. Four of the suspects were eventually freed for lack of concrete evidence; the other four received life sentences. The defense of three of the suspects was paid for by the Nation of Islam. Harris, who had been a close associate of the killers, steadfastly denied taking any part in the killings, and was given immunity from prosecution in return for his information and courtroom testimony.

According to one researcher, Clark Howard, whose book, *Zebra,* chronicled activities of the killer cultists, those arrested were lower-echelon members of the group. The leaders and most prolific of the killers are still at large.

Police in San Francisco were determined not to permit their city to become captive to the new horror of the

Stalker. Faced with a smaller geographic area and population than was the case for the Los Angeles lawmen, they moved quickly, throwing a protective blanket over the city. They were ready to bring down the Stalker.

One of their first moves was to saturate the city with the composite sketches of the suspect and fliers they received from Los Angeles. Hundreds of uniformed and plainclothes officers were assigned to patrol high-risk areas, and to lean on informants in the seamier parts of the city, particularly those in Hispanic areas.

"The whole department has been mobilized to apprehend the suspect," Comdr. Richard Klapp told reporters.

Captain of Inspectors Diarmuid Philpott said neighborhood patrols were beefed up and seventy officers had been assigned specifically to the investigation. Overtime was authorized so officers in district stations could join the all-out manhunt for the Night Stalker. Operating on the assumption that the Stalker was still in the area, Philpott asked residents to lock windows and doors.

Suddenly, panic was sweeping the Bay area as it had the Los Angeles area a month earlier. San Franciscans began organizing block watches, buying locks, and installing alarm systems. One hardware-store owner said his entire supply of window locks was sold out in a single weekend. "I'm telling everyone else to get a dog," he said.

The sale of deadbolts and other anti-crime devices not only took an abrupt jump, but prices doubled and tripled. The cost of deadbolts shot up from $1.99 to $3.99. Windows that formerly sold for $15 skyrocketed as high as $50. Alarm systems climbed from about $350 to as high as $1,500.

A large number of the people buying locks and alarm systems were older women.

"You bet I'm scared," Carol Parrish told a reporter. "I'm moving into the area where the Night Stalker struck. But I'm not moving in until the alarm system is installed and all the locks are on."

San Francisco police also began reexamining recent killings in the area to see if they might be linked to the Stalker. They uncovered two cases that had similarities to Stalker killings. Both had occurred earlier in the year.

One involved the bloody knife murders of two sisters who lived on Telegraph Hill. The sisters—fifty-year-old Christina Caldwell and seventy-year-old Mary Caldwell —were stabbed to death in their Greenwich Street apartment on February 20, 1985, almost a month before the March 17 slaying of Dayle Okazaki in Rosemead.

Theodore Wildings was shot in the head June 2 while he slept in a Cow Hollow apartment. His twenty-five-year-old girlfriend, *Nancy Brien,* was raped but escaped with her life in the attack.

Twenty-nine-year-old Wildings, who died in a hospital three days after the attack, was shot with a small-caliber weapon similar to guns used by the Night Stalker. *Brien's* description of her rapist matched that of the Stalker. The murders of the Caldwells and Wildings displayed two other trademarks of the Stalker—late-night entry through an unlocked door or window, and explosive violence. And Wildings's killer had exhibited yet one more chilling earmark of the Night Stalker—his cowardly precaution of murdering the male before raping the female.

Rose Marie Ovian, a young San Francisco engineer, learned she may have narrowly missed becoming a Stalker victim on August 15, two days before the Pan murder.

The twenty-year-old woman told authorities that she went to bed early that night. When she awoke, she found that someone had climbed a piece of scaffolding to gain access to a second-story bathroom window. The burglar had looted the upstairs and apparently tried to force open the locked door to her apartment. Later, she learned that fingerprints found in the apartment by police-evidence technicians matched those of the Stalker.

In combing the once-exclusive San Francisco Tenderloin district, police learned that a skinny Hispanic man closely fitting the Stalker's description often stayed at a seedy flophouse on Mason Street. The man had stayed at the hotel off and on for the past year and a half, paying the twenty-dollar-per-day rent in cash and using a variety of fictitious names. He had last stayed at the hotel during the week Pan was murdered.

The manager remembered that the man had worn dark jeans and a dark jacket covering a T-shirt. His only "luggage" was a shaving kit. He smiled a lot, the manager told police, showing "very bad teeth."

The mysterious transient left the hotel suddenly before noon, on Saturday, August 17. Pan was murdered that night.

The manager also recalled that there was a mysterious, unpleasant odor in and around the room when the skinny transient stayed there. "It smelled like skunk," he told police. The stink subsided in a few days after the roomer left.

Police investigators checked out the room and found a pentagram drawn on the bathroom door. They took pictures of the room from all angles and checked for fingerprints. Later, they removed the bathroom door from its frame and shipped it to Los Angeles to compare it to other pentagrams found at Stalker crime scenes.

Police also learned that a Hispanic matching the Stalker's description had sold a diamond ring and cufflinks to a man who lived in the El Sobrante area. The jewelry was identified by police as belonging to Pan. The El Sobrante man also produced other jewelry he'd bought from the Night Stalker look-alike. The jewelry was later identified as loot from burglaries in Southern California, most of them in the Los Angeles area.

San Francisco investigators obtained one of their most

valuable leads when they learned that a maroon or brown 1978 Pontiac Grand Prix with a damaged right fender, reportedly seen near one of the Stalker's murders in the Los Angeles County area, was also spotted near Lake Merced the day of the Pan murder.

Bay area police staked out the hotel and kept a close watch on the El Sobrante man. They were confident that they were very close to learning the killer's identity, and perhaps even making an arrest. The net was closing.

Shortly after the Pan homicide, San Francisco Deputy Police Chief George Eimil had released a brief statement advising that "certain similarities" in that murder appeared to link it with Night Stalker killings in the Los Angeles area. Despite increasingly frantic pressure from news-hungry reporters in both San Francisco and Los Angeles, however, neither the Los Angeles County deputy sheriff's department nor San Francisco police would provide more specific details about the similarities. They were playing it close to the vest and stubbornly refused to say more.

Then, in a surprise move that dismayed and angered police authorities, San Francisco Mayor Dianne Feinstein took matters out of their hands. She talked about the manhunt with reporters and told them that the similarities police were keeping such tight lips about included fingerprints that matched crimes in the Los Angeles area, and similar methods of operation that the cases all had in common.

Captain Block announced angrily at a news conference that the information released by the San Francisco mayor had threatened the success of the hunt for the killer. He labeled her actions as irresponsible political grandstanding, adding that he and other law officers were afraid the Stalker might now change his methods of operation and become more difficult to identify and apprehend. San Francisco police were angry, too. But the mayor was their boss, and they had to be more cautious about being openly critical. One San Francisco officer told reporters that the mayor was a "buffoon." But he spoke out only after he was assured that his identity would be protected.

The Stalker did not change his method of operation, but he did change his geographic location once more. He moved south.

Howard Evans walked into the living room and turned on the television. It was almost eight o'clock on Saturday night, Aug. 24, and the evening's prime-time programming would begin in a few minutes. But, because it was late August, he didn't expect to find anything more provocative than a few tired reruns. He could still hear his wife's voice from the kitchen. He turned up the volume.

Margaret Evans was still carrying on about locks and alarm systems. She was afraid of the maniac who was breaking into people's homes and killing, beating, and sexually abusing them. She was convinced that it would be a good investment in peace of mind to change all the locks in their house on Chrisanta Drive, in Mission Viejo, a quiet, suburban coastal community about fifty miles south of Los Angeles, and have a security system installed.

Her husband had scoffed at her apprehension. Nothing happened in Mission Viejo, he told her. If a suspicious stranger started wandering around these streets, someone would quickly spot him and notify the police. The Night Stalker had everyone in a state of panic. But *Howard Evans* wasn't going to waste a lot of money on something he didn't need.

A few hours later and two streets away, teen-ager Mickey Jensen was working on his motorbike in his parents' garage when he first noticed an orange 1976 Toyota station wagon pass. A little after midnight, it cruised slowly past again. Young Jensen frowned. He didn't recognize the car as belonging to anyone in the neighborhood. It was unusual for any car, much less an unfamiliar, nine-year-old clunker, to be cruising the upper-middle-class neighborhood at that late hour.

As Jensen mused idly about the curious old car, a few houses from the *Evans* home, on Chrisanta Drive, twenty-nine-year-old William Carns was drifting off to sleep. Lying alongside him was his fiancée, *Renata Gunther,* also twenty-nine.

Carns was a computer engineer who had moved to Southern California from Williston, North Dakota, where he worked for the Burroughs Corporation. The company transferred him to Southern California in 1983. He found the stucco single story brown house in the 24000 block of Chrisanta Drive in Mission Viejo. It was conveniently located only about three-quarters-of-a-mile from the Golden State freeway and only a few miles from where he worked, and he bought it. In a few months, he and *Renata,* a strikingly attractive woman he had met several months earlier, would be married and it would be their home.

It was just past 2 o'clock on Sunday morning, Aug. 25. Young Mike Jensen was growing tired. It was time to call it quits. He shut off the lights and prepared to close the garage door when he noticed the battered orange Toyota slowly cruise by once again.

There was something wrong here, he decided. As the car passed, he was able to make out the California license plate and wrote down the number. He would call police in the morning. But, once in the house, sitting in the kitchen, persistent thoughts about the car continued to bother him. A few minutes later, he telephoned the Orange County Sheriff's Department.

Sometime near 2:30 A.M., a slender figure dressed in Ninja black crept through an open window and moved silently through the darkened house occupied by William Carns and his girlfriend. In the bedroom, Carns was lying on his back, sleeping soundly. Alongside him, *Renata* tossed restlessly. The intruder, his feet clad in sneakers, sneaked up to the bed. Noiselessly, he slipped a pistol from his belt and, holding it a few feet from Carns's head, pulled the trigger three times. The computer expert's body lurched violently and flopped across *Renata,* awakening her immediately.

She rolled over in bed, her heart in her throat.

Before she could make a sound, someone had grabbed her by the hair and pulled her roughly out of bed. Then he jammed a gun in her face, slamming the metal barrel into her cheekbone. She gasped with the sudden pain.

"Shut up, bitch, or I'll blow your head off," the stranger hissed. In the darkness of the room, she could barely make out the black-clad figure. But she had felt the cold metal of the gun barrel, and the intruder's message was clear. She clamped her jaw shut. And she kept it shut, even when, his hand still in her hair, he dragged her to a bureau in another bedroom. Muttering to himself, he rummaged through the drawers until he found some neckties. He used them to tie her hand-and-foot, and tossed her carelessly onto a bed. As he tied her, he smirked. Then, in a raspy, chilling voice, he boasted, "You know who I am, don't you? I'm the one they're writing about in the newspapers and on TV," he hissed. Grinning, so that he showed a gap between his rotting teeth, he added ominously, "You know, if I kill one, I might let the other one live."

The young woman was helpless, paralyzed with horror, as she watched him rummaging through the room. He had the quick, certain moves of a professional burglar, searching for valuables. But he couldn't find anything in the room valuable enough and portable enough to steal. That seemed to enrage him. Cursing, he returned to the bed, bent down, then ordered her to lie on her back. She trembled as she listened to him unzip his pants and force her legs apart. She was ashamed, and tried not to think about what was happening to her. The odor from his mouth added to the disgust. Then, at last, the assault was over.

A little later she heard him leave the room. Then the sounds began again of drawers being pulled open, of her and Carns's personal property being rummaged through and spilled carelessly on the floor. He was swearing and shouting. Her terror built.

Shaking with fury at his bad luck in finding nothing to steal, the intruder stalked back into the room where *Renata* was tied up. Without a word he reached down with his huge hand and wrapped his bony fingers in her hair. Then he yanked her from the bed and threw her to the floor. This time he didn't even bother to untie her feet before he raped her. After he was through, she begged him not to hurt her anymore. She told him she had money hidden in a dresser. He cursed her and ordered her to "swear to Satan" that the money was there. Her eyes bulging with fear, horror, and pain, she framed the evil words. He smiled, revealing those awful, ruined teeth.

Renata showed him the money, and he snatched it from the drawer. Waving the handful of bills, he sneered, "This is all that saved you. This is all you're worth." But he still wasn't satisfied. He wasn't through with her yet. He ordered her to swear her love for Satan.

"I love Satan." She mumbled the words numbly. She repeated them when he ordered her to say them once more. He giggled, then forced her down to her knees. He pulled painfully at her hair as he brutally raped her mouth. Her mind reeled. He smelled and behaved like some vile thing that had crawled out of a cesspool. Her stomach knotted. She was dimly aware of the Stalker's cursing when he finally stepped back.

She braced for the bullet. Instead, he cackled one more time. Then he was gone. The neckties holding her hands and feet together had loosened sufficiently so that she was able to wriggle out of them in seconds. She staggered to a window in time to watch his dark form slide into the driver's seat of a battered old orange Toyota. Then *Renata* telephoned the police.

As she waited for them to arrive, still fighting the spasms in her stomach, she swore she would not rest until the degenerate fiend who had attacked her and her boyfriend was brought to justice. He was a monster and he belonged in San Quentin's death chamber. She would remember everything about him—his walk, his mannerisms, his posture, his hateful voice, his mocking smirk, the foul stench of his breath, and especially the way he looked at her when he had forced her to swear allegiance to the Prince of Darkness.

William Carns was rushed to a nearby hospital. The bullet fired by the intruder had smashed through his skull and injured his brain, and surgeons had to operate. Carns lived, but he had suffered permanent crippling brain damage. *Renata* was determined that her rapist would pay for that, too.

Despite the largest manhunt in the history of California, the Stalker's vile scorecard was continuing to grow.

Almost immediately, the Orange County Sheriff's Department linked the Carns shooting and the bestial sexual assault on his girlfriend to the rapist-killer who had been plundering suburban Los Angeles and San Francisco.

"We definitely believe it's the work of the Night Stalker," Orange County Sheriff's Lieut. Richard Olson told reporters.

People in Orange County reacted in the same way to news of the brutal attack in one of their communities as had residents in Los Angeles County and in San Francisco. There was a run on locks and alarm systems. Among the residents pushing to beef up their personal security was a thoroughly shaken *Howard Evans. Evans* was no longer writing off his wife's apprehensions as silliness. He wanted protection from the Night Stalker.

"He's got to have a bus [express] pass or a Disneyland E ticket or something because he's really getting around," a Los Angeles County deputy sheriff's detective suggested to reporters.

The Stalker was also digging a deeper hole for himself. Because he had to use state highways and expressways, the California Highway Patrol entered the case. The state police not only kept a close lookout for the orange Toyota, but they watched for anyone who might fit the Stalker's description. And they also distributed more of the posters and leaflets with the composite pictures of the Stalker suspect on them.

CHP Lt. Mike Maples said the highway patrol posted the posters and fliers in each of its offices and briefed all patrols on the killer. "We're on the lookout for him," Maples assured reporters.

A "summit" meeting of twenty-four investigators from thirteen police agencies was held in San Francisco. Attending the meeting, in addition to the Los Angeles County Sheriff's Department and the Los Angeles Police Department, were investigators from the Orange County Sheriff's Department, the California Highway Patrol, and the U.S. Park Police.

Then a forty-three-year-old grandmother from San Pablo named Donna Myers approached San Francisco police and told them she thought she knew who the Night Stalker was. Mrs. Myers was a friend of *Serafin Arredondo,* the man who had bought the jewelry from the Hispanic whom police suspected of being the Night Stalker. And she said she had noticed a striking resemblance between the composites and the man whom she and *Arredondo* knew.

She said the man was in his twenties, and that she had known him casually for several years. Sometimes when he was in the San Francisco area, he stayed at her home. She added ominously that he had rotten teeth and seemed to have an interest in the Devil and black magic.

Mrs. Myers said she didn't know his full name, but he used the name "Rick."

Police immediately sent a team of shotgun-carrying detectives wearing flak jackets to the Myers's house to stake it out. Heavily armed officers also continued to stake out the Hotel Bristol and *Arredondo*'s El Sobrante home.

While San Francisco police were distributing posters and leaflets with the Stalker's description and composites, Los Angeles detectives were following the dental-chart lead. The charts, obtained from the dentist whose business card had been found in the car stolen by the Stalker and used to abduct a child several months earlier, were sent to 4,000 dentists in the greater Los Angeles and San Francisco areas.

The dentist told detectives that the Stalker suspect was missing at least twelve lower teeth and that those that remained needed extensive work, including root canals. He felt certain that the Stalker was in constant pain and that he would have to seek dental help very soon.

In the meantime, the Guardian Angels, a gutsy anti-crime group known primarily for organizing unarmed vigilante-style street patrols in high-crime areas, began setting traps for the killer in Monrovia, where *Malvia Keller* had been murdered.

Members of the group continued to "house-sit" homes in the Monrovia area. They also escorted elderly San Gabriel Valley women, fearful of attacks by the Night Stalker, to and from their homes in the late evenings and at night.

Angels leader Curtis Sliwa reported that forty-two valley residents had requested Angels to stay in their homes. Other Angels patrolled streets in the Anaheim and Santa Ana areas in Orange County. A sixty-eight-year-old woman, Margaret Del Castillo, told reporters, "With an Angel, I will have a lot of confidence."

Twenty-seven-year-old Kathy Novell, who lived in a

yellow duplex with her four-year-old daughter, called the Guardian Angels after an attack by the Stalker two blocks away. "It will be a different feeling knowing that they're sitting on my living room sofa, ready to pounce," she explained.

The public usually appreciates the comforting presence of the Guardian Angels more than do police, who tend to resent them as intruders—even competitors.

Although police did not know it yet, they had already received their "major" break. It had been provided by sharp-eyed, quick-witted Mike Jensen and the Stalker himself.

When young Jensen reported the orange Toyota cruising his Mission Viejo neighborhood, just a few minutes before the Stalker struck William Carns's home, an Orange County sheriff's deputy made a note of the call and the license plate number.

Unfortunately, at the time there were no available patrols to check out the suspicious car immediately. But, when *Renata Gunther* telephoned police an hour or so later and told them her attacker had left in an orange Toyota station wagon, the pieces quickly fell into place for investigators. The manhunters now had a good description of a car thought to be driven by the Night Stalker. They even had the license plate number. And the clues were only a few hours old.

Assuming the Stalker did not own his own vehicle, the Orange County Sheriff's Department fed the description and license number into the state's computer in Sacramento to check them against stolen-car reports. Within seconds, there was a positive match. The old Toyota had been stolen in Los Angeles's Chinatown district while its owner was in a restaurant.

Police immediately put out an all-points bulletin for the vehicle. There was an outside chance that the Stalker might still be driving it. However, in the event that it was discovered abandoned, or unattended, officers were instructed not to touch it, but to wait for plainclothes officers who would stake out the vehicle.

Should they find it occupied, they were told to use whatever measures necessary to take the occupant into custody.

Two days after the Mission Viejo attack, the stolen orange Toyota station wagon was found in a parking lot in the Rampart area of Los Angeles. Detectives watched the car for almost twenty-four hours before deciding it had indeed been abandoned and the Stalker was not going to return for it. It was then taken on a flatbed truck to Orange County to be processed for evidence.

Instead of using the standard brush-and-graphite method of lifting latent fingerprints, the Orange County team used two new "breakthrough" techniques to retrieve latent prints from the vehicle.

The first involved standard superglue. Doors and windows of the Toyota were tightly closed and superglue was squeezed into a saucer, which was then placed inside the vehicle. Fumes from the glue permeated the interior, reacting to the moisture in any of the prints left in the car. Latent fingerprints turned white as the fumes did their work.

The other method involved an apparatus utilizing laser beams. The beams bathed the car's interior, and any prints, supposedly even those someone had tried to wipe off, were enhanced and raised. The Orange County Sheriff's Department was the only law enforcement agency on the West Coast with the new device.

The forensic team managed to raise a print, which they dispatched to Sacramento. Within hours, Orange County Sheriff Brad Gates knew the identity of the Night Stalker.

The prints belonged to Ricardo "Richard" Leyva Ramirez, a small-time thief, who used the nickname "Ricky."

The identification process had taken a "near miracle," state forensic experts in Sacramento told Gates. The new state computer, one of the first of its kind ever used, had been updated to include all persons with prints on file who were born after January 1, 1960. The Night Stalker was born in February 1960. Had he been born a scant forty-five days earlier, his prints would not have been in the computer.

With the prints, police were also able to secure a picture of Ramirez, taken during an earlier arrest. The fist of justice had, at last, come down on the Night Stalker. All that was left was to pick him up. Not always an easy task.

At a joint press conference attended by Sheriff Gates, Los Angeles County Sheriff Block, and Los Angeles Police Chief Daryl P. Gates, the Night Stalker's name was revealed publicly for the first time. The world learned that the foul-mouthed vandal who had been raping and killing California's citizens was Richard "Ricky" Ramirez. He was twenty-five years old.

For Sheriff Block, whose department had first recognized the presence of the Night Stalker as a serial killer and had led the manhunt, it was a satisfying feeling to look squarely into the television camera and say, "You cannot escape. Every law officer and every citizen knows who you are and exactly what you look like."

CHAPTER 9

Ricky

THE HUNT FOR ONE OF THE MOST HATED and feared killers in memory was picking up tempo. Now police had not only the name of the suspected killer but a photograph, as well, to replace the less-detailed artists' renderings. Police photographers had taken the picture themselves. Once the manhunters had Ramirez's name, they were able to check arrest records and learned that he had been picked up, fingerprinted, and photographed less than a year earlier.

To have a name *and* a picture in hand this quickly was almost more than the Orange County Sheriff could have dared hope for when he flew deputies to Sacramento with the print lifted from the orange Toyota. From past experience, he knew that attempting to match a single print with the millions on file was like looking for a needle in a haystack, unless there was a name to go with the print.

So far, he had been lucky. He'd had four unlikely breaks. The first was Mickey Jensen, the quick-witted teen-ager who not only noticed the Toyota cruising his street and had taken down the license number, but had also immediately reported it. The second break came when his deputies had, within minutes, put *Renata*

Gunther's description of the Night Stalker's car together with the car reported by Jensen. The third was finding the Toyota so quickly. And the fourth break was his forensic team's ability to lift a usable print from the car.

He was on a roll. What could it hurt to try for yet another break, especially when he'd heard that the State Department of Justice was about to activate a new supercomputer that was being touted as an electronic incarnation of Sherlock Holmes, Dick Tracy, and Columbo all wrapped into one?

Sheriff Gates gave credit where it was due. The hero of the breakthrough was a Japanese-constructed computer that had not only plucked the Night Stalker's prints and name from a few million possibilities, but had done so in a matter of minutes.

The Night Stalker's identity would still be a mystery, he admitted to reporters, without the revolutionary NEC supercomputer and identification system.

Before the new supercomputer, a typical computer search of the files containing millions of prints took more than six seconds per print, and often overlooked prints that were even slightly smudged—and the Night Stalker's print taken from the Toyota had been far from perfect. What's more, the old system was of very little use without the name of the suspect.

The NEC computer, however, not only possessed the capability of flashing through 650 prints a second, but could read even distorted or smudged fingerprints.

Made by Nippon Electric Company, it combined high-speed, custom-made silicon chips with a new technique for analyzing minute differences between one print and another. Besides plotting each point of identification in a fingerprint, the NEC computer was able to distinguish what was missing in distorted or blurred prints.

Fingerprints have been used to identify criminals since the turn of the century, with Britain's famous Scotland Yard being among the first police agency to use the technique. But the system was seriously flawed and seldom worked well unless police had more than one print and a name. Until the advent of computerized fingerprints in 1976, if fingerprint experts did not have a name from which to start their search, they had to sift through each print by hand, an almost impossible task.

Los Angeles police estimated it would have taken a single expert searching manually through the city's 1.5-million print cards sixty-seven years to come up with Ramirez's prints. It would have taken at least twice as long to sort through the 2 to 3 million prints on file at the California state identification bureau.

Using a radically different method of cataloguing prints, the FBI was able to convert its 17 million prints to digital form in 1976. Soon, police departments across the country began converting to computers, as well. But, again, without a name, the computer could take hours, even days, depending on the number of prints in a system, to come up with the right print. And, of course, it was quite likely to draw a blank if it had to work with a smudged or distorted print.

As more and more prints were added to their computer's files, law enforcement agencies began to complain that the machines were too slow and too undependable for routine police work. Until the NEC computer and identification system came along, law enforcement agencies, including the FBI, were facing a serious crisis, a crisis that threatened to relegate fingerprint identification without the name of a subject, to oblivion.

Although all TV detective-show fans know better than to pick up a pistol by the handle because doing so will smudge fingerprints, the fact is that investigators seldom get good prints from a handgun; and those they do get are quite often useless if they have to be fed into a computer without an accompanying name.

"Most of the dusting for fingerprints we do is for public relations purposes, to show people we are doing something to pursue the criminal," admitted an LAPD fingerprint expert in discussing the new identification system with reporters.

Still, as cumbersome and limited as it was, the old computer system did score some dazzling successes over the years. For instance, the Royal Canadian Mounted Police once used it to trace prints from a pizza box to a professional hit man who had gunned down a victim while posing as a delivery boy.

The San Francisco Police Department was the first to install the NEC fingerprint system in 1984 and almost immediately began picking up prints and identifications previous computer searches had missed.

The new system quickly began helping police to solve crimes that had been considered unsolvable for years. The San Francisco computer took only seven seconds to identify a man who had fatally shot a forty-seven-year-old woman during a 1978 robbery attempt. A glue-sniffer jailed for his own protection was fingerprinted, and the computer showed his prints were found at the site of a homicide several years earlier. In another case, a latent fingerprint from a burglary scene was run through the computer and matched to a man who eventually confessed to committing twenty-five unsolved burglaries. In its first four days of operation, the computer was used to crack thirty-four unsolved cases.

Eight months after San Francisco installed its NEC computer, the state of California decided to install one of its own. Technicians were still loading records from the old system into the new one when Sheriff Gates asked for identification of the Night Stalker's print.

Working all night, the technicians finished loading the system, and within three minutes of receiving its first assignment, the computer spewed out the names of five people whose prints most closely matched the one it had been given. At the top of the list, with a probability rating four times as high as the next nearest contender, was the name of Richard Ramirez.

"The job would have been impossible without the image-comparing capability of the new computer," one officer explained to a Los Angeles reporter. "In the past, we always needed the name of a likely suspect before we could compare prints found at a crime scene. We could never have provided Ramirez's name without the NEC system."

"When Ramirez's luck ran out, it ran out all at one time," said state fingerprint expert Frank Torelli. "We only loaded the fingerprints of persons arrested for felonies or serious misdemeanors born after January 1960. If Ramirez had been born just a month earlier, he would not have been in the computer's files."

Within hours after the joint announcement of the Night Stalker's identity by the Orange and Los Angeles county sheriffs' departments and the LAPD, newspapers were churning out special editions with Ramirez's picture splashed prominently on front pages, television stations were flashing his picture on screens at regular intervals, and police were updating their fliers and posters, substituting the photo for the composites. At the same time, state and local police were watching the streets, highways, and freeways in hopes of spotting Ramirez.

Police were confident it would be only a matter of hours, perhaps a few days at most, before they had Richard Ramirez behind bars.

Although the NEC system had canceled the Night Stalker's previous streak of incredible good luck in one clean stroke, the fact is that the Night Stalker's luck was running out, anyway. Bay area investigators were already locked into leads that would have eventually exposed the heartless killer.

Donna Myers and a friend proved especially fertile sources of information for San Francisco–area investigators.

Myers, who lived in a drab duplex in San Pablo, a ramshackle town north of San Francisco, confirmed that the man she knew as "Rick" was about six feet, one inch tall, weighed about one hundred fifty-five pounds, and had rotten, stained, gapped teeth.

What's more, she said, he was addicted to rock-and-roll music, especially the heavy-metal type, and was deeply into Satanism. Her description matched perfectly what the police already had on Ramirez.

From what investigators could determine from their lengthy interview with her the same day that Sheriff Gates flew the Stalker's fingerprint to the Justice Department computer, Donna Myers probably knew more about the Night Stalker than anyone in California.

Myers said she had met Rick six years earlier when she drove to El Paso, Texas, with friends.

"I had a new car, so I was anxious to take a trip," she recalled. "*Serafin* wanted to see his folks, so we decided to make the trip. Rick was a friend of *Serafin* in El Paso. He had an accent. I thought it was cute. He was also heavier and he dressed nicer in those days. I thought he was a real nice guy."

Rick used several aliases, according to Mrs. Myers, including Noah Jimenez, Richard Moreno, Richard Ramirez, Richard Munoz, Nicholas Adame, and Richard Mena. She never knew what last name was the correct one, but thought it was Ramirez.

When Mrs. Myers, and a companion returned to California, Rick followed them. Shuttling between Los Angeles and San Francisco, he slept in parked cars and alleys and, when he had the money, in flophouses.

"We would see him in San Pablo at least once a month," she told the investigators. He would do his laundry and stay the day.

He dressed in dark clothes, always dark clothes. He liked to eat junk food and yogurt—Pepsi, cupcakes, and banana splits—and he never brushed his teeth. He always carried a Walkman-tape cassette player and wore a black baseball cap with the logo of one heavy-metal group or another.

Rick often brought stolen cars to San Pablo. He specialized in Datsuns and Toyotas, for which, he told Mrs. Myers, he had a master key.

She said he showed signs of physical and mental deterioration over the past year. He lost weight and seemed jumpy all the time. She knew he had started using cocaine, first snorting it and then shooting it. His left arm had tracks running up the main vein. One day, she recalled, he broke a needle off in his arm. She had to take him to a hospital to have the needle removed.

Although Ramirez had long expressed a curiosity about Satanism, his interest had become an obsession during the last year.

"He really got into it. He drew a Satanic star on the upper part of his arm, and a witch's star on his stomach," Mrs. Myers recalled.

Rick also visited palm readers. He told his friends Satan was the supreme being and that Satan watched over him so he wouldn't get caught when he was committing crimes.

The woman said she had known for some time that Rick was breaking into people's houses and ripping them off. He often bragged of having stolen VCRs, microwave ovens, and jewelry. But, she insisted, she had no idea he was killing people—at least not until the last few weeks.

Once, when he came into her cluttered living room while the television was on, a police composite was flashed on the screen.

"Hey, Donna, do you think I'm the Night Stalker?" Rick asked.

"Hell, no, Rick," she remembered saying. "You ain't got enough guts to kill anybody."

But Rick seemed unable to leave the subject alone. Another time, he asked, "Ain't you afraid to be alone with me in the house?" Later, he asked, "Donna, what would you do if you broke into a home and found out people were home? Would you kill them, or what would you do?"

She said she thought he was kidding. "He always had a strange sense of humor," she explained.

Then, after the Pan murder, she brought up the subject herself. She told him he fit the description of the Night Stalker to a T.

"Yeah, I know," he replied. "That's why I had to leave L.A., 'cause they would think it was me."

A few days later, she discussed Rick with a friend, and they agreed it would be best if he told police about the jewelry Rick had sold him. Mrs. Myers sent her own daughter to police with some jewelry Rick had sold, as well. The jewelry, a pearl ring and a gold bracelet, had a California driver's license number engraved on it. Mrs. Myers considered that suspicious. As it turned out, police connected the jewelry to *Ruth Wilson,* who had been robbed and raped by the Night Stalker in Burbank during late May.

Checking on Mrs. Myers's statement that Ramirez had been seen with several cars, investigators learned from the state motor vehicle bureau that he had never held a California driver's license. But he had been arrested several times for driving without a license and, once, on suspicion of driving a stolen car. He also had one arrest on his California record for possessing a small amount of marijuana. The addresses he gave when arrested all turned out to be fictitious.

While police were seeking Ramirez, his former roommate, Earl Gregg, Jr., recognized one of his photos shown by the news media and called police in Lompoc. He said he believed a consuming cocaine habit had turned Ramirez into a burglar, driven him to carry out Satanic rituals, and had launched him on one of the most horrific murder sprees in the state's history.

The twenty-five-year-old Gregg, who had roomed with Ramirez for four months three years earlier, said the suspect had spent most of the past year in Los Angeles, where he began injecting cocaine.

It was the first confirmation police had that the Night Stalker was into heavy drugs. Gregg's information supported statements from several informants that Ramirez had been seen on skid-row streets several times during the past year, and had appeared "jittery" and unable to eat food he'd ordered.

Ray Garcia, a boyhood friend living in Oakland, told police he'd seen Ramirez on a number of occasions during the last year and added further confirmation that the suspect was a "coke head."

Another acquaintance, Mike Little, told reporters that Ramirez liked detective magazines, movies about murder, and drugs. When Ramirez first came to California, he drove around in an old-model Fleetwood Cadillac he'd bought. He often slept in the car, reclining the seats all the way back.

"I could not take his life-style," Little said. "First thing in the morning, he would roll a joint. He smoked lots of pot." Ramirez may have also used PCP, he added. PCP, also known on the street as "Angel Dust," is a powerful animal tranquilizer that causes brain damage and produces paranoia and violence.

Ramirez didn't eat well, but he had a sweet tooth, as many heavy drug users do.

"He would buy those big Hershey bars and eat one after another," Little recalled. "He ate a lot of candy and potato chips and drank a lot of Cokes. I would take him to a restaurant so he could eat, but he wouldn't touch his food."

In addition to his poor eating habits, Ramirez was also "messy and scuzzy," Little said, making a face. "He was a pig. . . . He never combed his hair or took a bath. And I never saw him brush his teeth."

Little often mocked Ramirez, calling him "Richie Richless" because he was so careless about spending his money.

Ramirez also liked to gamble. Until he became hooked on cocaine, he spent most of his money shooting craps. He was never seen with women. "Richie was into other things," Little said, shaking his head.

Besides gambling and drugs, Little remembered Ramirez's abiding interest in Satanic rock and any music that might be perceived as glorifying the Devil. "He loved Black Sabbath and Judas Priest," Little remembered.

One of Ricky's favorites was Judas Priest's *Breaking the Law.*

"If it's true that he did the things they say he did, then, as far as I'm concerned—that guy is history," Little said.

While the all-points bulletin was alerting law enforcement agencies across California and in the neighboring states of Arizona, Nevada, and Oregon, along with Ramirez's home state of Texas to be on the lookout for him, investigators were learning a great deal about the shadowy monster they had known only as the Night Stalker a few days earlier.

Richard (Ricardo) Ramirez was born on February 28, 1960, in one of the most isolated large cities in America. El Paso sits at the southwestern tip of the Texas Panhandle, where it is bordered on the south by the country of Mexico, on the west by the U.S. state of New Mexico, and to the east by the vast, isolated plains of west Texas. A mountain range splits the town—an Indian reservation is on the south side; and Fort Bliss, one of the U.S. Army's largest bases, is to the north. San Diego, California, is closer than Houston, Texas, and Albuquerque, the capital of New Mexico, is closer than Austin, the capital of Texas.

With a population of approximately one-half-million, it is America's largest border city. It is also one of the unhealthiest, with disease rates soaring well above the national average. Crime is also pervasive. Drug smuggling is among the highest in America, and the stolen-auto recovery rate is among the lowest. The thieves slip over the Rio Grande from the Mexican city of Juárez, while car thieves take their booty south into Juárez, where U.S. police can't touch them. The practice is so ingrained and so endemic along the U.S.-Mexican border that American authorities charge that many of the stolen cars are driven by Mexican federal police. The Federales reputedly place orders for the type and model of vehicle they want with car-theft rings operating in this country, and they're delivered across the border. The practice led to the U.S. indictment in 1982 of a top-ranking Mexican federal police officer. By 1990, U. S. officers said the stolen vehicle of choice of their Mexican counterparts was the Chevrolet suburban. The vehicle is roomy enough to accommodate large stocks of weapons and ammunition—as well as prisoners.

El Paso is a classic rough-and-tumble border city in other respects, as well. Economic classes are separated from one another as in few other American cities, except a handful of border towns. In El Paso, there is no "other side of the tracks." There, it is the "other side of the mountain." The Comanche, Franklin, Ranger, South Franklin and Sugarloaf mountains divide El Paso into the affluent west side, the blue-collar east side, and the poverty-stricken south side.

However, as bad off as El Paso may appear in comparison to other American cities, if a tourist really wants to see horrific economic deprivation, he has only to climb to the top of Comanche Peak, 6,186 feet high. From there he can look south to Ciudad Juárez on the Mexican side of the Rio Grande, the fabled river that serves as the pitifully porous border between the United States and Mexico.

Juárez is medieval squalor beyond the imagination of

most Americans, even those who live in New York's
South Bronx. There are winding dirt streets, cramped
slums, and grim industrial sites spewing noxious, poisonous smoke into the air.

The city's 1.2 million population, more than twice that
of El Paso, live mostly in mud hovels that pimple the
slopes of the Sierra Madre. Here and there, especially at
the higher elevations, can be seen fortressed mansions,
many guarded by barbed wire and gun turrets, which
shelter the city's ruling class—many of them drug dealers
who live off the misery of the less fortunate on both sides
of the border. In many ways, Juárez resembles Dante's
seven levels of Hell, with El Paso squatting like a bullfrog
at its gates.

Ramirez was born and grew up on Ledo Street, a
block-long economic and sociological concrete wound
hedged in by rusting cars and chain-linked fences, and
masked by El Paso's skyscrapers, shopping centers, neat
rows of homes, and miles of paved streets and boule-
vards. It sits under a brand-new expressway that constantly sprays a miasma of carbon dioxide and lead on
the residents below.

The two investigators sent to El Paso by the Los Angeles County sheriff to dig into Richard Ramirez's past
found the barrio where he grew up much the same as
he'd left it six years earlier. Youth gangs still fought for
turf and scarred abandoned lots, and festooned busi-
nesses, buildings, and store windows alike with spray-
painted graffiti. Police sirens still wailed constantly. All
that was missing were the trains that had previously
thundered to the railroad yards where Ramirez's father, a
resident Mexican alien, worked. But the noise from the
constantly passing cars on the new expressway more than
made up for the absence of the trains.

In 1985, lace curtains still adorned the white-stucco
house where Ramirez spent most of his youth, the youn-
gest of Julian and Mercedes Ramirez's seven children.

An incongruous mail-order picture of Jesus giving a blessing for peace was still tacked to a wall. That caught the cynical eyes of the California investigators, who were investigating the hideous atrocities thought to have been committed by the baby of the family who grew up there.

In his early years, Ricky Ramirez sought a peaceful sanctuary in El Calvario Catholic Church and, at the constant urging of his mother, regularly attended mass. The church is no longer there, demolished years ago to make way for the elevated highway where cars and trucks now clatter night and day.

By the age of nine, Ramirez was already becoming a loner, withdrawing slowly from his family and friends. Ray Garcia, a childhood friend and companion, much later recalled that young Ricky spent much of his time and money in the arcades and the 7-11 store, playing video games.

"When he wanted to do something, he did it," Julian Ramirez told investigators. Slowly, Ricky Ramirez withdrew from his parents and, later, when his drug problem became evident, Julian regretfully broke off with his errant son. Ricky's father told police that he had not spoken to the family black sheep for three years.

One of Ricky's sisters told the Los Angeles deputies that her brother had periodic seizures and convulsions, and said he suffered from epilepsy. Police, however, never found any history of epilepsy in his medical records, although others also said Ramirez sometimes suffered epileptic-like convulsions.

The teen-ager, who was later to terrorize California as the loathsome Night Stalker, never joined the gangs of marauding delinquents who roamed the streets of the Ledo barrio. But that doesn't mean he did not readily get himself mixed up in criminal activities. He hung around with a group that was heavy into smoking marijuana and stealing. At night, he slipped into homes in the more affluent parts of town, entering through unlocked windows and doors, as he would later in California. And he stole everything he could carry.

"He had this disease," Garcia told investigators. "Things would stick to his fingers. We used to call him Ricky the Klepto." He was also known as Richie *rabon,* Spanish for *thief,* and as *dedos,* Spanish for *fingers.*

Police caught him a few times and once sent him to a Texas youth camp for juvenile delinquents, where he received some counseling, before being released to attend junior high school. Before he was sent to reform school, Cesar Mendoza, a longtime assistant principal in El Paso's school system, said Ramirez was a "quiet guy who never was involved in violence or vandalism." But although he had been an average student at Lincoln and Cooley elementary schools, he came back from reform school a changed person.

After Ricky left the youth camp, Mendoza said, he constantly saw Ramirez for cutting classes and for having long absences from school. Charles Hart, a spokesman for the El Paso school system, said Ramirez's grades took a nosedive in junior high school. He failed in two tries to pass the ninth grade. Teachers said he always looked sleepy and tired during his last year at Jefferson High School. He'd simply sit and not make any effort to participate. He dropped out of Jefferson High when he was seventeen.

Ramirez cared nothing for work, either. As far as the L.A. investigators could determine, he never held or even sought an honest job.

In an interview with the *El Paso Times,* Julian Ramirez told a reporter that his son lost control of his life because of his heavy marijuana use.

A neighbor, who asked that her name not be revealed, told the *Times* reporter that she believed Ramirez's parents were not strict enough with him when he was young. She said the Ramirez children came and went as they pleased.

She recalled an incident when Ramirez was about twelve years old and threw a rock through a front window of her house. When she complained to Mercedes Ramirez, she said the boy's mother just shrugged.

Frances Bustillos, who grew up in the same neighborhood as Ramirez, said she knew him "pretty well." She remembered how he would suffer from seizures in elementary and junior high school. "He would go wild. No one could get near him."

She recalled playing softball and other street games with Ramirez, and riding the bus to school with him. He was just a typical kid when he was young, she said. However, when he was in eighth grade, he started hanging out with a bad crowd and began to get into trouble. He was caught breaking into houses, including her own, and was "really into marijuana" at the time. "I don't think he knew what he was doing half the time. Whenever I saw him, he was really stoned," she said.

The twenty-five-year-old Bustillos said she and her friends used to chase him away whenever he came near their homes. "Everybody, lock up your doors and windows, here comes Ricky *rabon,*" they warned. Ramirez apparently enjoyed the nickname. He felt it made him a celebrity.

Still another woman said she believed he left El Paso to live with an older brother whom he admired.

In addition to becoming fixated with marijuana, Ramirez developed an interest in martial arts and music when he was in junior high school, particularly the Beatles, Led Zeppelin, and Black Sabbath. Neighbors recalled seeing him in his backyard, practicing karate and walking around with a radio. He also liked reading horror stories and magazines that carried articles about rock stars.

Myers, *Arredondo,* Garcia, and Little said they could not remember his ever having had a girlfriend in California. But Garcia remembered that the girls in elementary school thought he was "cute." Alma Gaytan recalled that the girls in her class used to sigh "ahhh!" when he entered a classroom. However, although he dated occasionally, he did not have a regular girlfriend in El Paso.

Nohemi Navarrete, a criminology student at the University of Texas at El Paso, refused to believe the boy she'd known as a teen-ager could be the monstrous Night Stalker. The twenty-year-old woman told police she sometimes went out with Ramirez "for about a year." Navarrete was fourteen and Ramirez eighteen at the time.

She said the Richard Ramirez she knew believed in God and used to encourage her to study hard and stay in school.

Another boyhood friend, twenty-six-year-old Tom Ramos, told investigators he believed Bible study led to Ramirez's interest in Satanism. According to Ramos, an engineer, Ramirez emerged from a Bible-study group sponsored by the Jehovah's Witnesses with a fascination with Satan.

Ramos and another friend, twenty-six-year-old Eddie Milam, who used to attend the Bible-study classes with Ramirez, eventually became Jehovah's Witnesses. Ramos said Ramirez left the group after a few months.

"He said he could not live the way the Bible wanted him to live," Milam recalled, adding that Ramirez, although only thirteen at the time, was already smoking marijuana.

Ramirez's interest in Satan increased after participating in additional Bible studies; something not anticipated by the study group's sponsors. After reading about Satan, he would go to the library to check out books on Satanism and the occult. He speculated about Satan and the power he seemed to possess, and he empathized with the Devil's rebelliousness against God, the two friends said.

FBI records show that Ramirez was arrested three times as an adult in El Paso after he left school. The first two arrests were on marijuana-possession charges. The third was for reckless driving. He was driving a friend's car when he was picked up on the charge. Police found a toy cap gun, a ski mask, and a green wallet on the front seat next to him. The wallet had been stolen, but the victim, who said she felt it being taken from her handbag while she was in a crowd, could not identify the thief.

The arresting officer noted in his report that the tall, lanky seventeen-year-old fit the description of the man who had recently held up a Dairy Queen not far from where the Ramirezes lived.

The reckless-driving charge was dismissed, but one of the two marijuana charges brought three years probation. Shortly after he was placed on probation, Ramirez left El Paso with Myers and another friend.

In Los Angeles, he spent much of his time living in skid-row hotels on the east side. His sister, Rosa Flores, said he once worked as a street sweeper there.

Area merchants were in agreement in describing him as an extremely nervous person who kept to himself. He always wore dark clothes, dark glasses, and a baseball cap with the logo of AC/DC or some other heavy-metal group in front.

Ramirez frequented a fast-food restaurant called Fat Brat for breakfast. He always came alone and ordered his food to go. The owner of the restaurant noticed that he seemed to have money and was willing to spend it. A cook at Margarita's Place, a Mexican restaurant, said Ramirez often came in for lunch, or to eat late at night.

People in both Los Angeles and San Francisco who knew him said he developed an avid interest in AC/DC and its album *Highway to Hell.* One of the cuts on the album was the six-minute song "Night Prowler." The lyrics were to become known as the Night Stalker's "anthem."

As investigators talked to Ramirez's friends and acquaintances, they began to piece together the profile of a confused, angry loner who sought refuge in thievery, drugs, the dark side of rock music—and, finally, murder and rape. Law enforcement officers, from the lowest patrolman to top-level department heads and civilian criminologists, see hundreds of similar profiles every day. It was a troubled cultural mosaic common to many criminals, whose offenses might be either petty or heinous.

Many psychologists, psychiatrists, and sociologists, with their unfailing and remarkable hindsight, would claim they could have predicted the monster that was spawned from the economic, environmental, sociological, and psychological cesspool that was the Ledo Street barrio. But the claims, as usual, would come after the fact.

In these professionals' eyes, it is not the monster who is at fault, but the society that created the cesspool, or allowed it to exist. It is this sort of reasoning that has returned hundreds, perhaps even thousands, of monsters to the streets, to do what monsters do—maim, kill, and rape. It is a convenient and perfect cop-out.

The tunnel vision of the social scientists somehow fails to note that the majority of the monster's contemporaries, although exposed to similarly depressing circumstances, usually grow up to become reasonably well-adjusted adults. Some even go on to achieve remarkable successes, as did several of Ramirez's childhood friends in the Ledo Street barrio.

Law enforcement takes a more myopic view. Its business is to protect the law-abiding public by tracking down and removing serial killers and other homicidal rogues and lesser criminals from the streets. If a dog, cruelly mistreated in its youth, develops a hatred for humans and turns vicious, biting children or anyone else who comes within reach of its jaws, society does not click its collective teeth and elect to rehabilitate what cannot be rehabilitated. The animal is simply destroyed. A deplorable necessity, but a necessity, nevertheless.

Well, the social scientists clucked; *a human is not a dog. Humans deserve humane treatment.* But, having witnessed countless atrocities visited on humans by other humans every hour, every day, police tend to be more cynical.

The rare lawman given to philosophical musing might point out that the abuse and pain deliberately inflicted by humans on their fellow man is rarely repeated in the world of presumed lesser animals. Animals do not torture, mutilate, or rape their victims for pleasure before killing them. They simply kill them—as quickly and as efficiently as possible. When they kill, they kill from necessity. The Night Stalker killed for enjoyment.

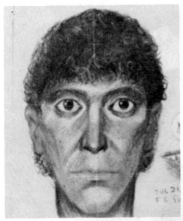

Police composite sketch of the "Night Stalker" suspect whose spree of rape, murder and robbery in 1984 and 1985 terrified Los Angeles residents. *(Author's collection)*

BK 7 8 6 7 4 0 7 1 2 1 2 8 4
LOS ANGELES POLICE = JAIL-F

Police photograph of Richard Ramirez after his August 25, 1985, capture in connection with the "Night Stalker" serial killings. *(Author's collection)*

Richard Ramirez, accused of being the Night Stalker, during his appearance in court in October, 1985, facing charges of fourteen counts of murder. *(AP/Wide World)*

Richard Ramirez flashes a pentagram—frequently used as a
Satanic symbol—while appearing in court. *(AP/Wide World)*

Ramirez displays a common Satanic gesture as Municipal Court Judge Elva Soper questions the experience and qualifications of Daniel Hernandez and Arturo Hernandez, two attorneys Ramirez wanted to hire for his defense. *(UPI/Bettmann)*

Jaime Burgoin (*left*) and his brother Julio (*right*). The brothers and other enraged citizens captured Richard Ramirez, accused of being the "Night Stalker" serial killer, in a Los Angeles neighborhood in August 1985. (*UPI/Bettmann*)

Richard Ramirez (partially hidden) and public defender Alan Adashek, then Ramirez's lawyer, appear in court in September, 1985, delaying entering a plea to several counts of murder, rape and robbery. *(UPI/Bettmann)*

Flamboyant defense attorney Melvin Belli at one point was considered by Ramirez and members of his family as the accused Night Stalker's defense. *(UPI/Bettmann)*

Accused Night Stalker Richard Ramirez arrives at court on October 4, 1989, in Los Angeles for sentencing. *(AP/Wide World)*

Ramirez, learning of his guilty verdict, responds to reporters' questions. Asked what he thought of the decision, he displayed a Satanic gesture and said, "Evil." *(AP/Wide World)*

Bernadette Brazal, a Night Stalker "groupie," attended Ramirez's trial daily and—although she never met him—wrote love letters to him, attempting to ignore the gruesome details of the testimony. *(Pat Tehan/*The Orange County Register*)*

CHAPTER 10

"El Matador"

AT APPROXIMATELY EIGHT-FIFTEEN A.M. ON Saturday, August 31, the Greyhound bus from Phoenix pulled into the Los Angeles depot. Among the yawning, sleepy-eyed passengers disembarking was a tall, thin Hispanic with curly black hair. He wore a pair of black pants and a black T-shirt emblazoned on the front with a Jack Daniels whiskey logo. He carried a black backpack hanging from one shoulder.

The man walked casually into the station. Inside, he stopped in the men's room. A few minutes later he emerged and passed several security guards without attracting a single suspicious glance. The guards paid no particular attention to him. Stepping into the early morning bronze smog, the lanky traveler glanced briefly across the street at the Los Angeles Police Department's Central Division station. It was the beginning of a typical bright, blazing hot Southern California day. He sauntered to the corner, where he boarded an eastbound Southern California Rapid Transit District bus.

The man who had for the last six months stalked more than two dozen California citizens, killing some, raping and molesting others, had walked right into the center of the intensive manhunt launched for him less than twelve hours earlier. His photo was on every television station and on the front page of every major newspaper in Southern California; nevertheless, no one as yet had given him so much as a second look.

Richard Ramirez, the bloody Night Stalker, had bragged more than once to friends and acquaintances that Satan watched over him and kept him safe from police. On that morning, his faith in the Prince of Evil's ability to shield him from the eyes of his enemies was greater than ever. But, if Satan had indeed protected him in the past, he had been doing a pretty poor job for the past several days.

First, there was the Jensen boy in Mission Viejo who had spotted the orange Toyota and taken down its plate number. Then there was the car recovered by police in Chinatown, and the fingerprint they were able to lift from it. Finally, there was the supercomputer in Sacramento that had not only plucked his print and identification from a staggering number of possibilities, but had done so in a matter of minutes.

There were also other instances where his demon protector had let him down, including problems with his friends, Donna Myers, *Serafin Arredondo* and others. But the most serious—indeed, fatal—letdown of all was Satan's failure to alert his disciple that law enforcement authorities knew he was the man they were looking for and that a massive, nationwide manhunt had been launched for him. Richard Ramirez had no idea he had been identified and publicly named as the Night Stalker.

It was, in fact, his very devotion to Satan that had led to his current predicament. After shooting William Carns and ravaging his girlfriend, Ramirez had returned to Los Angeles, dumped the car, and caught a bus to Phoenix to score some coke with the money he'd stolen from *Renata Gunther.*

The trip to Phoenix had been, for the most part, a blur.

High on the small stash of coke he still had with him, and with his Walkman fastened to his ear and the heavy-metal music scrambling helter-skelter through what the drugs had left of his brain cells, he had little awareness or interest in what was going on around him.

After replenishing his cocaine supply, he headed back on the Greyhound bus for Los Angeles near midnight on Friday. He was unaware that police had announced his identity and released his photo to the press at nine the previous evening. Within minutes, the story was on teletype and telephone lines, and speeding around the world.

Ramirez left Phoenix too early for the morning editions of that city's newspaper or its late-evening television news. He wasn't much of a newspaper reader, although he sometimes languidly watched television. And he might have even learned that thousands of police officers from Los Angeles to New York City knew who he was and what he looked like, from a radio broadcast—if he'd had a radio instead of the Walkman tape player.

In fact, if he had been a more sociable human being, he might even have picked up some information about his current predicament from other bus passengers, who had heard the news. But he was satisfied to be alone with his Walkman, his rock music, and his dark supernatural idol and protector.

Ramirez was the Devil's own, isolated from others of his species. He worshipped Satan in solitude, his mind and soul wallowing in the cancerous effects of the evil white powder and the profane messages from his tape player. He had hunted his fellow humans like a rogue grizzly turned maneater. Now they were about to even the score.

Several miles south of downtown Los Angeles, at approximately eight-thirty A.M., Ramirez walked into Tito's Liquor Store at 819 Towne Avenue. He selected a can of Pepsi-Cola, his favorite soft drink, from a cooler, then picked up a package of powdered-sugar donuts. As he walked toward the cashier, he noticed that several people glanced curiously at him. But he was used to that. The Walkman that seemed to be growing out of his ear, and his rotten teeth often drew curious glances.

At the cash register, he pulled three single dollar bills from his pocket and handed them to the cashier. He removed the ear plug to the Walkman from his ear as he waited for his change. Again, he was aware that several people were whispering behind him. He turned to look at them, but they quickly avoided his eyes. His heart quickened for a moment, but he dismissed the sudden alarm, attributing it to the effects of the cocaine he'd shot into his arm in the bus-station restroom.

That's when he first noticed the front page of *La Opinion,* a Los Angeles Spanish-language newspaper stacked next to the cash register. He saw the picture that dominated the page, but at first it didn't register. He looked again. His heart lurched so hard it seemed as though someone had punched him in the chest. He turned. The other customers were staring at him, wide-eyed and disbelieving. But this time, they did not look away.

"I tell you, it's him," a woman said to her husband. Her voice was loud enough to carry to where Ramirez stood, frozen in sudden fear.

He looked back again at the paper. Then he looked at the other papers—the *Los Angeles Times,* the *Herald Examiner,* the *Daily News.* It was his picture on the front page of each one. His old police mug shot was even on the front pages of the out-of-town papers: the *Sacramento Bee,* the *Orange County Register,* and the *San Francisco Examiner.*

Ramirez panicked. He bolted out the door, leaving the cashier holding his change. The Pepsi and donuts were abandoned, forgotten on the counter.

"It *is* him!" he heard the woman exclaim in a near scream.

"Who?" the cashier asked. He had been taken by surprise by the sudden commotion. He was puzzled and still clutched the change in his hand.

"The Night Stalker, damn it!" the woman's husband said. "Don't stand there, man. Call the cops."

It was hot. Ramirez could feel the sweat on his face. His armpits were already soggy. His heart was pounding in his chest, and his breath whistled through his mouth. He ran blindly, not sure where he was headed. A voice screamed in his head: *They know who I am. They know who I am! They're going to kill me. Get away. Got to get away.*

He bumped into someone. Ramirez couldn't see him because of the sweat, but he knew it was a man. "Hey, asshole, watch where you're going!" the man swore at him.

His lungs were burning. It felt as though he'd taken a deep drag on some green pot. He had to catch his wind. He slowed down. Slowly, his head and eyes cleared, and he saw he was on Mott Street. He looked around, feeling animal fear.

It was eight-forty-two. Although Ramirez didn't take the time to check street numbers or to look at his watch, he was in the 800 block of Mott, about two miles east of the liquor store he had fled twelve minutes earlier. Despite his physically ravaged condition, he had just run two six-minute miles, back-to-back. His heart felt as if it were going to leap out of his sunken chest. He stood, trying to catch his breath, his bony buttocks pressed against the side of a building. Panting from the fear and exertion, he leaned forward with his hands on his knees. It seemed there was only an instant's respite before he heard someone yell, "It's him! It's the Night Stalker! Call the cops!"

He started running again. Not so fast this time. He tried to clear his pounding head. His eyes darted here and there, looking for a way out. *A car,* he thought. *Gotta get me a car.* He thought of running into the street and stopping one, but they were moving too fast. He kept running. He saw two cars parked close together. One was locked. He checked the other; it was open. He crawled under the steering wheel, hoping to hot-wire it. His hands were shaking too much.

He heard the wail of a police siren. It seemed to be getting closer. It was coming his way. He started running again.

It was eight-fifty-seven. The Los Angeles Police Department was scrambling like fighter pilots on red alert. Black-and-whites screamed from all directions toward Indiana Avenue, about a mile southeast of Mott Street. Helicopters, like giant bumblebees, lifted into the air and veered toward the Boyle Heights area of the East Los Angeles barrio.

Frank Trevino's chopper was one of the first off the ground. As he turned the helicopter toward Indiana Avenue, listening to the voice-crackling in his earphones, he felt the excitement rush through his body like a drug. He had not felt this good in fifteen years, since Vietnam. He was suddenly a tiger stalking its prey. He had to check himself as his fingers reached instinctively for the triggers that were not there. There were no rockets to launch, no machine guns to fire.

Meanwhile, the man who, only a few hours earlier, had inspired such fear in others was now in the grip of panic himself. Running blindly, he cut off Mott Street onto Percy Street, looking for a hole to crawl into. He stopped in front of Bonnie Navarro's home, hesitating for a moment to catch his breath and wipe the sweat from his eyes. Then he opened the front gate.

Inside the house, in the living room, Bonnie Navarro was watching television when she heard the gate open. She frowned. In the background, growing louder, she heard the scream of police cars. Suddenly frightened, she jumped up and ran to the door. A man was approaching.

He kept looking to his right and left. There was fear in his popped eyes. She saw he was sweating. In fact, he was soaking wet.

When he saw her standing in the doorway, her hand on the screen-door latch, he cried, *"Ayudame* [Help me]!"

At first, Navarro thought he might be a mugging victim. She looked to the right, toward Mott Street, then to the left, toward Indiana Avenue. She could see no one. However, the police sirens were coming closer. In the background, she was able to distinguish the steady flap-flap-flap of helicopter rotors. Then she realized that the frightened man approaching her was being chased by police. Her throat tightened as she took a closer look at him. There was something familiar. . . . It was him—it was the Night Stalker.

"No!" she screamed, and slammed the door shut. Her twenty-year-old son, Frank, dashed from the bedroom. He raced out the door, but it was too late. The man in black had jumped the gate and was headed toward Indiana Avenue. The young man tried to calm his near-hysterical mother while he dialed the police.

Arturo Perez was sipping a cup of coffee in a donut shop in the 800 block of Indiana Avenue when he heard the screech of tires and a woman scream. He looked out the plate glass window and saw a car in a parking lot in front of the supermarket across the street. A man dressed in black was trying to open the door on the driver's side and pull a woman from the vehicle. She was fighting, punching, and slapping at her assailant—and screaming.

Arturo Benevidez, owner of Art's Barber Shop, was idly scanning a newspaper and talking to a friend in his shop, next to the supermarket, when he heard the screams. He looked out and saw the man trying to pull the woman from her car. It took only the merest glance for Benevidez to realize who the woman's assailant was. He'd been looking at the scumbag's picture in the paper only a second or so earlier. He ran out of the shop, into the parking lot, yelling, alternately, at the Night Stalker, then for help.

Perez had dashed out into the street only a few seconds before Benevidez. From the corner of his eye, he saw Benevidez bolt from his barber shop. Two other men were running around the corner from Percy Street. They, too, were headed for the struggling pair and the car.

"Mira! It's him. *El Matador!"* someone yelled. "The killer!"

The tall man in black, his face sweaty and dirty, turned and saw them. Eyes wide with fear, he backed away from the car and started to run. He jumped a fence on Indiana Avenue and was in the backyard of Luis Muñoz. There was no sound to be heard, but the trap into which Richard Ramirez had stepped into less than forty-five minutes earlier slammed shut.

Instinctively, Ramirez had headed for the barrio as soon as he realized he had been exposed. He knew these streets. He'd walked them off and on for the last five years. These were his people, Hispanics. The neighborhoods reminded him of Ledo Street in El Paso.

But he should have known better. Hubbard Street is a tough street in one of the toughest areas in Los Angeles County. Half in the city and half in the county, the area is ruled by gangs who battle one another for territorial rights. The young toughs strut along main streets like Indiana Avenue dressed in baggy-legged black pants that tighten at the ankles, topped by tight, snow-white undershirts, or patrol the streets in brightly painted "low-riders," preferably Chevrolets. The young men live by a "machismo" code that places heavy emphasis on personal pride, on their unique perception of "honor."

The violence and posturing, however, are seldom apparent on the side streets like Hubbard, Percy, or Princeton. These are the "neighborhoods." The working-class homes are well maintained, the lawns neatly trimmed.

Almost every house has some religious artifact—plaster Madonnas, wooden crosses, and wreaths with Jesus's image—on the front lawns or doors. Residents are territorial, family-oriented. Mess with one member of the family and you mess with the entire extended family, which includes sons and daughters, brothers- and sisters-in-law and cousins. Backyards are enclosed with wooden fences; front yards are shielded from trespassers with wrought-iron or chain-link fences.

Here, the older generations, the mothers and fathers, the aunts and uncles, are in control. Once many of them, too, strutted, cruised, and rumbled on Indiana Avenue and Whittier Boulevard. Now, they live more settled lives, holding jobs, working hard, and raising and caring for their families—though they still drink beer or tequila under the shade of fruit trees in their backyards on weekends and hot summer evenings.

Richard Ramirez jumped into all this when he vaulted the board fence surrounding Luis Muñoz's home. Muñoz was cooking hamburgers and spareribs on the outdoor barbecue when Ramirez landed a few feet away. Although now in his forties, with muscles no longer as tight as they once were, his waist no longer as trim as it had been, the carpenter was still a formidable man. And he was fully capable of protecting his backyard and home from uninvited strangers.

Understandably startled, he demanded to know what on earth Ramirez meant by jumping his fence. When Ramirez failed to answer, Muñoz smacked him alongside his head with the long-handled barbecue tongs he was holding. Ramirez, once the dreaded Night Stalker, was now reduced to a frightened, whimpering fugitive, and he didn't strike back. Instead, he begged Muñoz for some water. Muñoz responded by hitting him again with the tongs, and ordering him out of his yard.

Defeated, Ramirez dutifully began climbing back over the fence. He was exhausted, soaked with sweat. When he did not move as quickly as Muñoz felt he should have, the wiry carpenter hit him again with the metal tongs, this time across the wrist. The pain was sharp, blinding Ramirez for a moment. Then he dropped over to the other side, into another backyard. Fifty-six-year-old Faustino Piñon, dressed in slippers and workclothes, was working on the transmission of his beloved 1966 red Mustang.

Piñon was about to slide under the car when Ramirez picked himself off the ground and saw the Mustang. Scarcely able to keep his legs under him, partially blinded by the salt from his free-flowing sweat and the sharp pain in his wrist, he lurched toward the car and struggled behind the wheel. It was then that Piñon realized he was not alone. Incredibly, someone was trying to steal his car while he was working on it in his own backyard.

Instinctively, he rushed at Ramirez and caught him around the neck, just as the fugitive started the car.

"I've got a gun! I'm going to shoot you!" Ramirez screamed. His voice was shrill, hysterical. It sounded like the high-pitched screech of a tortured cat.

No way! Not after all the money and work Piñon had put into the car. Piñon grunted, tightening his grip on Ramirez.

The two struggled as Ramirez fought the car into gear. It started forward but Piñon caught hold of the wheel, causing the Mustang to crash into the fence. Ramirez shifted into reverse and slammed into Piñon's garage, causing the vehicle to stall.

Piñon finally wrestled Ramirez out of the car and onto the ground. Ramirez broke free. With the wiry carpenter's curses ringing in his ears, he raced down the driveway to the front of Piñon's house, onto Hubbard Street.

Across the street, Angelina de la Torres was getting into her gold Ford Grenada. She was on her way to a nearby mall to buy her daughter, Amber, a birthday present. Amber was four years old that day.

Angelina looked up just in time to see Ramirez, drenched in sweat, running toward her. The pretty, twenty-eight-year-old woman had never seen anyone so frightening. His eyes looked like those of the Devil. She grabbed the car keys and clutched them tightly as Ramirez stuck his head through the open window. He demanded that she give him the keys. She pulled away from him.

"Te voy a matar [I'm going to kill you]," Ramirez hissed, pointing his finger at her. Then he repeated, "Give me the keys. Give me the keys!"

But Angelina clutched them even tighter. It was then that she suddenly recognized him. It was the Night Stalker.

"El Matador! El Matador!" she screamed as loud as she could. Then she slid across the seat, wrenched open the door on the passenger's side, and jumped out.

Angelina's husband, Manuel, was in the backyard, preparing for Amber's birthday party that evening. When he heard his wife screaming, he ran to the front of the house. As he passed through the backyard gate, he grabbed an iron bar used to keep the gate closed.

Across the street, fifty-five-year-old Jose Burgoin had heard the commotion in Faustino Piñon's backyard. He looked out the window and saw Piñon struggling with a man dressed in black jeans and a black Jack Daniels T-shirt. He telephoned the police. Then, when he heard the would-be car thief run through the driveway separating his house and Piñon's, he headed for his door, yelling for his two sons, twenty-one-year-old Jaime and seventeen-year-old Julio.

As Burgoin stepped out the door, he could hear Piñon cursing the stranger for ruining his car. A moment later, Piñon appeared running up the driveway, his slippered feet slapping the concrete.

The two men heard a woman scream. Piñon stopped running and looked quizzically at his neighbor.

"El Matador! El Matador!" they heard Angelina de la Torres yell. They looked across the street and saw the stranger struggling with her. They watched, stunned into momentary inaction, as she scrambled frantically across the seat and escaped out the passenger's door.

"It's the killer. It's the Night Stalker," Jaime said over his father's shoulder, while he hurriedly stuffed his white undershirt into his pants.

Burgoin and Piñon started across the street together. "Let's get him," the elder Burgoin said in Spanish.

Jaime and Julio, following close behind, took off after the two older men. "Yeah," Julio said. "All right!"

But Manuel de la Torres reached Ramirez first, and whacked him once in the back of his neck with the iron gate rod.

Thirty-two-year-old de la Torres snarled from between clenched teeth as he swung the rod again, catching Ramirez across the shoulders.

Ramirez stumbled, fell to the ground, then got up. He started running as the Burgoins and Piñon drew near. Jaime caught up and punched him. Exhausted, dizzy, and barely able to breathe after his exertion, Ramirez somehow continued running. He was functioning on adrenaline manufactured by fear.

Incredibly, Ramirez then stunned his pursuers by suddenly stopping, turning and sticking his tongue out at them. Then he started to laugh. For a moment, everyone stopped. Ramirez laughed again, then continued to run.

"The son-of-a-bitch is crazy," one neighbor murmured.

And the last leg of the chase began.

About a block away, Manuel de la Torres was the first to catch up to Ramirez. He caught him alongside the head with the three-and-a-half-foot-long bar. Ramirez dropped to the ground. This time he stayed there. When he tried to roll away from de la Torres, Jaime and Julio pounced on him and held him down. A moment later, a deputy sheriff's patrol car, which had been trying to follow the chase across an empty lot and two backyards, pulled alongside.

Deputy Andres Ramirez knew he was driving too fast, even a little recklessly. But he didn't slow down even as he took the corner at Indiana Avenue and Hubbard Street so sharply that the car leaned to one side and the tires screeched in protest.

The police radio was filled with chatter. For the past five minutes, the dispatcher had been relaying what amounted to a step-by-step description of the quarry's rapidly changing location. Deputy Ramirez had been able to get a jump on the other patrol cars because he knew the area well and was able to anticipate where the chase would lead. He'd roamed those streets himself as a youngster.

As he rounded the corner, he suddenly slammed on the brakes. About fifty yards ahead, Hubbard Street was literally blocked by milling men, women, and children. Near the end of the street, he could see several men chasing another man.

One of the men caught up to his quarry and hit him in the head with what looked like a metal rod. The victim staggered against a fence, then dropped to his knees. The man with the rod raised it again, but before he could deliver another blow, two younger men dove on top of the stricken man, knocking him to the ground. Deputy Ramirez's heart leaped with excitement. The man who was now on the ground was dressed totally in black. Instinctively, the deputy loosened the pistol in his holster.

Andres Ramirez had prayed for this chance ever since he'd heard Richard Ramirez publicly identified as the Night Stalker the previous night. His fellow officers had teased him about having the same last name as the killer. They were even the same age: twenty-five years old. He'd taken the kidding as good-naturedly as he could, but inside he was fuming.

This foul beast, this pig, had brought shame to the Ramirez name. It had bothered him so much, in fact, that he'd asked his mother and father if they had any relatives in the El Paso area. They did not, he was told. Thank God. That had helped some, but not quite enough.

The crowd parted slowly as he approached, his car siren screaming, lights flashing. Someone smacked the side of his car with something. Punk kid. The deputy stopped the patrol car just a few feet away from where Jaime and Julio Burgoin held the Night Stalker. Officer Ramirez was shocked by what he saw. The killer's head was caked with dirt, sweat, and blood, but it was his eyes that held the deputy sheriff's attention. He had never before seen such abject fear in the eyes of a human being.

As Andres stepped out of the car, taking his handcuffs from his belt, the killer raised his hands toward him.

"Save me. Please. Thank God you're here. It's me. I'm the one you want. Save me before they kill me," he begged.

"He tried to beat my wife," the man with the rod said.

"All right, that's enough," Officer Ramirez said as sternly as he could. Although he could understand and empathize with the crowd's emotion, he had been trained to keep the peace, protect the public—even to protect such pitiful human rejects as the man lying in the street. Deputy Ramirez was permitted to share the crowd's disgust for the suspect. But he couldn't share in, or permit, further violence.

Richard Ramirez yelped in pain as the deputy sheriff cuffed him. Andres noticed the swelling on the killer's right wrist. Probably broken! He shoved his prisoner into the backseat of the patrol car, then climbed behind the wheel. It was then that he noticed the crowd had grown

—and seemed to be becoming unruly. Several hard thuds resounded against the metal sides of the patrol car. The deputy was about to radio for reinforcements when the crowd suddenly parted and a half-dozen patrol cars pulled up alongside him.

Relieved, and eager to satisfy any lingering doubts about identity, he turned to his prisoner in the backseat. "You're Richard Ramirez, aren't you?" He didn't have to ask the question. Even with his face smeared with filth and swollen from the blows he'd taken, there was no hiding those rotten teeth, the demon eyes, that evil face.

"Yeah, man. I'm Richard Ramirez." Then, to officer Ramirez's surprise, the man started to cry. He leaned forward, so that his head was almost between his legs. "Shoot me, man. Kill me. I don't deserve to live. Kill me now."

Deputy Ramirez didn't reveal his thoughts about that moment to reporters or writers. But he delivered his prisoner to his superiors, alive, and with no more bruises than he already had when he was rescued from the angry crowd.

By nine-forty-five A.M., Richard Ramirez was in a first-floor holding cell at Hollenbeck Division station. Officers, including Sergeant Frank Salerno, who had been the first to realize that a serial killer was stalking Los Angeles County, began to interrogate him.

At the same time, medics were checking his swollen wrist, and other cuts and bruises. "It's broken," Salerno said with a grin, his face devoid of any sympathy, as he looked at the wrist. The medics nodded their assent.

The Night Stalker may have been behind bars, but the people of East Los Angeles were not yet finished with him. The crowd that jammed the street outside the Hollenbeck Division police station by ten A.M. seemed unable to decide whether it wanted a public lynching or a street carnival.

There were scattered shouts of "Hang him! Hang him!" from some of the more than 600 people who pressed against the fence around the East Los Angeles station, hoping for a glimpse of the Night Stalker.

It was a hot, blistering day, and tempers seemed to rise with the temperature. At one point, it appeared the unruly, unpredictable mass of people might force its way into the station by sheer numbers and take back the prisoner. Police ordered the crowd back from the station, but it was only after officers broke out bullhorns to broadcast the dispersal orders—and called for reinforcements—that the mob finally began to back off.

Only a few minor troubling incidents marred the police success in avoiding a potentially nasty confrontation. One man carrying a long-bladed knife was briefly detained after he threatened to kill Richard Ramirez. Later, however, police released the man. They explained that he was drunk and hallucinating that the Night Stalker had killed his wife.

An overly exuberant group of youngsters climbed atop a black-and-white patrol car parked on the street and jumped up and down on the roof until they were chased away by police.

Participants and witnesses to the Night Stalker's capture received rousing cheers from the crowd as they were taken into the station for questioning. But the loudest applause was for Manuel de la Torres, his wife, Angelina, Faustino Piñon, and the Burgoins.

While some of the more cautious police officers described the scene outside the station as tense, most said it had more of a circus atmosphere, almost like spectators preparing to watch a parade.

Many in the mostly Hispanic crowd, in an impish mood, played with the army of news reporters who rushed to the station. Some joked—but others were dead serious, and in a mood for blood.

One woman told a reporter, "The police have had him

long enough. Now, they should turn him over to us. We'll make sure he gets justice."

A man shouted his agreement: "Yeah. Turn him over to us. I don't trust the court system."

There were others who were more relieved than vengeful. But they still had not forgotten the terror they'd felt while the Stalker was loose.

A woman said she had slept with a pistol under her pillow for fear that the Stalker would sneak into her house. "Now I can sleep safely at night." She smiled. "And I can put the pistol away."

A man said the capture of the Night Stalker meant he could get his apartment back. He said his sister was so terrified of the Stalker that she had moved in with him, leaving her home in Alhambra empty. "For two weeks, she has been driving me crazy. Sometimes I would think of leaving her window open so that the Stalker would get her and leave me in peace." He grinned.

While print journalists and TV camera teams moved through the crowd and pressed high-ranking lawmen for more information on the suspect and the capture, sheriff's deputies retraced Richard Ramirez's route in his desperate dash for safety after he was first recognized in the liquor store. They were searching for the handgun they believed he had thrown away. But after several hours the search was called off, without the gun being found. If indeed there was a gun, it could have been picked up by virtually anyone. Or it could be behind a bush, or under a car. They would try again the following day to locate it.

Sergeant Salerno was busy. In between interrogating Ramirez, he was also helping organize the prisoner's transfer to the central jail downtown. The crowd outside had not dissipated. Many were still calling for frontier justice. If there wasn't a tree from which to hang the bastard, a lamppost would do just as well, someone yelled. But the city and county officers were determined that their prisoner, no matter how hateful he might be, or how loathsome his crimes, would not become a Lee Harvey Oswald. There would be no Jack Ruby to gun him down while he was in police custody, as was the accused assassin of President John F. Kennedy. Los Angeles would not become another Dallas.

Protected by fifty specially armed and riot-armored officers, Ramirez was escorted down the back steps of the building to a brown, unmarked car. The group was led by Salerno and Sgt. Leroy Orozco of the LAPD. Salerno had directed the special Night Stalker task force for the sheriff's department, while Orozco had headed up the LAPD's task force.

Ramirez clasped his hands over his head to hide his face from the crowd as the car pulled away from the station and drove through streets roped off to keep people back. The convoy was escorted by two black-and-white police cars and six motorcycle officers on the two-mile trip to the county jail downtown.

It was a fitting experience for a coward who killed and terrorized helpless people in their homes with such ruthless savagery. He had been run down, beaten, knocked to the ground, forced to cower in the dirt while begging for mercy. And his captors and abusers were not even police. Instead, they were very ordinary people, much like those on whom he had preyed.

CHAPTER 11

Celebration

LABOR DAY SUNDAY WAS A DAY OF PEACE for the people of Los Angeles county. The Night Stalker, the dark beast who had held them in thrall for the past six months, was behind bars. What's more, he had proven himself to be just another two-bit cowardly punk who had cried like a baby when captured.

For many, Richard Ramirez's capture meant an end to citizens' needs for guns, locked windows and doors, curfews, and barking dogs.

One homemaker was especially happy about getting rid of the gun her husband had bought the previous month. The Whittier City resident said her husband had promised to sell the .357 Smith & Wesson as soon as the Night Stalker was behind bars.

"My father used to say a gun is more of a danger to its owner than it is to a thief. He was right. The second day we had the gun, my six-year-old son found it in my husband's nightstand drawer. Thank God, my husband is smart enough to unload it every morning before he goes to work. I shiver every time I think of what might have happened," she confided.

Fred Polous, an Anaheim postal worker, said he was

going to ship the Doberman he'd bought to his uncle, who owned a farm in Ohio. "That dog makes me nervous. I know he's supposed to be trained and that he's not supposed to attack unless I order him to. But does *he* know that?" Polous asked.

There were some, however, whose lives would be forever changed by the fear engendered by the Night Stalker. Some weren't even satisfied yet that Richard Ramirez was indeed the killer police had been seeking.

"They may have caught this one, but who's to say another one isn't going to take up where he left off?" a Valley resident explained. "Southern California is crawling with crazies. No, I think I'll keep locking my doors and windows, keep the gun under my pillow, and set the alarm system every night before I go to bed."

"You notice, the police refer to this Ramirez guy as a suspect. A *suspect.* I don't think they're positive he's the right one. You know, they make mistakes like that all the time," said Fred Heim, an Orange County realtor.

In the East Los Angeles barrio—especially on Hubbard Street—Sunday was festival time, despite the sweltering afternoon heat. The neighborhood was suddenly famous. Manuel and Angelina de la Torres, Faustino Piñon, and Jose Burgoin and his two sons, Jaime and Julio, had become instant celebrities. Details of the roles Hubbard Street residents had played in running the feared Night Stalker to ground were already becoming known from coast to coast.

Los Angeles Mayor Tom Bradley, a former Los Angeles policeman, had personally called de la Torres to thank and congratulate him. Calls from all over the country kept the phones of the principal heroes busy most of Sunday with messages of praise and congratulations.

Three-year-old Richard Perez, Piñon's grandson, told everyone who would listen, "My grandfather is a hero. My grandfather is a champion."

Reporters and television crews roamed the streets for

the better part of the day, looking for interviews. First, they sought the de la Torreses, the Burgoins, and Piñon. Later, anyone who would talk to them was good enough. As camera crews, news photographers, and reporters milled about on the streets, talking to anyone who would admit they spoke English and agreed to answer questions, most residents sat under fruit trees or on front steps, drinking beer and watching the passing show.

One reporter asked Jose Burgoin if he was frightened, chasing the dreaded Night Stalker.

"Of course I was scared," Burgoin said, looking suspiciously at the reporter as though he suspected the young woman might not be too bright. "But one does what one has to do at a time like that. I didn't think of it until later."

When he returned home from the police station the previous evening, after Ramirez had been moved to the county jail, Manuel de la Torres was asked if he felt like a hero.

"No," he said flatly. "All I'm thinking about now is my daughter's birthday party. Today is her fourth birthday."

He talked with reporters Sunday morning, but eventually grew bored with the same questions being asked repeatedly. So he withdrew to his backyard to enjoy a few beers and instructed Angelina to tell the reporters he wasn't home.

Angelina described the Night Stalker as she first saw him. "He looked mad and ugly . . . wet and sweating and smelling very bad. They should send him to the gas chamber just for being so ugly."

Maria Cortez was asked whether she thought the Stalker was in league with the Devil. "This thing about the Devil is a lot of malarkey," she scoffed. "They'd better not let him off on that. He's guilty."

Tito Fuentes laughed. "If he was the Devil's disciple, he sure picked the wrong neighborhood." He pointed to the madonnas on the lawns and to the pictures of Christ on doorways. "Jesus lives in this neighborhood. We don't allow no devils here."

Sixteen-year-old Felipe Castenada said, "He should never, *never* have come to East L.A. He might have been a tough guy, but he came to a tougher neighborhood. He was Hispanic. He should have known better."

Piñon's wife, Reyna, said, "I suppose when you think about it, we all could have been killed." She said she and her neighbors were disappointed and angry when they had learned on television that the Night Stalker was Hispanic. "But he wasn't going to get any mercy from us, just because he was Latin."

In the days that followed, however, some bitterness and petty bickering began to deflate the euphoria Hubbard Street residents had enjoyed. There was the matter of the $70,000 in combined rewards offered by a variety of municipalities, including the city of Los Angeles, Los Angeles County, and San Francisco, as well as the state of California.

When Manuel de la Torres was first asked if he would apply for the reward, he told a reporter that he had not thought about it. A few days later, after the names of de la Torres, Piñon, and the Burgoins were being bandied about as prime candidates to split the reward money, several people from Hubbard Street also made application for it.

While no one contested de la Torres's worthiness to share in the reward, potential claims by Piñon and the Burgoins were questioned by some. One man told reporters that neither Piñon nor the Burgoins was anywhere nearby when he and de la Torres had run the Stalker down. Another man said he'd knocked the Stalker down, so that de la Torres was able to hit him.

Although he tried to avoid hard feelings with his neighbors, de la Torres said he and the Burgoins, father and sons, had been the first to catch up to Ramirez. He was not sure as to who else was there, he said. "I didn't take roll call. No one was thinking about rewards at that time."

Anyway, he pointed out, it was far too early to be fighting over the bounties on the accused killer. One of the stipulations for payment of the various rewards was that the Night Stalker be convicted. The way things usually worked out in California courts, it would probably be at least a year, likely far longer, before the trial would even get under way.

In the meantime, Los Angeles County District Attorney Ira Reiner and his staff were working to prepare their charges against Ramirez. Reiner immediately appointed as chief prosecutor Deputy District Attorney P. Philip Halpin, a veteran who had prosecuted the infamous "Onion Field" cop-killing case twenty years earlier.

Halpin responded by spending Sunday and Labor Day methodically constructing the beginnings of what he hoped would be an airtight case that would funnel Ramirez into California's gas chamber. Although Halpin had until the close of the business day on Wednesday to file charges, he filed them as soon as the courts opened Tuesday morning.

The first charges filed involved the May 9 robbery and burglary of eighty-five-year-old Clara Cecilia Hadsall, in Monrovia; and murder, robbery, and sexual offenses in the May 14 attacks on *Harold Wu* and his wife, *Jean*.

Within the next few weeks, Ramirez was charged with fourteen counts of murder, nineteen counts of burglary, six counts of robbery, five counts of attempted murder, two charges of kidnapping, seven charges of rape and fifteen sexual-assault charges, which included five acts of forced oral copulation, seven of sodomy, and three lewd acts with children.

Halpin presented his initial list of charges against Ramirez, along with the names of victims, to the court. The list included:

- June 28, 1984—Jennie Vincow, 79, Eagle Rock. Murder, burglary.
- March 2, 1985—Thomas Sandova, Eagle Rock. Robbery.
- March 17—Dayle Okazaki, 34, and *Angela Barrios*, 20, Rosemead. Murder, attempted murder, robbery.
- March 17—Tsai-Lian Yu, 30, Monterey Park. Murder.
- March 20—Eight-year-old girl, Eagle Rock. Burglary, kidnap, rape.
- March 27—Vincent Zazzara, 64, and his wife, Maxine, 44, Whittier. Two counts of murder, burglary.
- May 9—Clara Hadsall, 85, Monrovia. Robbery, burglary.
- May 14—*Harold Wu*, 66, Monterey Park. Murder, robbery, sexual charges.
- May 30—*Ruth Wilson*, 41, Burbank. Burglary, sex charges, robbery.
- June 1—*Malvia Keller*, 83, and sister, *Blanche Wolfe*, 80, Monrovia. Murder, attempted murder, robbery.
- June 27—Six-year-old girl, Arcadia. Burglary, robbery, sex charges.
- June 28—Patty Elaine Higgins, 32, Arcadia. Murder, robbery.
- July 2—Mary Louise Cannon, 75, Arcadia. Murder, burglary.
- July 5—Sixteen-year-old girl, Sierra Madre. Attempted murder, burglary.
- July 7—Sixty-three-year-old woman, Monterey Park. Burglary, rape, robbery.
- July 7—Joyce Lucille Nelson, 61, Monterey Park. Murder, burglary.
- July 7—*Linda Fortuna*, 63, Monterey Park. Burglary, robbery, sex charges.

- July 20—Maxson, 66, and Lela Kneiding, 64, Glendale. two counts of murder, robbery.
- July 20—*Chitat Assawahem.* 32, Sun Valley. Murder, robbery, burglary, sex offenses.
- August 6—Christopher, 38, and Virginia Petersen, 27, Northridge. Attempted murder, burglary.
- August 8—*Ahmed Zia,* 35, Diamond Bar. Murder, robbery, burglary, rape.

The prosecutor said he planned to file additional charges in the coming days and weeks, and that San Francisco was expected to file murder, attempted murder, and robbery charges in the Pan attack.

During this period, Halpin added the June 28, 1984, murder of seventy-nine-year-old Jennie Vincow in Eagle Rock to the list of the Night Stalker victims. The Vincow murder occurred 9 months before that of Dayle Okazaki on March 17, 1985, and wasn't tied to the serial killings until reasonably late in the investigation.

The Vincow murder was an abominable killing. Only the victim could have known the true horror, pain, and fear she suffered—and, of course, she could not tell anyone.

Jennie Vincow lived alone in a modest, one-bedroom apartment on Chapman Street. When police officers found her, she had been dead for several hours. Her throat was so viciously, severely slashed that she was almost decapitated. Her body had been ripped by so many knife wounds that it was more in pieces than together.

Blood was splattered all over the bedroom and the bathroom. Smears in the bathroom indicated that the killer had attempted to wash his hands before leaving. Blood dappled the bedroom floor in sickening, congealed pools. It formed crusty, soggy scabs on rumpled bedclothes. Ugly rust-colored smears streaked the walls.

The room was a grisly chamber of horrors, filled with the smell of death. Drawers were scattered throughout the apartment, their contents spilled helter-skelter as the murderer had frantically ransacked them, apparently seeking jewelry, cash, or other valuables.

Entry to the apartment was easy. The killer had simply removed a screen from a front window. Police dusted the apartment and picked up five good partial fingerprints from the window and screen.

Later, an autopsy disclosed that the widow had been raped, either before or after her attacker had almost ripped her frail body apart and nearly slashed her head off. Investigators theorized that she had either surprised the burglar in the act of ransacking her apartment, or that the intruder was a killer-rapist who simply used the burglary as an excuse to commit the heinous crime and to cover his tracks.

The body was found by the victim's fifty-year-old son, Jack Vincow. He and his mother lived in separate apartments in the same building complex. Vincow told investigators that he had visited his mother on the afternoon of June 27, and that they had spent several pleasant hours together. When he left, Vincow promised to visit her the following day.

Twenty-four hours later, he walked into his mother's unlocked apartment and into a scene from hell. He was alarmed by the incredible disarray in the usually neatly kept apartment and, with his heart pounding in fearful apprehension, Vincow searched for his mother. He found her mutilated body, sprawled obscenely on the bed. Her neck had been slashed so severely that at his first horrified glance, he thought she had been decapitated.

There was nothing he could do for her. shaking with horror and grief, he called out, "Mother! Mother!"

Later, he recalled, "When I saw her, she was already dead. I shouted out to the manager that my mother had been murdered and for him to call the police."

* * *

Immediately after Ramirez's capture, it seemed as though the accused Night Stalker was going to do most of Deputy Prosecutor Halpin's work for him. During the first day and night of his incarceration, both at the Hollenbeck-division station and at the Los Angeles County Jail, the once-fearsome Night Stalker developed a severe case of verbal diarrhea.

Ramirez was scarcely in the holding cell at the Hollenbeck station when he told Det. George Thomas, who was guarding him, that he was the Night Stalker. "I did it, you know," he said. "You guys got me. The Stalker."

Several minutes later, while Salerno, Sergeant Orozco, and other detectives were questioning him, Ramirez broke down and, with tears streaking his sallow, sunken cheeks, he said he was sorry. Then he asked police officers to kill him.

"Of course I did it. You know that I am a killer. So what? Give me your gun. I'll take care of myself," Ramirez told his interrogators.

"You should [give me your gun] . . . I am a killer . . . So shoot me . . . I want the electric chair . . . They should have shot me on the street . . . Hey, I want a gun to play with, Russian roulette . . . I would rather die than spend the rest of my life in prison."

Police officers said that he blurted out the damaging statements spontaneously, before they had a chance to go through the obligatory reading of his constitutional rights to protection against self-incrimination as outlined in the so-called *Miranda Warning*.

At the same time, he rambled on about being under the control of the Devil, claiming that he had no control over his actions because he was Satan's slave.

Noticing the disgusted skepticism of the investigators, he suddenly screamed, "You think I'm crazy. But you don't know Satan." Then he laughed in an eerie cackle that ended in a coughlike grunt.

A few weeks later, although he had been ordered by a

court-appointed attorney to say nothing more, Ramirez bragged again to sheriff's deputy Jim Ellis, who had been assigned to watch him in his cell and make sure he didn't commit suicide.

As Ellis took notes, the Night Stalker told the deputy that he loved to kill. "I love to kill people. I love to watch them die. I would shoot them in the head and they would wiggle and squirm all over the place, and then just stop. Or I would cut them with a knife and watch their faces turn real white. I love all that blood," Ellis recorded Ramirez as saying.

Ellis reported that Ramirez also told him that he had "a lot of opportunities to do [in] different people," including sheriff's deputies, LAPD officers, and a Whittier police officer. According to Ellis, Ramirez added that the next time he had any chance to "do" anyone, no one would escape. He would "do" everyone. He also boasted that he was an uncatchable "super criminal" who had killed twenty people.

"One time I told this woman to give me all her money. She said no. So I cut her and pulled her eyes out," the deputy quoted Ramirez.

Maxine Zazzara, who was slain with her husband on March 27, 1985, in Whittier, had her eyes gouged out. Police never recovered the eyes and were still looking for them when Ramirez was arrested.

Ramirez also admitted that he had killed Peter Pan in San Francisco.

During his first night at the county jail, the serial-killing suspect told investigators that he had a locker at the Greyhound bus station and gave them the key. Police found two handguns and some cocaine and jewelry in the locker. The two guns were apparently not used in any of the murders, a police spokesman said.

Investigators drew another blank as they continued the search for a small-caliber weapon, probably a .22 or .25, which they believed Ramirez had ditched on his flight down Hubbard Street. Several of his victims had been shot with a small-caliber pistol, which explained why some of the Night Stalker's victims survived, despite the fact that he had blasted away at them from almost point-blank range.

While the residents of Hubbard Street were celebrating on Sunday, law enforcement officers, with the help of police cadets, combed the neighborhood, using metal detectors, in renewed efforts to find the gun.

The search was unsuccessful and police announced a $5,000 reward for anyone who turned in the weapon. Most investigators speculated that if the gun was dumped in the Hubbard Street area, it had probably been found by someone. And it was more likely that the finder would keep it as a gang weapon, or for holdups or drug rip-offs. Hubbard Street wasn't Marshalltown, Iowa.

Sheriff's Lieutenant Dick Walls said that without the handgun it might not be possible to link Ramirez to some of the homicides he was responsible for.

Police were, however, more fortunate in recovering a .22-caliber semi-automatic pistol from a woman in Tijuana, Mexico, after following leads from informants, and from Ramirez himself. The woman said she'd been given the gun by a friend of Ramirez's. Tests revealed the pistol was the murder weapon used in the slaying of *Harold Wu*.

Recovery of jewelry and other identifiable loot from crime scenes was also essential for helping establish links between Ramirez and the host of murders and robberies authorities were charging him with. In this respect, they did exceptionally well.

A bracelet and gold ring turned in by Donna Myers's daughter in San Francisco was linked to the Peter Pan murder, after police found Ramirez's fingerprints on the jewelry. Another cache of jewelry was recovered from a Los Angeles "fence" who admitted he bought the stolen property from Ramirez.

The search for other stolen jewelry was extended to El Paso, where the police department secured warrants to permit searches of the homes of Ramirez's parents and one of his sisters.

When they learned the Night Stalker had family in the Texas border city where he was born, Los Angeles investigators immediately suspected he might have sent home some of the jewelry he'd stolen. After two informants in San Francisco confirmed their suspicions, they asked El Paso police to obtain the search warrants.

Investigators also suspected that Ramirez might have mailed the eyes he'd gouged from Mrs. Zazzara to El Paso. These, along with a variety of weapons, were included in the list of items sought when the search warrants were prepared. Police were also hopeful of finding bloodstained clothing, tape recordings, videotapes, or photographs of victims. Police suspected that the Night Stalker might have taken pictures of some of his victims to keep as macabre mementos.

The hunch and tips on the jewelry proved correct. Investigators, both from Los Angeles and from the El Paso police department, recovered more than 300 pieces of jewelry from the home of the Night Stalker's sister, Rosa Flores. The jewelry included rings, necklaces, earrings, gold chains, and brooches. The items, found stashed in shoe boxes, filled an inventory eighteen pages long.

Searchers, however, failed to turn up Mrs. Zazzara's brown eyes, any weapons, or other physical evidence, aside from the jewelry, which might link Ramirez to the killings in California.

Although the jewelry was found in Rosa Flores's home, El Paso police said she was not considered an accessory to her brother's crimes, and no charges were filed against her.

Rosa Flores, in fact, would not believe her brother was the Night Stalker. Even if she was wrong and he was the killer, she added, he had to be sick and not aware of what he had done. Like her father, she blamed her brother's actions on the drugs he'd taken. She said when Ramirez telephoned his brother, Julian Ramirez, Jr., from jail, he denied involvement in the slayings.

"He laughed and then asked Julian how was the weather outside. And then he laughed some more and said he didn't do it. That sounds a little psychotic to me," she pointed out.

Mrs. Flores said her brother was especially upset by the charges that he had forced sexual abuse on several young boys. "He thought that was disgusting," she told a newspaper reporter.

Police turned up nothing at the home of Julian and Mercedes Ramirez, his parents.

A few days later, police showed victims and surviving relatives a total of 2,000 pieces of jewelry, televisions, stereo gear, cameras, luggage, and clothing recovered from El Paso and other sources. They were asked to identify them if they could.

At the same time, about thirty witnesses and victims of attacks by the Night Stalker went to the Los Angeles County Jail to view a lineup. Authorities would not say at the time whether any of the survivors—some accompanied by nurses—or other witnesses were able to identify either Ramirez or any of the stolen property.

On Monday, when Halpin filed his initial charges against the Night Stalker, Los Angeles Municipal Court Judge Elva Soper appointed a public defender to represent Ramirez. Several days later, an El Paso attorney, Manuel Barraza, said he had been hired by the Ramirez family to represent the accused Night Stalker.

Among the first moves he expected to make, Barraza told reporters, was to ask for a change of venue on the grounds that his client could not receive a fair trial in Los Angeles because of the widespread publicity and prejudice. He singled out a statement made by Los Angeles Mayor Tom Bradley, while awarding commendations to policemen who arrested Ramirez. Bradley had remarked that, no matter what happened in court, he knew the defendant was guilty, the lawyer complained.

For a man who had himself been a high-ranking police officer, it was an admittedly inappropriate remark, at the least, for the mayor to make, and Barraza said he expected it to give him a "lot of leverage" in winning a positive ruling on his motion to hold the trial outside Los Angeles.

On September 9, Ramirez was scheduled to enter a plea on the first murder, rape, and robbery charges filed by Halpin. But the public defender's office, already staggering under a backlog of previous cases, cited a lack of time to examine adequately the mass of police reports. A delay was granted by Judge Soper.

Los Angeles investigators also contacted police from Phoenix, after Ramirez told them he had spent several days there following the Carns attack. Phoenix police said Ramirez had not been charged with any crimes during the few days he was in the Arizona city, but said they would investigate the possibility that he may have come there to buy drugs or fence stolen goods. Arizona investigators said they also had several murder and rape cases that appeared to fit the Night Stalker's method of operation, and would check those out as well.

El Paso Police Lieut. Ricardo Cuellar said his questioning of Ramirez's high-school friends and acquaintances revealed no serious involvement with Satanism or Satanic groups. He told reporters that despite claims from a few religious leaders and journalists, few true incidents of Satanic practices were confirmed to have occurred in the El Paso area.

In the Southwest the work of *curanderos* peasant Mexican healers who call on a blend of Christianity and ancient Indian religious customs and practices are often mistaken by the uninformed as evidence of Satanism. Mexican witchcraft, or *brujeria,* which is closely related to *Curanderismo,* can involve occasional negatives spells or curses, experts explain, but the widespread religious practices are generally benign.

Cuellar told reporters the El Paso Police Department had never investigated any crimes in the city involving Satanic practices, although he conceded that it occasionally did get reports of Satanic ceremonies in the desert nearby. Sometimes there were even unsubstantiated claims of human sacrifice. But they always turned out to be nothing more than some kids getting together for a beer bust.

"Kids like to fantasize, to talk to impress others. To the best of our knowledge, that's what Ramirez was doing when he used to tell others about his Satanic involvement when he was a teen-ager here," the police lieutenant said.

America's most famous Satanist, Anton LaVey, founder and leader of the Church of Satan in San Francisco, and author of the *Satanic Bible* and *Satanic Rituals,* claimed he'd met Ramirez in 1983. But LaVey remembered the young man was "the model of deportment. I suppose that shows even murderers may not be all bad. Maybe he did his murders for reasons other than Satanism. Maybe he was disturbed or had an ax to grind," LaVey suggested.

Critics claimed to reporters that LaVey's books, which have sold a half-million copies, encouraged violence by persons with axes to grind.

"Anything can be misused," LaVey responded. "When I was a kid, every time there was a murder, the murderer would say something like 'God made me do it.' A lot of psychotics are doing what they're doing and saying they're Satanists as a way of getting themselves off the hook. There are crazies, and there always will be crazies. And whatever is around that they can lay the blame on, they will do it." LaVey's *Satanic Bible* specifically prohibits animal and child sacrifice, but talks approvingly of "symbolic" human sacrifice.

"When I met Richard Ramirez, he was one of the nicest, most polite young men you'd ever want to meet," LaVey told the press.

Richard Walker, an El Paso psychologist, who said he had examined more than one hundred killers and rapists, described Ramirez as fitting many of the same patterns he had noted in other murder suspects. Serial killers are turned on when they see others helpless and in agony, he said.

Walker explained: "They are average men with some kind of a hangup. They have low confidence and don't enjoy anything." They are also usually loners, he added. "People with close relationships don't kill."

CHAPTER 12

Lawyers and the Media

NOW THAT THE BEAST WAS CAGED, THE NEXT —and most difficult—step was to see that he paid the price for his awful crimes. In the case of the Night Stalker, it was to prove a most difficult step, indeed.

Considering the number of charges, the physical evidence, eyewitnesses, and Richard Ramirez's own statements to police, Los Angeles County District Attorney Ira Reiner's expectation that he would have the Night Stalker on death row within a year seemed reasonable.

Neither he nor anyone else could foresee the legal and media circus the case would become. But that's exactly what it would be—a nightmarish marathon that would last four years, cost the state almost $2 million in trial and other legal costs, involve a half-dozen defense attorneys, and almost 3,000 jury interviews.

The case appeared to be off to a running start when Reiner appointed veteran Deputy District Attorney P. Philip Halpin to prosecute the case within hours of Richard Ramirez's arrest. The forty-eight-year-old hardnosed veteran prosecutor responded by working over the Labor Day weekend. On Tuesday morning, twenty-four hours before he was required to, he filed murder, robbery, burglary, and sexual charges against Ramirez.

Judge Elva Soper kept things rolling by appointing Allen Adashek, an experienced public defender, to represent Ramirez.

But from that point on, everything went downhill. It would be almost six months before Ramirez would even enter a plea to the charges. Another eighteen months would pass before the start of the preliminary trial. And the trial itself would not get under way until January 1989—more than two and a half years after his dramatic capture and arrest.

Problems with defense attorneys began a week after Ramirez's arrest. Serious conflict between Adashek Manuel Barraza, the young El Paso attorney hired by the Ramirez family, quickly developed.

Barraza, a bright young man, just thirty years old, had a thriving, if not especially lucrative, practice among El Paso's poor Hispanic population. His secretaries were his sister, Sally, and his wife, Lourdes. Sally was married to Joe Mena, who grew up across the street from the Ramirezes on Ledo Street. He was a good friend of Ramirez's sister, Rosa Flores.

Sally Mena explained to a reporter from the *El Paso Herald Post:* "The Ramirez family had no money to help out their son. His mother could not go to Los Angeles because she did not have enough money, so the family was raising donations."

Joe and Sally Mena contributed, then told Barraza about the family's plight. Barraza responded by making a personal cash donation. He was then asked to defend Ramirez. He knew the Ramirezes could not afford the defense costs of a notorious murder trial, and he certainly didn't have the financial resources to pay for it out of his own pocket.

He was a young lawyer, only in practice a few years. And the Night Stalker case was the kind that promised to be totally time-consuming. The case was high profile, and he would be faced by a skilled, high-powered prosecution team with seemingly unlimited resources from the nation's second-largest city in its efforts to win convictions against his client. Barraza didn't even have a license to practice law in California. But he took on the case.

"He's always trying to help people too much," his sister told an El Paso newspaper reporter. "He takes cases without people paying him. He tries to help people, but they take advantage of him. People owe him thousands of dollars."

Barraza knew what it was like to not have much money. He knew what struggle was all about. But he had been lucky enough to have good family role models. He was the eldest of seven children and the only college graduate in the family. When he was growing up, his father had supported the family by cutting hair in his two-chair barber shop. The elder Barraza was still cutting hair in the same shop when his son was offered the Ramirez case. Although he did not make enough to send his son to college, Manuel Barraza, Sr., encouraged his son to make the most of his intelligence.

Married at nineteen, young Barraza worked his way through the University of Texas at El Paso, and graduated with a law degree from the University of Texas at Austin when he was twenty-three. He was admitted to the Texas bar at twenty-four.

"Mom and Dad could not give him much money, so he did it himself by working part-time and getting scholarships," Sally Mena explained proudly.

Eleven days after Ramirez had been run to ground by the residents of Hubbard Street, Barraza flew to Los Angeles—at his own expense—to talk to his infamous client.

After talking to him, Barraza said he learned that Ramirez was suffering from mood swings ranging from euphoria to deep depression.

"At first, he was really euphoric to see me. When I

came into the jail, it was very uplifting for Richard. He surprised me. He was really upbeat," Barraza told a reporter.

But by the time their two-hour conference had ended, Ramirez had slipped into a depression, Barraza said.

The next day, Barraza announced that he could not personally defend Ramirez after all because the case might last as long as two years. "The case will be a long one. It is a monster. I'd have to give up my Texas practice." Reality had intruded.

Barraza nevertheless said the trial should be moved somewhere else. He didn't believe Ramirez could receive a fair trial in the Los Angeles area. There had been too much publicity and widespread press coverage.

Barraza also told the press that throughout their two-hour meeting, Ramirez insisted that he was innocent— that he was not the Night Stalker. And despite his decision to pass up the job of defending Ramirez, the Texas attorney said he expected to meet with him once more before returning to El Paso. He suggested a joint meeting among himself; Ramirez's court-appointed public defender, Allen Adashek; and the defendant.

Adashek didn't appreciate the Texas lawyer's help with the case, and he didn't mince words about it when he talked with news reporters. He told them frankly that he saw no need for a joint meeting between himself, Barraza, and the defendant. Adashek said that he was Ramirez's attorney, and if Barraza expected to take over the legal chores he would have to be appointed by the court.

Experienced courthouse and crime reporters were well aware that such a move was highly unlikely, since Barraza didn't have a license to practice in the state. At most, he could help with the groundwork, including certain trial preparations. And he could sit in at a trial and offer advice to a California-licensed defense lawyer, but he could not submit motions or function as the attorney of record without a state license.

Although he might be considered a small-town lawyer by Los Angeles standards, and be from out of state, Barraza wasn't one to take a perceived snub lightly. He was scrappy, a fighter. After his second meeting with Ramirez—the meeting boycotted by Adashek—he advised the news media that he had decided to continue representing the defendant until he personally selected a California lawyer to take his place.

"A lot of people want to do it just to make a name for themselves. I don't want someone who will drop out of the case once he makes a name for himself," Barraza explained.

He said he would recommend to the public defender's office that Adashek be removed from the case. "I think his interests are in conflict with Richard Ramirez's," he told an *El Paso Herald Post* reporter.

The Texas attorney said he had offered Adashek some evidence he'd gathered in El Paso, but the public defender rejected it. His most serious criticism of Adashek, however, was accusations that the public defender wrongly allowed Los Angeles police officers to grill Ramirez after being appointed his attorney.

On Thursday, September 14, the burgeoning contest between the two lawyers tilting over the accused Night Stalker's defense chores heated up a bit more. When Barraza went to the county jail to talk to Ramirez, he was told that his client refused to see him. Outraged, Barraza complained to reporters that Adashek was turning his client against him.

"The first time I saw Richard, he was really friendly with me," he said. But after meeting with Adashek for three hours, Ramirez "didn't know which way to go. He was just confused."

Although he refused to discuss his own three-hour meeting with Ramirez, Adashek told an El Paso reporter by telephone that the accused serial killer made his own decisions. He also denied Barraza's charges that he was turning Ramirez against him. "I told [Barraza] that I was happy to work with him and to receive any information he had. But he got angry and stormed out," the public defender explained.

It did seem that, for someone who had announced he was turning down the job of defending the accused Night Stalker, Barraza was getting himself awfully worked up.

At the end of the week, on Friday, September 15, Julian Ramirez, Jr., and his sister, Rosa, drove the 900-mile trip from El Paso to Los Angeles to visit their jailed brother.

On September 28, the day before Ramirez was due to be arraigned on thirteen new charges, Rosa Flores told reporters that her brother wanted to plead guilty because he was afraid he would not get a fair trial, and feared he would be killed in the county jail.

The following day, Ramirez did not appear with his attorney for the arraignment, but was kept in a cell just outside the courtroom. No public explanation was offered by either Adashek or Halpin for his absence. But, later in the day, Rosa Flores told a Los Angeles *Daily News* reporter that her brother wanted to fire Adashek and hire famed attorney Melvin Belli.

She said her brother believed that Adashek kept him out of the courtroom because the public defender knew he wanted a new lawyer. She said her brother had yelled from the holding cell, "I'm guilty. I want Melvin Belli."

A Los Angeles county sheriff's spokesman admitted Ramirez was kept in a high-security area, not so much because they feared he would try to escape, but for his own protection. Other inmates were said to have made threats against him. Public defender Henry Hall, Adashek's co-counsel, said inmates were also threatening Ramirez in the lockup area outside the courtroom.

Ramirez's fears—and those of his jailers—were justified. Criminals have a moral code of their own; a somewhat similar, yet twisted reflection of what is considered normal by society. Murder, robbery, burglary, drug-dealing, kidnapping, and arson for hire are, for the most part, considered "respectable" crimes.

There are some gradations, though. Murder in the commission of an armed robbery or burglary is okay. So is murder for hire, murder to inherit money, or murder for revenge. Less acceptable is the murder of a child or murder resulting from some mental derangement—such as those committed by some serial killers, for instance.

Occupying the bottom of the criminals' social scale are most sex crimes. The rape of a child, especially a child under the age of ten, is a heinous crime in the criminal code of justice. It often carries with it the convict death penalty.

In prison, there are no officially appointed or elected courts or judges, and there are definitely no trials. If a suspect has been charged with a crime against a child, and if the evidence presented in newspapers or on television is strong, his peers may judge and carry out the punishment.

There are no appeals, no extenuating circumstances, no pleas of insanity. A convict condemned by his fellow inmates immediately becomes the target for a razor-sharp spoon or deadly piece of bedspring wielded by some outraged psychopath who has appointed himself a righteous executioner.

High-profile criminals, such as serial killers, may also become the targets of fellow convicts anxious to enhance their own reputations as tough guys or prison celebrities through an act of assassination.

As a vicious rapist, a despoiler of children, and a ruthless serial killer, all rolled into one, Richard Ramirez was a prime candidate for swift prison justice—and spontaneous termination. He was aware of his situation. He'd learned the code from his years on the "streets." It was most likely the reason he had complained so bitterly to his sister when news reports disclosed that he was accused of raping young girls and sodomizing boys.

He was officially accused of additional sex offenses, including rape and other crimes involving three children, when sixty new charges were filed against him by the district attorney.

Mrs. Flores said her brother "really freaked out" when he heard that sex charges involving assaults on children had been filed. Among the new counts was the rape and kidnapping of an eight-year-old Eagle Rock girl, and the sodomizing of an eight-year-old Sun Valley boy. Either one could have earned Ramirez a shot at quick prison justice.

Ramirez complained bitterly when he was kept in a holding cell outside the courtroom during arraignment proceedings on the latest charges. Judge Elva Soper upheld his confinement in the holding cell, but pointed out that it was for his own protection, and he could listen to the courtroom procedures over a loudspeaker. Although it was unlikely that a fellow jail inmate could get to him in the courtroom, he would be a more accessible target for an outraged relative of one of the victims.

There was another reason for restricting the defendant to a holding cell during the proceedings. His behavior during early courtroom appearances was bizarre. At his first appearance, he flashed a pentagram scrawled in ink on the palm of his hand to photographers and spectators. The pentagram was inverted, point down, to denote it was a symbol of Satan or the Black Arts. The inverted pentagram is sometimes referred to as the Baphomet, a goat-headed figure with human female breasts that is a universal figure of Satanism.

Ramirez fidgeted constantly and turned to stare at spectators in the courtroom; he argued angrily, and sometimes loudly, with Adashek and Hall, and taunted bailiffs and other law enforcement officers. He wasn't an easy, pleasant, or cooperative defendant to represent.

The judge was becoming concerned by the unremitting and extensive press coverage, much of which seemed bound to prejudice Ramirez's chances for a fair trial. It was difficult to fault the media corps for doing their job. After all, perhaps no one in the often bloody history of the Golden State had committed more shocking or horrific crimes. Not even Charles Manson's crazed clan of homicidal flower children had instilled more widespread fear. Nevertheless, the judge imposed a wide-ranging gag order that prohibited attorneys, investigators, and witnesses from discussing the case in public, and especially with the press. As might be expected, the press strongly objected to what it perceived to be a violation of the First Amendment.

Melvin Belli visited Ramirez at the jail the week before Halpin filed the sixty new charges. Present at the meeting, in addition to Belli and Ramirez, were Adashek, Barraza, and the defendant's sister, Mrs. Flores. Belli, who had defended Lee Harvey Oswald's killer, Jack Ruby, in 1964, refused to reveal publicly anything about the meeting. But Barraza said Belli had discussed defense strategies.

Ramirez's thirty-year-old sister, Rosa Flores, said her brother was growing disenchanted with Adashek. "It's been coming on because Adashek tells him one thing, and then tells him another and another," she claimed. She also criticized the public defender for restricting visits with Ramirez unless he personally approved the visitors.

Robert Ramirez, another of the Night Stalker's brothers, and a Tucson, Arizona resident, added his criticism of Adashek. "They don't let Richie make his decisions on what he wants. They just brainwash him so he doesn't know what's going on," he complained.

According to Barraza, Belli would not decide whether he would take the case until the following week. The seventy-eight-year-old Belli, like Barraza, was concerned with the length of time the case seemed likely to consume. But the El Paso lawyer said Belli liked "the challenge of a case where everybody's against the guy."

More skeptical observers, including more than a few reporters, merely smiled when Barraza talked of Belli's lofty-sounding reason for wanting to take the case. As far as they were concerned, it was just another act, a publicity-generating, ego-pleasing grandstand play. The wily lawyer knew how to play the press and the public, and was milking the situation for all the publicity he could squeeze out of it.

The Night Stalker's hopes of landing the famous Belli were dashed for good the following week, when the flamboyant San Francisco attorney announced he would have to turn down the case because of time and money. It was probably just as well for Ramirez, because Belli's record as a criminal lawyer was only average. In addition to Ruby, his criminal defendants ranged from self-appointed social activists from Berkeley to topless dancers. In the opinion of some of his fellow lawyers, his defense of Ruby was less than brilliant. His real skills were in personal-injury cases, which had made him a wealthy man, and had earned him the title "King of Torts."

"I wish I could defend him," Belli told reporters in San Francisco. "I like the guy. That may prove he's nuts, I'm nuts, we're all nuts. But I like him."

Belli explained that the case would cost him too much money and too much time away from his practice. He said Ramirez's medical and psychiatric bills alone would cost at least $300,000. "And that's just part of it. Unfortunately, the only person with the money to defend this case is the public defender," he added.

The squabble over who would defend Ramirez had taken on the atmosphere of a circus act. It was more like the old days when Mr. Satanist himself, Anton LaVey, was helping out as a cage boy with the Clyde Beatty Circus, and later as an assistant lion tamer. But although LaVey had flirted with many professions, he wasn't a lawyer, so he couldn't be called on to defend the nice polite boy he recalled once chatting with. But there were other lawyers in the wings, and some had nearly as much flair for drama as LaVey—and Belli. There was more, much more excitement and legal game-playing to come before a trial would get under way.

There were two main reasons for the time-consuming bickering and confusion:

The district attorney and the court were determined to make certain that Ramirez's civil rights were in no way violated. The state appeared to have an airtight case, and Reiner didn't want a conviction overturned by an appeals court. Consequently, his deputy, Halpin, was bending over backward to make certain that there were no foul-ups, procedural or otherwise, that could either interrupt the trial or provide grounds for reversal of a conviction and a new trial.

The other problem was Ramirez himself. He was clearly unable or unwilling to help direct intelligently or emotionally his own defense. He may have been capable of understanding the charges against him, but he displayed little understanding of what it would take to mount an effective defense. What's more, like many criminals, he did not demonstrate the emotional stability and patience to deal with the ponderous workings of the legal system and its pedantic bureaucracy.

His behavior was more like that of a spoiled child than that of a twenty-five-year-old man. Throughout the pre-trial proceedings and, later, the trial itself, he would pick his lawyers based on whether he liked them at the moment, and whether they catered to his petulant whims. He didn't seem to be concerned with, or aware of, the various gradations of competency within the legal community.

He developed a dislike for the overworked Adashek because he was brusque, with a no-nonsense attitude. The public defender's office was swamped with work and, although Adashek believed in what he was doing, he simply had no time for his client's whimsical shifts of mood.

Equally important, Adashek was also a non-Hispanic and, in his client's twisted view, part of "the system" that wanted to send him to the gas chamber. Perhaps Ramirez had already forgotten that it had been Hispanics who ran him down before he was rescued by police. The Night Stalker was no hero to people of Hispanic descent. He was no Benito Pablo Juárez, no Pancho Villa, not even a Zorro. He was a villain who coldly murdered sleeping men in their own homes, then raped their wives and children.

Among streetwise petty criminals like Ramirez, public defenders are usually considered to be inexperienced or incompetent lawyers not good enough to survive in private practices or find a decent position with an established law firm. What's more, they frequently work closely with the district attorney to arrange plea bargains that encourage the criminal to accept responsibility for a lesser crime that carries a lighter sentence. "Public defenders will always get you some time," according to the prevailing street wisdom.

If Ramirez had been charged with burglary or even armed robbery, a cautiously negotiated plea bargain might have been a reasonable and practical avenue to pursue, given the overwhelming evidence the state had accumulated against him. But Ramirez was facing "heavy" charges—the heaviest, in fact. He was smart enough to know he wasn't going to be allowed to plead guilty to something like manslaughter, instead of first-degree murder; or to indecent assault, instead of rape. He was on a one-way road. Either he found a way to beat the charges altogether, or he would be facing the gas chamber. Prosecutors wouldn't dare ask for, or accept, anything less.

Although both the judge and the prosecutor had to guard zealously Ramirez's right to a fair trial, both were concerned about the endless delays tied to his inability to settle on a lawyer. And prolonged delays seldom helped the prosecution. Witnesses' memories grew vague, or they moved away and were reluctant to return, or to interrupt their lives and revive dismal memories for a lengthy trial. Evidence can be lost or damaged. The longer the delay, the more problems can develop. And, according to the American system of justice, the state must prove the defendant guilty. The defendant is not required to prove himself innocent.

"Any time a trial is delayed, you have the potential of the unavailability of witnesses," explained Chief Deputy District Attorney Gilbert I. Garcetti. In this case, Garcetti said, delays were especially dangerous for the prosecution because so many of the witnesses were elderly. They might die or become physically or mentally unable to testify.

Then, too, as time passed, Ramirez's physical appearance might change. Among precautions taken by the district attorney was an order to have impressions made of Ramirez's teeth. Given their poor condition, or possible injury in jail, Ramirez could lose more of his teeth. And his rotted teeth were one of the most dramatic characteristics by which many witnesses were able to identify him.

There were other problems, too. Too much publicity, especially more sensational journalism, could make the impaneling of an unbiased jury difficult. At the moment, their most serious problem along these lines seemed to be posed by Barraza, Rosa Flores, and other members of her family.

It seemed that they were relaying statements Ramirez made to them directly to reporters. Some of the statements repeated by the family were inflammatory and seemed certain to prejudice people against the defendant.

In an interview, Hall labeled Barraza's public discussions of his private conversations with Ramirez as unseemly and unprofessional. The same was true for Rosa

Flores, he added. As an example of the dangers in relaying conversations with Ramirez to the press, he cited Mrs. Flores's claim that her brother had said "I'm guilty. I want Melvin Belli."

If Barraza was indeed interested in helping Ramirez, he should stop encouraging his client to drop the public defender, many legal experts felt. As Belli pointed out, defending the case would be extraordinarily expensive and the only available agency with the financial ability to mount an effective defense was that of the public defender.

Ramirez was nevertheless determined to get rid of Adashek. On Oct. 10, Municipal Judge Soper approved Ramirez's request to fire Adashek, and to hire Joseph Gallego, a private attorney from Oxnard. Given the defendant's adamant refusal to cooperate with Adashek, and his apparent distrust of the public defender, the judge had little choice but to concede to the demand.

Gallegos, who had twenty years' experience as a practicing lawyer in northern California, had himself been drawn into an embarrassing personal brush with the law in 1976. He served sixty days in jail and received five years' probation for shooting a prostitute in the hand during a dispute, nine years earlier, according to Vincent O'Neill, a Ventura County deputy district attorney. Gallegos claimed Ramirez knew of the incident, and it should have no bearing on his ability to defend his client.

Among Gallegos's previous major murder cases was the 1979 defense of a member of the Nuestra Familia, a powerful Mexican-American prison gang. His client was convicted and sentenced to twenty-seven years in prison.

Judge Soper expressed concern about Gallegos's fee arrangements, especially since the Ramirez family apparently had little money, and their attempt to raise a defense fund through contributions had little success. She could not understand how the family could hope to finance an expensive defense unless they sold book and movie rights to Ramirez's life.

If those rights had been assigned to Gallegos in payment for his services, and to reimburse him for the considerable out-of-pocket expenses he was certain to incur in defending his client, Gallegos could be guilty of a conflict of interests.

California judges had been especially concerned about such conflict-of-interest charges since the conviction of another notorious serial killer, Juan R. Corona, was reversed upon appeal. Corona's lawyer had a book contract agreement before the verdict was announced—leading to the reversal. Corona was convicted at his second trial. Gallegos advised the court that the rights to Ramirez's biography had been assigned to his sister, Rosa Flores.

California law, adopted several years earlier after public outrage over a big-money book deal signed in the wake of the Son of Sam serial slayings in New York, also requires that profits based on a crime be turned over to the victims. James Schwartz, an assistant state attorney general, said he knew of no case in which "a defendant attempted to assign his rights in order to shield the money from the victims." But, if the Ramirez family tried that to pay their legal fees, his office would fight it, he said.

Gallegos refused to disclose just how he expected to be reimbursed and how he expected to pay for other costs, which, as Belli had indicated, could eat up as much as $300,000 for medical and psychiatric services alone.

Despite the judge's quite understandable concern, there was no legal way to force Gallegos to reveal if he expected to be paid from the sale of book and movie rights by the Ramirez family.

William Genego, a criminal law expert at the University of Southern California, said in an interview with reporters that "there is often a conflict between what is motivating a lawyer and what is in the best interests of his client." There are many ethical rules "prohibiting this kind of conflict of interest," Genego added, "but it's hard to prove because a lawyer can always raise the sanctity of the lawyer-client privilege."

Gallegos explained that Ramirez had selected him to head his defense because he needed someone who had criminal trial experience and could speak Spanish. He added that he agreed to take the case because "I have devoted my life to the practice of law . . . and I want to make sure Mr. Ramirez—especially because he is of Latin descent—gets a fair trial."

He said he expected the trial to take a year. The judge postponed Ramirez's date for entering pleas to sixty-eight felony charges until October 22.

Even as Judge Soper was dismissing Ramirez's public defenders and okaying the fifty-six-year-old Gallegos as their replacement, Rosa Flores was in the courtroom with Barraza and two other lawyers, Arturo and Daniel V. Hernandez of San Jose. A few minutes earlier, outside the courtroom, Arturo had told reporters that he and Daniel Hernandez had been retained to head the Night Stalker's defense. The Hernandezes were not related, but each practiced law in San Jose and sometimes shared cases.

Judge Soper, however, refused to recognize Arturo Hernandez when he attempted to address the court. Later, Arturo Hernandez expressed confidence that Ramirez would change his mind about accepting Gallegos as his new counsel after he had met with Mrs. Flores, Barraza, himself, and Daniel Hernandez at the county jail. Apparently referring to Judge Soper's earlier snub in the courtroom, Arturo Hernandez added, "It's sad we have to fight to defend someone."

The credentials of the two lawyers were not impressive. Neither had much experience. Arturo had less than three years' practicing law; Daniel had a few months more than three. Arturo said he first met Ramirez's sister while he was attending law school in El Paso. Her endorsement of him as Ramirez's attorney was backed by her brother, Robert Ramirez, Arturo told reporters. He also said he and his partner had been recommended by Belli's office.

Rosa Flores explained to reporters that her brother had not been aware of Gallegos's criminal record. "How can he defend [my brother] with a felony record behind him?" she asked. She said she had hired the Hernandezes to replace Gallegos.

"I feel that Dan and Art would make proper defense attorneys for my brother," she added. "I want them because of their track record."

Her last statement was a rather curious one, reporters learned later. Not only did the Hernandezes have barely six years' legal experience between them, but they had tried only a few murder cases—none involving a possible death penalty. Arturo was thirty-one, while Daniel was ten years older. Further investigation revealed that Daniel had been cited for contempt for failure to appear in court by judges in Santa Clara County.

Earlier in the year, Daniel Hernandez was fined by two judges for failing to make court appearances. In those cases, he had sent the court doctor's slips, similar to those taken to school by children, advising teachers that they must miss class. Daniel Hernandez's excuse slip actually said that he "couldn't attend physical education." He was fined $1,000 in one instance for failing to appear in court, and $1,500 for another non-appearance.

After the $1,500 fine, Daniel Hernandez told reporters outside the courtroom that he had experienced heart problems for the past three years, and said he was being treated by a doctor. A doctor's examination later found no indications of a heart problem, although he did have "moderately high blood sugar."

What concerned Halpin and Assistant Prosecutor Alan Yochelson even more was a first-degree murder conviction case Daniel Hernandez had defended several months earlier. Although the conviction was upheld in the District Court of Appeals, both the trial judge and the appeals court agreed that Hernandez's performance had been "deficient in several respects." Not the least among these was the question of Hernandez's competency during trial.

Other deficiencies listed by the appellate court included Hernandez's lack of preparation for motions, questioning of defense and prosecution witnesses, failure to subpoena witnesses properly to get them into court, and eliciting opinions of the defendant's guilt from some of the witnesses.

As a result of these "deficiencies," the prosecutor in that case had to take on a double work load to assure that both sides of issues were presented to guard against a possible appellate court reversal of any conviction obtained. In other words, the prosecutor was forced to do his own difficult job, and much of his opponent's, as well.

Because a death-penalty case is exceptionally complex —an automatic appeal is filed after a conviction and sentence of execution—the points on which it can be overturned are many. A defendant who can show ineffective representation by his counsel has a good chance for a reversal and a new trial.

Don Braughton, a Santa Clara County assistant district attorney who had prosecuted cases in which Daniel Hernandez was the defense attorney, said the lawyer "just sort of blossomed with cases" about a year after he had put out his shingle in San Jose. One of Hernandez's brothers was a deputy chief of police and another a retired deputy chief of police in San Jose, the assistant DA added.

Braughton estimated that Daniel Hernandez had handled "about fifteen trials," many of them murder cases, but none involving a possible death penalty, by the time the law partners were hired by the Ramirez family. "His problem was not getting cases. His problem was servicing the clients he had," Braughton said of Daniel Hernandez.

Arturo Hernandez was more of a mystery. Records showed that he had graduated from the University of Santa Clara School of Law, and was admitted to the California Bar on July 13, 1983. No one could be found by reporters who seemed to know much about his legal experience. Braughton said he had seen him around the Santa Clara courthouse making minor appearances, but was not familiar with his trial experience.

On October 22, the two Hernandezes appeared in Judge Soper's courtroom to ask that they be officially named as Ramirez's defense lawyers. Also present were Halpin, Yochelson, Gallegos, and Ramirez. In the spectators' gallery were Ramirez's fifty-eight-year-old mother, Mercedes, his sister, Rosa, and his brothers, thirty-seven-year-old Julio and thirty-four-year-old Robert.

As he had on previous appearances, Ramirez behaved like a hyperactive child, variously hopping from one foot to the other, craning his head this way and that to see who was in the courtroom, shaking his body so that his chains would rattle, mumbling, smirking, glaring, and grinning. Occasionally, he would flash the pentagram tattoo on his hand at photographers. He seemed impatient with the court proceedings, fidgeting constantly, like a child in church on Sunday.

Judge Soper wanted to know everything she could about the Hernandezes' qualifications—as well as how they expected to be paid. She expressed doubt that they could adequately represent Ramirez.

Suddenly, Ramirez interrupted. Speaking up in a shrill, agitated voice, he commanded, "I want these two lawyers."

The judge and attorneys attempted to ignore the first outburst, but when Ramirez again interrupted and demanded, in a loud, bold voice, that the Hernandezes be appointed as his attorneys, Halpin suggested that the defendant should confer with Gallegos, who was still his attorney of record.

"I don't want to confer with him!" Ramirez shouted. He was behaving like a petulant teen-ager.

A few minutes later, Halpin questioned the Hernandezes' right to address the court—they had not yet been appointed defense counsel.

Ramirez responded for them, yelling, "They do to me!"

Judge Soper pointed out that the new attorneys did not meet even minimum requirements set by the Los Angeles Bar Association for attorneys in death-penalty cases. The standards included ten years as a state bar member and the handling of at least fifty criminal trials, forty involving felony charges, and thirty of those cases completed before a jury.

The judge said she had grave doubts about the propriety of the newest suggested change of counsel and delayed a decision for two days. She also appointed an independent Los Angeles lawyer, Victor E. Chavez, to review the Hernandezes' proposed contract with Ramirez and to advise the defendant on the pitfalls of retaining inexperienced attorneys.

Daniel Hernandez told Judge Soper that he objected to her making the question of the qualifications of him and his law partner a public matter.

"It is the duty of the trial judge to protect the defendant's right to effective counsel," she replied. And the court also had a duty to the people as well, Judge Soper added. "It has a duty to see that this case is brought to a speedy trial. It cannot be done if at every hearing the defendant requests a new attorney."

The judge again postponed Ramirez's pleas to the staggering list of charges filed against him. Although he had been in custody for seven weeks, he still had not entered pleas on any of the charges. It was the fifth such postponement.

The prosecution was dismayed at the snail's pace at which the proceedings were moving. Halpin complained that one state witness had already died of natural causes. "We must go forward," he urged, with some impatience. He suggested that if delays inspired by Ramirez's giddy lawyer-juggling continued, the court should enter "not guilty" pleas for the defendant, and set a date for a preliminary hearing.

Ramirez's family continued to feed information to the press. On Wednesday, Julian Ramirez, Jr., a truck driver from East Los Angeles, said his brother would plead guilty to murder if the prosecution would drop the molestation charges. On Thursday morning, however, Julian said his brother had changed his mind. "He changes his mind real quick," he explained.

Two days later, Judge Soper learned that Chavez had been rebuffed by Ramirez in his attempt to talk with him. Ramirez had also refused the judge's offer to share any information the court might have on the Hernandezes, or to seek any additional information he might want on them.

"I never had a chance to talk to him," Chavez explained. "I sat there in county jail cooling my heels . . . he refused to see me."

Reluctantly, Judge Soper approved Daniel V. and Arturo Hernandez as Ramirez's defense attorneys, again expressing her doubts as to their competency.

Ramirez immediately leaped to his feet and hoisted his handcuffed wrists as high as possible to display the pentagram—an encircled and inverted five-point star—crudely drawn on his left palm. Below the Satanic symbol, he had inscribed the numerals "666," the numerical sign of the Beast of Revelation, the Antichrist.

Judge Soper reacted to the outrageous performance by ordering Ramirez removed from the courtroom. As bailiffs led the smirking, heavily chained defendant toward the nearby holding cell, he shouted loudly, "Hail, Satan!"

It was the same perverted two-word salute that several victims of the Night Stalker had been forced to repeat while on their knees, pleading for their lives.

It seemed that the light-fingered sneak thief from El Paso, turned monstrous serial killer in Los Angeles, had worn down the judge, lawyers, and everyone directly concerned with moving the case through the courts. It was a sweet victory for the accused Night Stalker. But sweet can sometimes turn sour overnight.

Daniel Hernandez entered pleas for his client of not guilty to fourteen charges of murder and fifty-four other counts. Ramirez also faced one murder charge, one of attempted murder, and associated other counts in the slaying of Peter Pan and in the assault on Mrs. Pan in San Francisco. Other charges, including attempted murder and sexual assault, were still pending against Ramirez in Orange County as well, for the attacks on Carns, on his girlfriend, *Renata Gunther,* and for the burglary of their home.

Before adjourning the hearing, Judge Soper extended her gag order to include the Ramirez family. And she set the defendant's next court appearance for Friday, December 13, before Judge Candace D. Cooper, who was to preside over his preliminary hearing.

Members of Ramirez's family later denied that he had shouted "Hail, Satan!" "We'll see" was what he really yelled, they insisted. However, a court stenographer who was sitting only a few feet away from the defendant confirmed that Ramirez had, indeed, shouted "Hail, Satan!" And other spectators in the courtroom agreed. The accused serial killer had responded to his victory with a public "thank you" to the dark god he served.

Ramirez's defense attorneys refused to be interviewed by reporters after the hearing, citing the judge's gag order. Daniel, however, complained briefly again about Soper's making public the information about their qualifications. "The court . . . went out of their way to explain to the public what was discussed in private. We don't see that as a very kosher thing to do," the lawyer griped.

Replaced so quickly by the Hernandezes as Ramirez's defense attorney, Gallegos was no longer bound by the gag order and he told reporters that he interpreted his former client's display of the pentagram and the shocking salute to Satan as a kind of boyish exuberance to show that "he's happy that this part of the proceedings" was over.

"I wish them all the luck in the world," he added of the new defense team. "They're certainly going to need it."

While all the patience-frazzling lawyer juggling and confounding legal maneuvering was going on, court officers and journalists became aware of a surprisingly large number of young college-age women among the regular spectators. It appeared that the Night Stalker had a fan club, his own giddy following of groupies.

Most of the women crowded into the front row of spectators' seats, immediately behind the railing shielding the defense and prosecution team from the public—and in front of the scramble of reporters. When a newspaper journalist asked them about their seemingly obsessive interest in the case, most explained that they were college journalism students.

One of the girls elaborated on her interest in the grisly case, and in the accused serial killer, by explaining that she was interested in writing about the human side of the affair for her campus newspaper. Others stated simply, and straightforwardly, that they thought the gaunt, pasty-faced accused rapist-killer with the pentagram tattooed on his palm was "cute."

Nevertheless, after a Los Angeles–area newspaper columnist published a piece about the Night Stalker's cheering section, only a few appeared in court the next day. Three were carrying textbooks and notebooks, and told anyone who asked that they were covering the proceedings for college-class projects. But others were shockingly frank about the spiritual and romantic links they were convinced they had formed with the accused serial killer. One grotesquely dressed young woman insisted that she was destined to acquire occult protection from a serial killer who was Hispanic. Another groupie announced that she was engaged to him and they were going to marry.

Bernadette Brazal was one of the pretty Richard Ramirez–watchers among the gaggle of coeds who didn't claim to be a writer, or would-be journalist covering the case out of professional interest, and she made no bones about her reasons for being there. She told a reporter for the *Orange County Register* exactly why she was there. Posing her remark in the form of a question, she asked herself about her interest in the accused Night Stalker: "Do I love him? Yes!" she said in reply. "In my own childlike way."

She was the most loyal of all the young women who appeared in the courtroom, sitting patiently through the wearisome, laborious rounds of motions, counter-motions, rulings of law, and all the other legal gobbledygook that eats up tremendous amounts of time and money in pre-trial proceedings in the American courts. To most, without a legal background or interest, or at least a journalistic reason for being there, pre-trial hearings can be brutally boring.

But the pretty, olive-skinned girl with the lustrous, long black hair was usually there, sitting near the front of the Los Angeles Municipal Court gallery to add her unswervingly faithful support for the defendant. She told a columnist that she thought the gap-toothed wreck was good-looking enough to be a male model, or a movie star.

In the interview, reprinted in other papers through an Associated Press report, she confessed, "I feel such compassion for him. When I look at him, I see a real handsome guy who just messed up his life because he never had anyone to guide him."

At twenty-three, the comely coed was about the same age as some of the women who had been beaten, raped, sodomized—or murdered—by the brutal serial killer that the press—and even the police—now routinely referred to as the Night Stalker. She admitted she tried to ignore some of the more grisly testimony and other references to the crimes he was accused of committing. She said she was convinced he was innocent.

The young media-arts student at California State University in Los Angeles said she hadn't yet met Ramirez, but had written him daily love letters since he was first locked up, and had included fifty photographs of herself. She said she told him that she thought he was cute, but should be a good boy and stop listening to bad rock music by AC/DC.

When Ramirez refused to answer her letters, it hurt her feelings, so she didn't send him a Valentine on Valentine's Day. And she also stopped talking about love in her letters.

Nevertheless, she continued obediently to show up in the municipal court gallery for his hearings—and when he behaved and was a "good boy," earning access to the courtroom himself, she would wink, smile, or wave back whenever he glanced her way and nodded in recognition.

Another young woman had more success getting to Ramirez in his cell, after becoming intrigued with him, his crimes, his plight—and his eternal soul. A born-again Christian, she wrote to him in jail, and he replied. He even agreed to a meeting, which grew to a series of confrontations.

She apparently attempted to convince him to "accept Christ" in the letters, according to her minister, but Ramirez was more interested in a personal relationship.

The twenty-five-year-old single girl, converted from Judiasm herself, eventually gave up on Ramirez as a potential convert and asked her minister to contact tabloids like the *National Enquirer, Globe,* and the *National Examiner* in efforts to sell her story.

She said she had a file of forty-three letters written over a three-year period to her by Ramirez. Some were very detailed and revealing, highly suggestive and sexual in nature. A large percentage were devoted to Satanism.

Courtroom groupies, prison pen pals, and others eager to befriend accused or convicted killers are neither unique nor a new phenomenon. They are especially likely to emerge and show up when particularly notorious killers are on trial. The cheerleader corps that writes letters, appears in courtrooms and in jailhouse visiting rooms to support high-profile murderers are as likely to be pretty teen-agers or girls in their twenties as they are to be middle-aged matrons and grandmothers. Savage sex killers attract the most avid followings.

Kenneth Bianchi and his cousin, Angelo Buono, each had cheerleading sections during the sensational trials for the Hillside Strangler murders they committed. Ted Bundy, the Love Bite Killer, who was finally executed in January 1990, after ten years on Florida's death row, had dozens of groupies who attended his trial and wrote love letters to him in prison.

Even John Wayne Gacy, Jr., the barrel-bodied, sadistic Chicago-area contractor who sexually abused, tortured, and murdered at least thirty-three young men and boys, became involved in a long-distance love affair with a twice-divorced mother of eight. The romance began after he was convicted and imprisoned on death row at the Illinois State Prison at Menard.

And courtroom and prison groupies are not limited to females, although that is most often the case. When a lovely female North Korean terrorist was in prison awaiting trial in the Republic of Korea for helping blow up a Korean Air Lines jetliner that claimed 115 lives, she received hundreds of love letters and marriage proposals.

Although at the time Kim Hyon Hee was the most hated woman in South Korea, most of the letters to her were from South Korean or Japanese men.

And when former barmaid Betty Beets was being convicted of the murder of one of her two husbands found murdered near Dallas, Texas, most days after court proceedings were adjourned she returned to her cell to find love notes, cigarettes, candy, or other gifts left for her by male admirers.

Many of the men and women who initiate close relationships with notorious killers claim they have fallen in love. Some relationships begin through the mail, or with smiles, winks, and nods in courtrooms, and sometimes lead to prison marriages that may or may not be consummated.

Other devoted admirers of sex killers and mass murderers profess Christian soul-saving motivations or opposition to the death penalty.

But it seems that despite all the excuses of romance, soul-saving, and anti-death-penalty activism, most prison groupies are motivated by an obsessive desire for titillation, and a chance to share in the notoriety of a feared or hated human being.

As proceedings in the Night Stalker case choked, coughed, and sputtered through the tedious hearings, Deputy Prosecutor Halpin continued to fret over the delays. "This case should be rolling," he complained. "There's no reason to delay justice. I hope the issue of who's going to represent Mr. Ramirez is finally settled."

The impatient, sometimes crusty prosecutor, dapper with his graying, neatly trimmed beard and hair, and dark suit and vest, was not to get his wish. No more than a few days passed before the Hernandezes took the next step that was to continue delaying the trial.

The defense attorneys announced that they would ask for a change of venue to have Ramirez's trial moved from Los Angeles to San Francisco. They said the extensive publicity and hysteria would make it impossible for Ramirez to get a fair trial in Southern California. Although Ramirez also faced murder and attempted murder charges in San Francisco, they claimed it would be easier to find an unbiased jury in the Bay area.

The new defense team accused the press of painting Ramirez as a "monster." Daniel Hernandez said he and his co-counsel found Ramirez "to be very personable, friendly, and relaxed. He was very coherent. We had no problems with relating to him," Hernandez said.

One of their immediate priorities, the two attorneys said, would be to overturn a court order that prevented Ramirez from most contact with the outside world. He was permitted no phone calls and no newspapers, magazines, television, or radio in his cell.

At Deputy Prosecutor Halpin's request, the December 13 court date was moved up to October. He hoped to convince Judge Cooper to set a date for the preliminary hearing prior to December 13.

Daniel and Arturo Hernandez responded by requesting a six-month delay before the preliminary hearing, claiming it would take them a week to prepare for each of the fourteen murder charges against Ramirez, and additional time to gather and correlate their information.

Judge Cooper denied the request, calling it excessive, and set the preliminary hearing date for February 24. She said the defense was entitled to a "reasonable amount of time to prepare . . . [but] I think six to seven months is excessive, and I don't intend to grant it."

She added that late February was approximately four-plus months from the time the new defense team accepted the case. "I think that is ample time for investigation," she said. "As far as the holidays go, sir, you gentlemen are simply going to have to work for the holidays."

Judge Cooper also scheduled hearings for December 13 and January 20 to consider whether the defense lawyers were receiving all the evidence they requested from Halpin and other law enforcement authorities.

Halpin tried his best to thwart a defense request for thousands of reports on tips provided law enforcement agencies during the massive search for the Night Stalker. He explained that nearly 12,000 clues were recorded during the manhunt, and that he considered the request to be time-consuming and irrelevant to the defense.

The judge, however, ruled the Hernandezes could have access to the reports, although not to the identities of informants who had requested anonymity.

While the seemingly unending courtroom squabbling flared around him, Ramirez watched in apparent amusement. He was heavily shackled with chains on his ankles, linking his legs, and other chains around his wrists were attached to his waist. There would be no flashing of his pentagram-imprinted palm to spectators. He acted cocky and confident, although restless and uncomfortable in the chains.

Ramirez grinned broadly at Sheriff's Detective Gil Carillo, who was one of the leading investigators in his case and who was watching the proceedings. Once, as he was being led from the courtroom to a holding cell after an adjournment, Ramirez smirked, then uttered a deprecating slang greeting in Spanish to Carillo. The poker-faced detective ignored him.

After the hearing, Arturo Hernandez complained to reporters about Judge Cooper's refusal to grant the six-month delay for the preliminary hearing. "I think that's totally unfair," the lawyer grumped.

It seemed that everyone involved with preparations for the Night Stalker trial would be doing more work than celebrating during the forthcoming Christmas and New Year's holidays.

CHAPTER 13

A Waiting Game

SOMETIMES IT SEEMED MORE LIKE A POKER game than a murder trial. Deputy District Attorney Halpin was sitting with four aces, playing the final hand of the night. He knew he had the pot, and wanted to play out the hand before it was time to quit. The other players knew he held a winner, but they kept stalling, keeping an eye on the clock.

It was clear that Halpin believed the preliminary hearing should have been completed by this time, and a date set for the trial itself. As he had said repeatedly, most often in recent weeks, time was of vital importance.

With the passage of time, the memories of victims and witnesses, even investigators, grew dimmer and more unreliable, open to impeachment by the defense. Worse, victims and witnesses die, move away, or refuse to testify. After all, many of the victims and witnesses in the Night Stalker case were elderly. Eighty-five-year-old Clara Hadsall, the Stalker's seventh known victim, had already died from natural causes in late October. It was even possible that some important piece of evidence could be lost.

And, in a surprising turn of events, Joseph Gallegos,

the attorney who had replaced the public defenders and briefly represented Ramirez, died of a heart attack in his Oxnard home. Had Gallegos remained as counsel for the accused Night Stalker, and suffered his attack later in the proceedings, the effect on bringing the already convoluted case to trial and a conclusion could have been devastating. But with Gallegos's replacement by the Hernandezes, although as personally tragic as his death might have been to his family, it was no longer pertinent to the trial or fate of Richard Ramirez.

But time was definitely on the side of the defense. Given the prosecutor's pat hand, time's inevitable attrition, and a possible mistrial, in fact, seemed to offer Richard Ramirez his best chances. If Halpin became too impatient with the seemingly interminable delays, chances for trial miscues or some inadvertent violation of the defendant's rights increased—and, with them, the unhappy specter of a mistrial.

The judges were equally aware of the dangers, and they were especially wary of possible civil rights violations. At times it appeared they bent over backward in their efforts to avoid any miscues or errors that might later provide the defendant with possible grounds, no matter how flimsy, for a mistrial.

All Halpin could do, for the most part, was to continue to prepare and polish his case, grit his teeth, and wait. As frustrating and potentially damaging as delays could be, a mistrial would be a disaster.

At times it appeared that Ramirez was enjoying every minute of the friction, delays, and attention. But the game-playing could be put to serious purpose. His courtroom antics, his wearisome juggling of lawyers, and his family's seemingly imprudent statements to the press all appeared to be designed to test the patience of the prosecution and the court, and to prod them into making a costly mistake.

The endless delays, the dizzying parade of lawyers, and

the tolerance of the court with what seemed to be the antics of a spoiled child were also beginning to gall the public. It was difficult to understand why Ramirez was permitted to continue his shameful legal shenanigans. He seemed to be making a fool of the justice system and the public. The public wanted swifter justice.

The press was grumbling, too. They questioned the wisdom of the court for allowing so many changes in legal counsel and for the ceaseless postponements. They were especially critical of the decision to allow nearly a five-month delay before the preliminary hearing. Outraged editorial writers debated the logic of a justice system that gave so much more consideration to the rights of criminal monsters like the Night Stalker than to his victims.

The growing outrage of the public and the demagogic indignation of the press added to the problems Halpin and the courts had to contend with. The more impatient people became, and the more the press reflected that impatience, the more difficult it would be to assure Ramirez of an impartial jury and a fair trial.

Judge Soper had tried to ease the dangers and threats to a fair trial by issuing the gag order forbidding people connected with the case, including attorneys and witnesses, to discuss it with the public or the press. Public Defender Adashek had obtained a court order restricting Ramirez's contact with the public. Judge Cooper greeted the new year with a ruling that no cameras or microphones would be allowed in the courtroom for the preliminary hearing, still set to begin on February 24.

She justified her ruling by pointing out that the presence of a television camera during earlier hearings had apparently helped inspire some of the bizarre courtroom behavior by Ramirez.

"I have no doubt the interest in this case is going to continue," she declared. "This high level of interest, together with certain actions of Mr. Ramirez, has caused me to exercise my discretion" to ban cameras from the courtroom.

The judge cited as examples the incidents when Ramirez displayed the pentagram and number 666 on his left palm, and his "Hail, Satan!" salute.

Not surprisingly, the electronic broadcast media—television and radio—complained the loudest. The ruling affected them most directly. But the print media quickly rallied to their support. The media generally considers restrictions on one element of the press to pose a threat and a challenge to all.

Attorneys for the Radio and Television Association of Southern California, joined by the three national television networks, said they would appeal Judge Cooper's formal ruling.

"The print media is allowed in with the tools of its trade, and the broadcast media is not," a spokesman for the association complained to reporters. He cited First Amendment protection for the press and "the public's right to know." The Night Stalker trial was a big story, and television news-show producers wanted their cameras in the courtroom for the action.

Deputy District Attorney Halpin endorsed Cooper's ban on cameras and microphones—except for the small microphones on tape recorders used for note-taking purposes only. He said he would have no objection to television cameras if the entire hearing was telecast unedited, an option that was economically impractical for television stations. He added that, if he had a choice, he would close the hearings to both the public and the news media.

Then, in a surprise move, Municipal Court Presiding Judge Maxine Thomas transferred Ramirez's preliminary hearing from Judge Cooper to Judge James T. Nelson.

Judge Nelson was an experienced jurist and had attracted national attention when he presided over the preliminary hearing for Cathy Evelyn Smith, the drug user and dealer who was arrested in the death of comedian

John Belushi. Miss Smith was charged with murder, accused of giving Belushi the lethal speedball of cocaine and heroin that led to his death by overdose. The former rock-and-roll backup singer eventually served eighteen months of a three-year prison sentence for involuntary manslaughter before returning to her home in Canada.

Both Judge Nelson and Judge Cooper were experienced and capable jurists. And the announcement of the shift of judicial assignments gave no indication whether the flap over the ban on television cameras was involved in the decision. But Judge Cooper was clearly and openly disappointed about her abrupt removal from the proceedings.

When Judge Thomas announced the change, she explained that the transfer was being made to avoid taking up so much of Judge Cooper's time with a case that was so complicated and expected to last for so many months.

But Judge Cooper said she had been looking forward to the proceedings because it was such a fascinating case. The Night Stalker pre-trial proceedings offered personal and professional challenges that would be difficult to turn down for any jurist who loved his or her work. It had all the necessary elements to become a keystone in a distinguished judicial career, attracting attention in both the legal and public arenas.

"I was told the case was being transferred because the preliminary calendars were full," Judge Cooper advised the press. But she added that when she was initially assigned to the case (by then Presiding Judge Malcolm H. Mackey), it was understood that she would be temporarily spared from presiding at the normal preliminary hearings that come daily before the courts. "Either way she [Judge Thomas] goes, she's down a court," the disappointed jurist objected. "That's no net gain, in terms of workload."

Nevertheless, Judge Cooper was permanently removed from the case. And among other things, the judicial shift, in effect, nullified her ban on television cameras and microphones in the courtroom during the preliminary hearing. She was no longer the judge of record. But she defended the ban, pointing out that a case that involved such "intense public interest" offered special risks because of the close scrutiny.

"It's a lot easier to blow it, frankly," she said of the chances of winding up with an adverse decision on appeal, "on a highly visible case."

The new judge quickly served notice that some of his decisions might be no more palatable to the press than those of his immediate predecessor. Judge Nelson suggested that he might accede to a motion by Ramirez's defense and close the preliminary hearing altogether to the press. He explained that the sensational case had already generated "as great a degree of pre-trial publicity as I've ever seen in this county."

The possibility of tainting the potential jury pool because of such widespread prior knowledge of the case among the public was considerable, he warned.

The media came out of its corner slugging, determined to keep the proceedings open so that it could report on one of the Los Angeles area's most hair-raising and lurid murder trials in a decade. Not only the press from Los Angeles, but the national media and journalists from throughout the world, had plans to cover the trial.

On the day of the preliminary hearing, Judge Nelson's first order of business was consideration of the defense motion to close the proceeding to the press. The defense team argued that continued widespread pre-trial publicity would seriously damage their client's chances for a fair trial.

But several news organizations had put together a formidable array of attorneys to oppose the defense motion and, after listening to their arguments—as well as the defense's—Judge Nelson ruled that the preliminary hearing would remain open to the press and public.

"The court finds it is not necessary to protect the right of the defendant to a fair trial by closing the preliminary hearing," he declared. "Taint there will be, but a fair jury will be found."

And the new judge marked up yet another win for the media when he did not continue or reinstate his predecessor's ban on television cameras or microphones.

It was a clear press victory, another win for the First Amendment. But even the media conceded, in editorials and columns and on broadcast programs, that it would be difficult to find an intelligent juror in Southern California who had not heard of Richard Ramirez and of his homicidal alter ego—the Night Stalker.

While losing the effort to ban the press from the hearing, the defense was also pursuing a challenge to a tape-recorded statement that Ramirez had given to police shortly after his arrest on August 31. They charged that his interrogators had improperly coerced him into making the statements, while ignoring his repeated requests for an attorney.

In a written motion submitted on the first day of the hearing, the defense team claimed that police had badgered their client into implicating himself by warning that it would "haunt his mother to her grave" if he didn't tell them everything he knew about the sordid Night Stalker rape-and-murder spree.

Consequently, the lawyers claimed, as a result of the statement they were challenging, police were able to seize several pieces of evidence, including two handguns, other weapons, jewelry, and various property stored in a locker at the Greyhound bus terminal. If the statement could be discredited and disallowed, the handguns and other items seized as a result could not be used as evidence in court. Judge Nelson would rule on it later.

When the motions were disposed of and testimony in the preliminary hearing was at last ready to begin, the prosecution's first witness was Jack Vincow. His seventy-nine-year-old mother, Jennie Vincow, was the Night Stalker's first known victim. He found her dead in her apartment of a slashed throat and multiple stab wounds on June 28, 1984.

Neatly dressed, and speaking in a clear, audible voice, Vincow told the court he saw his mother alive for the last time the afternoon of June 27. He found her mutilated body almost twenty-four hours later, when he entered her unlocked apartment for a visit.

In the living room, "I saw everything was thrown around on the floor." When he entered the bedroom, he found his mother's corpse on the bed, her throat slashed so violently that her head was almost severed from her body, he added.

A week later, on March 13, Ramirez was taken to the Orange County seat in Santa Ana, where he entered pleas of innocent to attempted murder and rape charges in the attack on William Carns and his fiancée, *Renata Gunther,* in their Mission Viejo home. The orgy of violence was believed to have marked the Night Stalker's last crimes in California before his arrest five days later.

Ramirez agreed to postpone a preliminary hearing in Orange County until after completion of the proceedings already under way in Los Angeles.

The prosecution received its first setback a few days after the hearing in Los Angeles resumed, during testimony of Joseph Duenas. It was Duenas who had witnessed the slaying of Tsai-Lian Yu, when the Night Stalker pulled the screaming woman from her car and stabbed her to death.

Duenas said the man he saw kill Yu fit Ramirez's physical description and pointed him out in the courtroom. But during cross-examination by the defense, Duenas conceded that he could not be positive in his identification.

After three weeks, the confounding delaying tactics of

the defense team were severely testing the crusty Halpin's already thin patience. The defense persistently challenged almost every move and every aspect of the prosecution's case, suggesting that the evidence to convict was woefully inadequate. They claimed the case was marred by violations of Ramirez's constitutional rights during questioning, a prejudiced police lineup for witnesses and victims, and careless investigative techniques.

"I think if the rules were followed, we would have a tremendous case in our favor," declared Daniel Hernandez. The acrimonious legal tilting began to swing from the purely professional to the intensely personal.

The Hernandezes complained bitterly on several occasions that Halpin had referred to them as "clowns." Halpin publicly accused the defense attorneys of putting on a performance for newspaper and television reporters.

At one point, the antagonism between Halpin and the two defense counsels grew so heated that Judge Nelson interrupted to scold both sides. "Unless you are all very anxious to share the same cell, I would ask that you stop using this to cast aspirations at each other," he snapped.

Halpin dismissed the defense strategy with more than a smidgen of open contempt, calling it little more than a desperate smoke screen. He said he was presenting only the minimum amount of evidence to have Ramirez bound over for trial. "I have to at least create a suspicion in the judge's mind that this guy committed these crimes," he explained. He was too savvy, too experienced, to give away his whole case at the preliminary hearing.

Daniel Hernandez's cross-examination was obdurate and tough. It was especially extensive, probing, and relentless for a preliminary hearing. When the defense was questioning witnesses, he never allowed a statement to go by unmolested when it could be challenged, or an objection lodged. He didn't permit assumptions. When it was his turn to cross-examine, he bombarded witnesses with salvos of questions. He wouldn't ask one question when he could ask two or three. He argued over seemingly minor and arcane legal points. If he couldn't fire cannons, he used pistols. The defense was clearly determined to discredit the evidence police had gathered, and to suggest that the horrid crimes of which their client was accused just may have been committed by someone else.

Hernandez also complained to Judge Nelson that law enforcement agencies were not being as fully cooperative as they were required to be in the sharing of evidence. Consequently, he was forced to be especially thorough while questioning witnesses, in order to obtain as much information as possible.

He said he had to fight to get photographs of crime scenes from police. And when they were at last turned over to him, he found 6,000 uncataloged pictures on his hands. A police spokesman testified that no one was trying to make things difficult for the attorney. It just happened to be the way such evidence was stored, the law officer said.

During the three-week hearing, more than thirty witnesses testified. *Angela Barrios,* whose roommate, Dayle Okazaki, was killed, and she herself shot in the hand, was one of those who testified. Police had found the Night Stalker's baseball cap with the AC/DC logo in her garage.

Speaking calmly and with conviction, Miss *Barrios* identified Ramirez as the man who shot her in the hand, and who later pointed his gun at her outside the condominium she had shared with her roommate.

During cross-examination by the defense, *Angela Barrios* and other witnesses conceded that they had seen Ramirez's photograph on television and in newspapers, and had heard he was the object of the Night Stalker manhunt before they attended a lineup conducted by the sheriff's department on September 5.

The defense lawyers objected to the prior identification

of Ramirez, and claimed a sheriff's deputy had held up two fingers during the lineup. Ramirez was in the second position in the lineup.

Judge Nelson overruled the objections. He also said Ramirez's questioning by police and sheriff's deputies, after he had requested an attorney, was not an issue to be decided by the court at that time.

As the drama unfolded around him, Ramirez appeared to be enjoying himself. He often carried on animated conversations with his lawyers, sometimes laughing aloud, during crucial testimony. He laughed a lot, and joked with his attorneys, even cackling loudly, during crucial testimony.

Once he laughed loudly after a young widow's testimony had caused several spectators to cry as she tearfully described how her assailant had raped and beaten her while her slain husband lay nearby, then sexually molested her son. When the judge asked Arturo Hernandez why the defendant was laughing, Hernandez replied that it was a private joke and did not concern the sordid recollection of witnesses.

Sometimes, Ramirez sneered openly at the prosecution. At other times, he scanned newspapers for accounts of testimony and studied photographs of crime scenes. He smirked, twisting his heavy lips cruelly over his ravaged teeth, when he came across a death-scene photo he especially liked.

Whenever he seemed to grow bored with talking to his lawyers, scanning the photos, or taunting the prosecutor, he turned to smile at Bernadette Brazal, his most faithful fan.

If Ramirez found the first month of his preliminary hearing amusing, there was reason to complain during the second. His defense attorneys appeared in the courtroom without their client at the end of the first week in April, explaining to Judge Nelson that Ramirez no longer felt like attending the remainder of his preliminary hearing. He preferred to "stay at home," in his jail cell, they reported.

Nelson was not sympathetic, nor was the prosecution. The judge said that Ramirez had to attend the hearings. Halpin was more adamant. "I don't want to take the chance on some sort of procedural problem later," he explained. Even the slightest error of judgment or law might someday lead to a successful appeal of a conviction, leading to a reversal and an order for a new trial. Neither the state nor the court could afford to take chances—although it might be quieter and significantly improve the decorum of the courtroom without the defendant's alternately clownish and sinister presence.

Daniel and Arturo Hernandez were free to file a written motion and request a court hearing with witnesses if they wished to try to change his mind, Judge Nelson said. But, for now, Ramirez must attend the proceedings. California state law did not give the defendant an absolute right to waive his presence at the hearing, Nelson explained. Granting such a request to permit a defendant to sit out a portion of his preliminary hearing in a capital case would be without precedent.

The defense attorneys said Ramirez had several personal reasons for his request. These included:

- An uncomfortable holding cell at the Los Angeles Traffic Courts Building, where the hearing was being held.
- A nagging toothache resulting from some unfinished root-canal work undertaken on his snaggled and rotting teeth by county dentists.

Ramirez had also undergone other dental work since his arrest, some of it so extensive that police officers and the prosecution worried that it might have so altered his appearance that it could affect the ability of witnesses to confirm his identification in court.

- He was uncomfortable in the courtroom because the press and other observers stared at him when witnesses testified about the gruesome details of the crimes committed by the Night Stalker.

When reporters asked why the dental problems should qualify as a valid reason to skip court, Daniel Hernandez replied with a comment about his own attitude toward dental problems. "I'd rather be at home if I had a toothache," he said.

In response to a similar question about the Night Stalker suspect's timid reaction to stares, Daniel's teammate, Arturo, remarked, "It would be normal for anyone" to feel self-conscious about people staring at them.

Reporters did some perplexed staring then, at one another, as if uncertain whether they were being put on, or if they should take the attorneys seriously. A reporter observed to a colleague that the two Santa Clara lawyers sometimes made extremely curious remarks—in court and out.

The holding cell Ramirez was kept in just outside the courtroom was a stark, unlit five-by-five-feet enclosure. Up to that time, Ramirez had remained three to six hours a day in the cramped pen, waiting for court appearances or for transfers back to his cell at the county jail.

After inspecting the holding cell, Judge Nelson ordered Ramirez kept in a much larger cell near the courtroom.

Ruth Wilson, the Burbank woman who was raped and sodomized at gunpoint by the Night Stalker on May 30, just over one year earlier, was still outraged when she faced Ramirez in the courtroom in mid-April. She had suffered absolutely vile torment, and it was a degrading ordeal she could never wash clean from her mind. And she would never forget the pasty, dope-ravaged face of her abuser, no matter how much dental work he might have had done.

When Halpin asked her to identify her assailant, she glared for a moment at Ramirez, then coldly nodded her head in his direction. "He is sitting on the end there, in blue," she gritted.

She was the second witness to identify Ramirez positively; *Angela Barrios* was the first. Halpin now had established sufficient proof to be sure of trying Ramirez on at least one charge each of murder and rape. Ramirez had also been linked by a witness to the Satanic pentagram, which was drawn in blood on the kitchen wall where *Angela Barrios* had found the body of her slaughtered roommate, and to the baseball cap with the AC/DC emblem.

Speaking evenly in a steady, deliberate voice, *Mrs. Wilson* described how she had been awakened at about one A.M. by a flashlight shining in her face, of how she was dragged into her twelve-year-old son's room, and how the armed intruder terrorized the boy by putting a gun to his head.

She told about her brutal rape and sodomizing while she was bound and gagged, and how her attacker had turned her apartment topsy-turvy in his ruthless search for valuables. And she recalled how, despite her pain, humiliation, and terror, she nevertheless got him to talk to her for about twenty minutes before he left. That's how she got such a close, clear look at his face.

As testimony and the weeks passed tediously, Ramirez lost interest in the proceedings. His courtroom behavior was generally tense. His attorneys described him as "antsy." His behavior now was even more bizarre than before.

Sometimes, during especially lurid testimony describing the sordid crimes, he would rattle his chains, giggle, stare eerily at witnesses, or flash chillingly evil grins. At times he locked his sinister eyes, which looked about as inviting as cesspools, in staring contests with spectators, court officers, or frightened witnesses. Finally, to minimize the intimidating stares, bailiffs ordered Ramirez to look straight ahead and to avoid all eye contact with anyone called to give testimony.

Ramirez doodled. His scrawlings were primitive and childlike in their construction. But his compositions revealed a look into hell. Once he drew a caricature of Deputy District Attorney Halpin, which the defense attorneys showed in court. The caricature bore a remarkable likeness to Halpin's face—however, it was attached to the body of a bitch dog.

Some journalists and other observers questioned the wisdom of the defense attorneys and the defendant in the seeming nonstop taunting of the prosecutor.

Halpin was an exceptionally formidable man, a hardworking, no-nonsense professional. He was dead serious about his job—his current assignment, in particular—and he wasn't in court to play games or to become the butt of an accused serial killer's crude attempts at humor. Halpin was no sitting duck, and could take care of himself in the no-holds-barred, rough-and-tumble of big-time criminal law. In fact, some observers suggested that at times it was he who intentionally provoked the two defense attorneys. He was openly contemptuous of them.

A few courtroom regulars speculated that Daniel and Arturo Hernandez would eventually change their client's plea to "not guilty by reason of insanity."

Up to this point, however, none of the various defense attorneys or any of the three judges had questioned Ramirez's ability to comprehend the courtroom proceedings, although on the surface there appeared to be ample reason to do so. To the contrary, even his own attorneys maintained that their client was so attentive and comprehending that he sometimes helped prepare their cross-examination of witnesses.

The defendant had recently observed his twenty-sixth birthday, and he was young and alert.

Despite his apparent quickness of mind, however, the

crimes the defendant was accused of committing did not appear to be those of a rational man. Courtroom observers asked themselves: Could it be in any way possible that the mangled bodies, ravished women, devastated psyches, and ruined families left behind by the Night Stalker were the work of a man who was sane? And since his arrest, the defendant's erratic behavior, both in his cell and in the courtroom, might also raise legitimate doubts about the soundness of his mental state.

But launching a successful insanity defense is neither as easy, nor as commonly used, as most people outside the criminal law community think. Some surveys have shown that Americans believe that as many as fifty or sixty percent of people accused of felony crimes resort to the insanity defense, but professional studies show that the number is closer to two or three percent—and most of these defendants are unsuccessful.

The most notorious and widely remembered case in which an insanity plea was successfully used was that of John Hinckley, Jr., who was acquitted in June 1982 of the shooting of President Ronald Reagan. Legislators in several states responded to the broadly criticized acquittal by changing their laws. They either banned the insanity defense altogether, or created a "guilty but mentally ill" provision in their criminal codes that permitted prosecution after an accused offender was deemed cured of his ailment. An insanity defense was no guarantee of an acquittal, nor was it a convenient easy way out for accused killers and their attorneys. There would be no insanity plea for Richard Ramirez.

But the fact that the accused Night Stalker's attorneys weren't planning an insanity defense for him didn't stop his disgraceful courtroom behavior. On May 1—the day when witches celebrate spring and fecundity by prancing around Maypoles, and communists celebrate the workers' revolution—Ramirez's arrogance and occasional taunting of court officers reached a breaking point.

The court had already warned him not to stare at witnesses as they walked to and from the stand. There was solid reasoning behind the order; it was aimed at preventing Ramirez from intimidating witnesses. Testifying could be a devastatingly emotional experience for some of them, in particular women who were so ruthlessly brutalized by the Night Stalker attacks. And it was feared that the cold, unblinking stare of the man accused as their attacker could destroy their composure and fragile hold on self-control before they even reached the witness stand.

Nevertheless, when Esperanza Contreras Gonzalez, who had been subpoenaed as a prosecution witness, walked hesitantly by the defense table to testify about a gun her boyfriend purchased from Ramirez, and which she turned over to police, serious trouble erupted. Ramirez disregarded the order. He turned and fixed his beady, dark eyes on her.

Bailiff Steve DePrima reacted instantly. He sprang across the room, grabbed a handful of Ramirez's hair, and jerked his head toward the front of the courtroom. As DePrima gruffly repeated that Ramirez was to look toward the front of the courtroom as he had been previously admonished, the defendant struggled and tried to knock the bailiff's hand away. Two more husky bailiffs hurried to help DePrima, jumping on Ramirez and knocking him to the floor in the struggle.

It was an uneven contest, as uneven as the chances of the unprotected women and children savaged in the Night Stalker attacks after their husbands and fathers had been killed. This time the man accused of those attacks was pitted against three healthy, husky, and determined court officers.

Lawyers were scrambling for cover, witnesses had leaped from their seats, and the courtroom was in a state of pandemonium, as the bailiffs dragged the wildly struggling and cursing defendant back to his holding cell.

Arturo Hernandez rushed after the struggling men and reached the holding cell moments after Ramirez had been roughly dragged and pushed inside. Peering through the peephole, the lawyer shouted, "You don't have to hit him anymore! He's not moving around!"

Much later, after some of the court decorum had been restored, Arturo Hernandez blamed the shocking outburst of violence on DePrima. He claimed that the bailiff had been antagonistic and hostile toward his client ever since the preliminary hearing started.

Chief Bailiff Tom Beattie, however, defended his subordinate's rapid and decisively firm action. He blamed Ramirez for provoking the incident because he had failed to follow the instructions of the bailiff. "We constantly have to tell him to keep his face straight ahead," Beattie said.

Beattie removed DePrima from the Night Stalker case, but said no disciplinary measures would be taken against the bailiff. The exit of DePrima didn't end the acrimony over the unprecedented courtroom fracas, however.

The defense team was outraged. Arturo Hernandez accused Halpin of trying to provoke him into a physical confrontation with the bailiffs. Hernandez said that as he was shouting at the bailiffs to stop hitting his client in the holding cell, Halpin had suggested to him: "Why don't you wait until they come out, and beat them up?"

But the violent outburst had provided a singularly exciting day that broke up any monotony that might have been threatening to set in at the marathon hearing. And after the incident, Ramirez was noticeably reluctant to turn and stare at witnesses as they walked to or from the witness stand.

Six days after the startling confrontation, the preliminary hearing finally ended. On May 7, Judge Nelson ruled that sufficient evidence of crimes had been presented to establish a prima facie case. He ordered Ramirez to stand trial on a total of forty-one criminal charges.

The charges included fourteen counts of murder, five attempted murders, fifteen burglaries, four rapes, three acts of forced oral copulation, and four counts of sodomy.

Under Halpin's skilled, methodical direction, six witnesses had identified Ramirez as their attacker during the frenzied fourteen-month orgy of murder, sexual assaults, and burglaries that had raged through the suburbs of Los Angeles.

Judge Nelson dismissed eighteen other charges, including allegations of raping or otherwise sexually abusing three young boys and girls. The parents had objected to subjecting their already emotionally scarred children to suffering the additional trauma of testifying at the hearing. None of the charges that were dropped involved homicide.

Ramirez's reaction to the judge's order that he stand trial was predictable. Most defendants faced with a similar outcome would scowl in angry disappointment, break down in tears, or shake their heads in feigned—even genuine—disbelief. Ramirez, clad in his rumpled blue prison jump suit and hobbled by the restraining leg irons, responded by curling his lips in a diabolic smile over his new dental work and pumping a clenched fist into the air as if he had just won a great victory.

Two weeks later, Ramirez formally entered pleas of innocent to fourteen counts of murder and thirty-one other felonies. The original thirty-six felony counts Judge Nelson had ordered him to stand trial on had been trimmed when Halpin decided not to pursue five more-difficult-to-prove charges of robbery. In proving a burglary charge, it is necessary only to show the defendant had illegally entered a house or apartment. To prove a charge of robbery, it is often necessary to recover the stolen goods and show they had been in the defendant's possession.

With the preliminary hearing and the defendant's formal pleas to the charges disposed of, the prosecution and defense attorneys began jockeying for a trial date. Settling on a date that was both agreeable and practical for the concerned parties, the defense, the prosecution, and the court would be no small matter.

Although the prosecution and the court are required to do everything they can to adhere scrupulously to the dictum of a defendant's right to a speedy trial, the defense has considerably more freedom in seeking and obtaining delays. And defense lawyers are especially likely to exercise their prerogative in complex murder cases.

A few weeks after the conclusion of the preliminary hearing, Los Angeles County Superior Court Judge Dion Morrow set the accused Night Stalker's trial date for September 2, 1987. In setting the early date, the jurist rejected complaints by the defense team that they could not be ready for trial on what they claimed was such short notice. Two months later, the judge complied with their pleas for more time, and reset the trial date for December 2.

The Hernandez defense team took advantage of the additional time to continue its legalistic guerrilla war, delaying hearings, filing for dismissal by claiming a lack of prosecution evidence, requesting countless private meetings with Judge Morrow that excluded the prosecution, and moving for change of venue from Los Angeles County. And Morrow himself was forced to delay several hearings because of conflicts with proceedings in other murder cases on his court calendar.

In early November, Ramirez's jailers seized twenty police photographs of Night Stalker crime scenes they found in the defendant's cell. He had been showing them off to other inmates and to jail guards. Nineteen of the photos were of Maxine Zazzara, the attorney murdered with her husband during one of the Night Stalker's most monstrous nights of necrophilic madness. One ghastly picture of the forty-four-year-old woman's nude, mutilated body with its eyes gouged out was fastened to the wall of Ramirez's cell, like a ghastly pinup from *The Texas Chainsaw Massacre*.

The defense lawyers protested angrily and branded seizure of the photographs as "outrageous" interference with their client's right to counsel. Daniel Hernandez said the defense had given Ramirez the photos because he needed them to study and help prepare for his defense.

But Ramirez admitted that he had used the grotesque photographs to intimidate fellow inmates. They had been threatening him and calling him a punk. Being called a punk in prison or jail has even worse connotations than the same uncomplimentary label carries on the outside. A prison punk is literally a homosexual, or someone who is too frightened or too weak to protect himself from anal and oral sodomy by other prisoners.

"I wanted to scare them, to show them there was blood behind the Night Stalker," Ramirez said in explaining why he passed around the photographs. "After they saw the pictures, they went away scared."

In November, Halpin filed a motion to have Judge Morrow removed from the case and replaced by another jurist, even though a change would almost inevitably result in more delays. A new judge would need time to acquaint himself or herself with the complex case. Halpin explained that he believed that Morrow simply had too many other cases on his docket.

"We have a critical situation," Halpin explained to reporters. ". . . the incredible pain that this delay is inflicting on the survivors in this matter. Every day that we delay causes them more trauma, and we don't have the right to do that.

"If we could have gotten anything going, if we had accomplished anything in these months since July, I would never have considered filing this motion," he declared. "I have never filed one before in my life. I consider it repugnant."

The Deputy DA said he had earlier asked Morrow, in

view of his pressing workload, to refer the case to the master calendar court for reassignment. But the judge had refused.

Ignoring the mountain of motions, special conferences, and pleas for more time, the Hernandezes were among the first to criticize Halpin for seeking to delay the trial. The lawyers and everyone else connected with the case who were part of the legal establishment knew that at this stage of the proceedings, a delay of the defendant's "right to a speedy trial" could become the basis for a successful appeal of conviction and order for a new trial if the prosecutor's action could be shown to be unjustified. Halpin had not made his startling move before careful consideration.

Morrow agreed to step aside, and forty-eight-year-old Superior Court Judge Michael Tynan was assigned to the case.

Tynan was appointed to the Los Angeles Municipal Court in 1981 by then-Governor Jerry Brown, and was appointed to the Superior Court in 1984. Before his appointment by Brown, he had been a public defender for thirteen years. He was experienced, organized, and firm.

Tynan wasted no time in letting everyone connected with the case know who the boss was going to be. He laid down the law and announced firmly that he would not tolerate any unnecessary delays. He suggested that the two Hernandezes find themselves living accommodations in Los Angeles for the lengthy trial ahead, rather than continue to commute the roughly three hundred miles up the California coast to their homes and offices in San Jose.

The tough talk aside, the delays continued. For one thing, the trial could not begin until the defense motion for change of venue was decided. And, although Morrow had been removed as the trial judge, that question would still be decided in his court.

There were other motions to be dealt with, as well,

including the defense effort to have the case dismissed, the motion to suppress evidence obtained as a result of the controversial videotaped confession shortly after Ramirez's arrest—and yet another defense motion to try the charges against Ramirez separately.

The Hernandez team backed up their argument that their client could not get a fair trial in the Los Angeles area by showing hours of local television news program videotapes in the judge's chambers. They had collected thick sheaves of newspaper clippings about the case as well. And they disclosed a poll they had commissioned that showed ninety-four percent of Los Angeles–area residents had heard of the Night Stalker. The poll indicated that fifty-two percent of those approached already considered Ramirez to be guilty.

Judge Tynan scheduled hearings on these and other motions still pending in the distressingly intricate case for the first three months of 1987. Halpin responded to the judge's action by describing himself as "depressed but not surprised" that the trial would not begin until spring—at the very soonest.

The new year started out on a more cheerful note for the disconcerted prosecutor, however, when Judge Morrow turned down the defense request to shift the trial from Los Angeles. Despite the pre-trial publicity, the chances of finding twelve unbiased jurors in Los Angeles County were greater than anywhere else in California because there was a potential pool of 5 million people from which to select, he explained.

From that point on, however, matters veered sharply downhill again. Four trial dates were consecutively set, then reluctantly changed. Tynan systematically denied several of the defense motions left pending after his ruling on the venue change. But as soon as he dismissed one, it seemed the defense filed another to take its place.

Despite the judge's best intentions and the prosecutor's increasingly insistent urgings to get the proceeding under way, spring gave way to summer and the court was still tied up in the seemingly interminable pre-trial maneuvering.

Halpin wasn't the only one who had lost his patience with the never-ending delays, however. Authorities in Orange County were sick of the waiting and, in July, moved to bring Ramirez to Santa Ana for his preliminary hearing on attempted murder and rape in the vicious Mission Viejo attack on Carns and his girlfriend. But their efforts, too, were quickly bogged down in a barrage of defense activity.

It was autumn and children had trooped back to classes weeks earlier, when, on September 11, in Los Angeles Superior Court, Judge Tynan rejected yet another defense bid for a lengthy delay. This time the Hernandezes claimed they had uncovered startling new evidence that would clear their client of the terrible charges against him.

If after so long a time they had, indeed, uncovered such earth-shaking facts about the Night Stalker case, they could use the information at their client's trial. Judge Tynan had endured enough. He set the trial date for February 1, 1988.

When the defense duo unsurprisingly made a last-minute bid in early January for yet another delay, the judge sharply refused their request. Tynan ordered the San Jose attorneys to be ready to go to trial on February 1. In what had to be an understatement, he declared, "I'm getting very tired of these delays."

The two San Jose attorneys didn't tire that easily, however. They still had a few legal tricks up their sleeves. In response to a defense appeal, the State Appellate Court issued a ruling ordering the LAPD and Los Angeles County Sheriff's Department to provide the defense attorneys with access to police information about similar murders that had occurred about the same time as those attributed to the Night Stalker. They hoped to show, they claimed, that similar crimes as those attributed to the Night Stalker had been committed at times and places far removed from Richard Ramirez.

The two law enforcement agencies, accompanied by the Los Angeles County district attorney, immediately protested. Noting that the defense was asking for specific types of murders, those with similar methods of operation as the Night Stalker, police pointed out that information simply wasn't compiled or filed that way. Combing their files and breaking down the information into categories such as those outlined by the Night Stalker defense would be almost impossibly time-consuming and costly, they argued.

The prosecutor declared that the request had no relevance to the case, and was just another trick to delay the trial.

Although law enforcement authorities appealed the ruling, Los Angeles DA Ira Reiner eventually agreed to concede to the defense demand. Collecting and correlating the information would indeed be costly and time-consuming, but the alternative would be acceding to more potentially detrimental trial delays while the county's appeal was argued in the higher court.

Judge Tynan scheduled the trial to begin at the end of June. The Hernandezes said they were ready—and promised no more delays.

Then, two weeks before the trial was to begin, the defense team charged Tynan with bias and asked that he be replaced by another trial judge. They claimed that, in a closed hearing in his chambers, Tynan had called them a security risk and ordered that they be searched before visiting with their client.

The closed-chamber flare-up had occurred after Ramirez was discovered with an unauthorized rock-music tape, which he said he had picked up from the defense attorneys' table in the courtroom as he was led back to the holding cell.

Tynan angrily denied the charge of bias, but the accusation had to be dealt with, nevertheless. Orange County Superior Court Judge Phillip E. Cox was assigned to rule on the bias charge and on the motion for the removal of his Los Angeles colleague from the case. The Hernandezes asked for a two-month trial delay while Tynan's fate as the trial judge was decided. Their motion was denied.

The attempt to replace Tynan backfired on the San Jose lawyers. Not only did Cox turn down their request, but he suggested they had set up his colleague. He sternly charged that the two defense attorneys had deliberately created a situation, "in violation of their professional ethics," which they attempted to use to disqualify Tynan.

Restored as trial judge, Tynan reset the trial date for mid-July. The chastened defense attorneys promised they would be ready.

Selection of a jury at last began on July 22, from an initial pool of seventy prospective jurors. Deputy DA Halpin was ecstatic, despite Tynan's gloomy predictions that he anticipated serious problems finding twelve unbiased men and women to sit on the panel. Selection of the twelve jurors and twelve alternates was expected to take six months.

On August 2, Deputy District Attorney Halpin announced that threats had been made on his life by Ramirez. According to Halpin, Ramirez had told a jail deputy of a plan for someone to bring a gun into the courtroom, "get it to Ramirez, and have Ramirez shoot the prosecutor and then turn it on the courtroom."

Halpin said he had enough proof for the threat that he would use it as evidence in the trial.

Disclosure of the threat on his life came after Halpin complained he was the only one who had been searched before coming into the courtroom that morning. He said it was the first time in his career that he'd ever been searched.

"It seems a strange approach [to security], at best, to search the district attorney when he comes into the courtroom and no one else," he observed.

Halpin was particularly upset by Judge Tynan's previous order against searching prospective jurors. Anyone could get a badge, pose as a juror, and bring in a weapon, he warned. Other courtroom shootouts had occurred before, and security was a problem to be seriously dealt with.

Sergeant Frank Salerno and Tynan both admitted threats were made, but they refused to elaborate publicly.

Tynan had ruled that attorneys for both sides in the case must be searched before entering the courtroom as a result of the incident involving the contraband rock tape that had passed into Ramirez's hands.

Jury selection crept inexorably along into December and to the year-end holidays. The original juror pool of seventy was quickly exhausted and more than 1,500 prospective jurors were eventually examined and interviewed by the prosecution and defense. Hundreds were excused because they could not afford to spend an estimated two years in court. More were dismissed because they admitted they already believed Ramirez was guilty of the Night Stalker murders.

Another disturbing trend became noticeable midway in the proceedings. No Caucasians and no Asians were being selected for the jury. Those that were acceptable to the prosecution were inevitably struck—or dismissed— by the defense.

One prospective white juror was overheard reassuring another prospective white juror, as they awaited their turn at oral examination by the attorneys, that there was "nothing to worry about. If you haven't got a tan, they won't pick you." Prospective panelists of all races joked among themselves about needing a tan to be selected.

It could have been worse. A year before the proceedings reached the jury-selection stage, the defense had tried to convince Judge Morrow that the panel should include non-English-speaking Hispanics. Daniel Hernandez claimed, "They share a common cultural background with the defendant."

Judge Morrow was still presiding. He was as aware as anyone that the defendant was American-born and English-speaking. And he had no time for what some critics might consider frivolous motions or requests. He wasted little time in ruling that jurors sitting in the Night Stalker trial would not be selected for their inability to speak English.

During the drawn-out jury-selection process, a black man already selected for the panel was especially overheard by prospective jurors telling another selected juror that he would not support the death penalty for a minority until more whites were sentenced to death. The remark was reported by one of the prospective jurors to Judge Tynan.

The black man vehemently denied making the racist remark, but Tynan nevertheless removed him from the panel. The judge explained that he could not afford to take a chance that the black man had made the statement.

Daniel Hernandez responded to the incident with the black juror by moving for a mistrial. He declared that all the jurors had been tainted by claims that the panel was selected on the basis of race, and that others had heard the black man's biased statements about the death penalty. Tynan denied the motion.

Although Halpin orally charged the defense with deliberately keeping Caucasians and Asians off the jury—California law forbids the systematic exclusion of any ethnic group—the deputy DA did not ask for a mistrial. It had been difficult and vexing enough moving matters to this stage. The prosecutor wasn't about to start tossing monkey wrenches into the procedure.

But Daniel Hernandez was less hesitant about such

interruptions. He asked for a mistrial. This time he claimed that black women were being excluded from the panel by the prosecution.

The accusation was puzzling to Halpin, who pointed out to the court that at that stage of the proceeding four black women had already been selected for the jury.

Judge Tynan denied the motion for mistrial, and scolded Hernandez.

"I find these kinds of accusations troubling," the judge said. "Mr. Halpin is known as a hard-nosed, tough prosecutor, and he may have some rough edges. But no one in this building would call him dishonest or deceptive . . ."

The antipathy between the pugnacious Halpin and the two defense attorneys, particularly Daniel Hernandez, was becoming increasingly obvious and acidic. At almost every opportunity, it appeared, they were hurling gratuitous insults and challenges. At last, Tynan interrupted the bitter verbal sparring and admonished both of them —as Judge Morrow had done before—to behave themselves. But even though it was closer to New Year's Eve than to the Fourth of July, the fireworks were just beginning.

By early January 1989, a twelve-member panel of six blacks and six Hispanics had been selected. Seven members of the panel were women. A couple of weeks later, on January 29, the twelve alternate jurors were impaneled.

At last, three-and-a-half years after Richard Ramirez's dramatic capture and arrest, the trial of the reputed Night Stalker was set to begin.

CHAPTER 14

Trial

LIKE A SKILLED SURGEON PREPARING TO EX-
cise a malignant tumor from a patient, Los Angeles
County Deputy District Attorney Philip Halpin coolly
and methodically set about his task of removing the
Night Stalker cancer from the society he had plagued for
too long.

In an even, almost monotonous tone, Halpin began a
low-key, no-frills chronology of the grisly facts and chain
of evidence relating to the thirteen slayings and other
crimes in Los Angeles County with which Richard Ramirez was charged. In his opening statement to the jury,
which lasted two and a half hours, he recalled how the
crimes were discovered—a dying man calling "Help me"
after dialing 911; a teen-ager with her head smashed in
crying for her father; an innocent three-year-old padding
next door in pajama-clad feet hours before dawn to sum-
mon a neighbor's help for his ravished mother and his
murdered father.

The bodies of one couple were discovered after they
failed to arrive for their weekly pre-church Sunday morning breakfast with their family. They were found in their

bed—"one sprawled over the other." The man was nearly decapitated.

There was the forty-one-year-old mother who staunchly and silently endured rape and sodomy in hopes that the Stalker would not harm her twelve-year-old son, who was locked nearby in a closet. After the assaults, she courageously engaged the attacker in conversation for twenty minutes so that she could later help identify him for police.

Halpin also spoke of the surviving victims who wouldn't be in court, one of them a woman in her eighties. Mrs. *Blanche Wolfe* had not spoken since 1985, almost four years previously, when she was savagely assaulted, and her sister had been brutally murdered and branded with a Satanic pentagram.

"She cannot speak and she is fed through a tube, but she is still alive. Therefore, the defendant is only charged with attempting to murder her," the prosecutor explained calmly to the jury.

As the jurors and court spectators watched and listened to the prosecutor in rapt silence, tears formed in eyes. Others, including survivors and friends of victims, who had waited nearly five years for this story to be told, gritted their teeth in anguish, frustration, rage, and hatred.

Occasionally their eyes shifted from the prosecutor, who looked, behaved, and sounded surprisingly like a sedate professor delivering a routine and boring lecture to a class of college students. At those times attention was riveted on the subject of his discourse: a tall, gaunt, young Hispanic man seated at the defense table, Richard Ramirez, the one-time sticky-fingered El Paso sneak thief accused of some of the most savagely sordid outrages in American criminal history.

The rotting snaggleteeth that had been a trademark of the Night Stalker and made his ravaged mouth look like a worked-out coal mine were gone. The devastated bicus-

pids and molars had been replaced or repaired with fill-
ings, root canals, and caps. The lumpy blue LA County
Jail jump suit he had worn throughout the exhausting
pre-trial hearings was also gone.

Now he was dressed in a spiffy charcoal-gray pinstripe
suit that had been bought for him specifically for the
trial. The piercing black eyes victims described as demonic were hidden by stylish sunglasses. Only his
shaggy, dark hair that brushed the collar of his new suit
was still there. But it was no longer dirty, tangled and
matted. It had been washed, neatly combed and styled.

Richard Ramirez's new courtroom image had been
skillfully and professionally crafted. He looked as if he
might have stepped into a business board meeting as a
junior executive, or breezed into any swinging upscale
singles bar to troll for a girlfriend or a one-night romantic
fling. Ultimately, of course, his behavior, not his ward-
robe, would eventually determine his courtroom persona.
And, of course, the evidence and testimony would inexorably shape the jury's attitude—and judgment of the
well-dressed young man who was fidgeting so nervously.

Beside him at the defense table, to attempt to control
and direct his behavior, while hopefully convincing the
jury of twelve men and women that their client was every
bit as normal and civilized as he appeared, were his lawyer, Daniel Hernandez, and Richard Salinas, a paralegal.

Co-counsel Arturo Hernandez was not present. No
public excuse was offered for Arturo's failure to accom-
pany his client on the critical opening day of the trial.

Superior Court Judge Michael Tynan's courtroom was
packed for the opening day, with reporters, photographers, and television cameramen avariciously hogging
more than one hundred of the limited spectator seats, and
taking up standing room, as well. More than thirty reporters were packed into the first few rows alone. It was a
media event, almost as big as the wedding of rock super-
star Madonna and actor Sean Penn. It was bigger than

Freddie Krueger, Jason, or Norman Bates, but this wasn't *Nightmare on Elm Street, Friday the 13th,* or *Psycho.* This was about real-life horrors.

The Los Angeles–area press was there, of course, and other major California media. The three major television networks filmed segments on the trial opening. It was covered by the national U. S. news wire services, Britain's Reuters, and National Public Radio, as well as by reporters from *The New York Times,* the *Chicago Tribune,* the *Philadelphia Inquirer,* and several other individual newspapers. Perhaps the smallest news organization to dispatch its own reporter to the trial was the 50,000-circulation *El Paso Post Herald* from the defendant's hometown.

Grim-faced uniformed bailiffs and a phalanx of stolid, unsmiling men dressed in dark suits, which seemed to have all come from the same clothing-store rack, also helped swell the audience. The plainclothesmen were detectives from the Los Angeles County Sheriff's Department and the LAPD and officers from other agencies who had worked on the case either as members of the tasks forces or independently.

They included a sprinkling of lawmen from nearby Orange County, where the Mission Viejo attacks occurred, and from San Francisco. Generally, they made themselves conspicuous by their efforts to make themselves inconspicuous.

Occasionally a clanking sound would be heard coming from the defense table when Ramirez made a sudden movement, causing metal to brush against metal. Nearly hidden from the jury and spectators by the table and by his own chair, the metal chains shattered the image of the rising young executive that his natty appearance attempted to convey. Whenever the leg chains rattled, the eyes and attention of every bailiff and detective in the courtroom suddenly shifted toward him. The sound was like a powerful magnet.

Everyone entering the courtroom had to file past metal detectors at the door, and several reporters and other observers were stopped and asked to empty pockets or purses, or to remove jewelry before they were allowed to pass. Security in the courtroom was very, very tight. Although courtroom shootings were rare, they were not unheard of.

In 1970, radicals Ruchell Magee and Jonathan Jackson shot and killed a judge, two convicts and a boy, with four guns smuggled into a Marin County, California, courtroom in an airline bag by Jackson. In 1982, attorney Oscar Fonseca was shot dead in a Toronto, Canada, courtroom, in another dramatic and bloody incident.

The forty-nine-year-old judge, Michael Tynan, sat stoically on the bench, his handsome face framed by plain thin-rimmed glasses as he, too, listened intently to the prosecutor. This was his first major death-penalty case, and it had already severely tested his patience.

During the nearly two and a half years since he had replaced Dion Morrow as presiding judge, he had been required to deal with a mind-numbing litany of defense-instigated delays. Some of them, such as the motion for non-English-speaking jurors, seemed to be outrageously obstructive and frivolous. But rulings had to be made, nevertheless.

On the other side, there was the increasingly impatient badgering of the prosecution to get the trial under way, as well as a host of other problems, including the unfortunate courtroom fracas between the defendant and the bailiffs and the report of a death threat against the prosecutor.

Attempts to mediate and restrain the constant bickering and open belligerence between the opposing attorneys were particularly wearing. As scholarly, calm, and low-key as the prosecutor now appeared to be, as he calmly addressed the jury in his opening statement, he was a fighter who gave up no unnecessary ground. He could be as bellicose and irascible as an oil-field bully when it came to the acidic legal in-fighting and matching of wits bound to occur in such a high-profile murder trial. He was openly and volubly contemptuous of his opposition, especially quick to tangle with Daniel Hernandez.

In their defense, Ramirez's attorneys had to know they were fighting an uphill battle against tremendous odds. An incredible amount of evidence had been gathered against their client, not the least of which were his own statements. And the crimes he was accused of were horrendous—Jack the Ripper–like outrages that had held millions in terror and served chilling notice that there was no such thing in Southern California as a nice, safe middle-class refuge from the runaway crime and violence of big cities; that pleasant homes in orderly, neat communities offered no guarantee of safety.

The defense attorneys weren't oblivious to the odds, and they weren't oblivious to the heavy pressures and responsibilities they had undertaken with the case. They smarted under the glib barbs of the prosecutor and, at times, it was difficult for them to hold their own in the "no prisoners taken" atmosphere of the courtroom quarreling. The prosecution complained that the defense team had repeatedly shown up in court "unprepared for even the most menial task." Once, in frustration, Arturo Hernandez angrily invited the prosecutor outside the courtroom to settle their differences in the hallway. Halpin declined, making no effort to hide his contempt.

Finally, the judge had the press to deal with. The media's desire to stay close to the dramatic murder case was understandable. But there were times when the heady competition in the media for exclusive stories—thirty years ago they would have been called "scoops"—appeared to the more understandably conservative and cautious criminal justice establishment to be, at best, needlessly sensational; and, at worst, wildly irresponsible.

Not even the powerful American press had the right to jeopardize a defendant's right to a fair trial.

When the trial opened, Judge Tynan refused to follow the lead of one of his predecessors in the case, Judge Candace Cooper, who banned cameras and microphones at the beginning of the preliminary hearing. But he warned still photographers that the picture-taking would stop as soon as he entered the courtroom to take the bench. And he firmly informed them that there were to be no photographs taken of jurors or civilian witnesses without their permission.

As the judge was laying down the ground rules to the press, he interrupted the recitation long enough to scold a photographer who was moving around seeking a better angle for a picture. "This really isn't a photo opportunity," the judge sternly admonished. "It's a trial."

Nevertheless, when jurors filed into the courtroom, the judge had to shoo photographers from the jury box so that the members of the panel could take their seats.

Despite the large number of seats monopolized by the press on the opening day of the trial, there was still room for scores of the merely curious public. A young man with teased burgundy hair was admitted. So was an East Los Angeles College ethnic-studies and humanities professor, who said it was like "going to see a rock star." A sixty-six-year-old salesman told a reporter that if he were Ramirez, "I wouldn't look so conspicuous with a smile and smirk on my face. I've seen Halpin in court before," he added judiciously. "He can be a mean s. o. b."

At the jury box, Halpin was telling the panel that Ramirez was linked to many of the murders through fingerprints, glove marks, and footprint identification. Eyewitnesses had identified Ramirez from police lineups as their assailant. At least four different handguns were used and identified in the killing spree.

Symbols of Devil worship were found near some of the victims, the prosecutor said. In one of the most gruesome descriptions, Halpin recounted the double murder of the Whittier couple, Vincent and Maxine Zazzara. Vincent Zazzara was shot in the head. His wife's throat was slit. "And Mrs. Zazzara's eyes had been gouged from her head," Halpin told the quiet, intent panel.

Using a large map of Los Angeles County, mounted on an upright frame, he showed the jurors exactly where each of the crimes had occurred, giving a detailed account of each one, beginning with the June 28, 1984, murder of Jennie Vincow.

The deputy district attorney wasted no time in advising the jury that he wanted guilty verdicts and sentences that would send the craggy-faced defendant to California's gas chamber.

"We have alleged these murders are in the first degree, were premeditated, and occurred during burglaries or other crimes," Halpin declared. We are asking for the death penalty in this case. This is where your work begins," he told the jury of seven women and five men.

Defense Attorney Daniel Hernandez announced that he would reserve his opening remarks until after the prosecution concluded its case. Halpin estimated that would take about four months.

Spectators and reporters were anxious for the fur to begin flying in the long-awaited trial. But Halpin disappointed them by filling the first week of the trial with a staid, methodical, and controlled performance. The hours passed slowly as a parade of witnesses appeared, one after the other, offering a stream of dreary technical testimony.

The technical data were interrupted and spiced up only occasionally with an eyewitness account, but the drama was clearly missing. As the days passed, the reporters with their notebooks and cameras began to drift away, seeking other more immediate and tempting fare for their audiences. The youth with the purple hair was also soon missing, and the throng of other curiosity-seekers thinned noticeably. It was going to be a long trial, and people had their lives to live.

Much of the real action during the first weeks of the trial was offstage, in private huddles between attorneys and the judge at the bench. That was where the heat was, and most of it was directed at Daniel Hernandez. The judge was tangling heatedly with Hernandez, as was Halpin. After watching the action at the bench for a couple of days, one courtroom wag observed that it was becoming difficult for an outsider to tell who was on trial, Richard Ramirez or Daniel Hernandez.

The discussions were supposed to be out of earshot of the jury, but they often became so animated that they carried throughout the courtroom. In fact, one juror called out during one exchange, "I can hear you!" One of the most common remarks was some variation of "Let's keep it down."

At one point, Judge Tynan ordered Hernandez, whose co-counsel, Arturo Hernandez, had not shown up in court since the start of the trial, to "shut up." Tynan also told him he "was doing a lousy job" of trying to explain the relevance of a particular line of questioning.

In his cross-examination of a relative of one victim, Hernandez asked if he had checked into a mental hospital for a brief stay. Tynan stopped Hernandez and admonished him that it was "almost cruel" to pose questions about past mental health to a man who had already suffered such a loss.

A forensic expert had testified at the preliminary hearing that Ramirez's fingerprints were found on a window screen at the apartment of the dead woman.

In another exchange, Hernandez complained that Halpin was not keeping him apprised of the order of witnesses. That comment temporarily jiggled Halpin's composure.

The prosecutor said he was "damn tired" of Hernandez's accusing him in front of the jury of being dishonest. Halpin told the judge that he had bent over backward to keep the defense up to date on every detail of the case. Tynan concurred with the deputy DA.

Hernandez explained that Halpin was deviating slightly from the previously disclosed chronological order in which he was supposed to present his case, and that was causing problems for the defense.

Tynan was unsympathetic. "Mr. Hernandez, you are a lawyer," the judge said sternly. "You are expected to be possessed of a certain amount of flexibility and preparedness. Now this kind of whining that you are not prepared because someone came in a little early is really not commendable."

During another particularly labored bench huddle, Hernandez apparently perceived something amusing about the situation and laughed. It was Tynan, however, who had the last laugh. "You can laugh all you want, but I'm ruling against you," he snapped.

Following the embarrassing confrontation, Hernandez, who always made a point of meeting reporters after hearings and other court appearances, slipped out the back door. But reporters cornered Halpin as he was walking out the front door of the courthouse, and asked him to critique his opponent. The prosecutor refused to be drawn into a discussion.

During the next few weeks, the trial progressed smoothly. But if Halpin, who had sweated and fretted for three and a half years to move the proceedings to this point, expected the relative smooth sailing to continue, he was headed for a painful disappointment by the events of February 28.

Daniel Hernandez appeared in court on that day, a Monday, with a doctor's report claiming the defense attorney was suffering from nervous exhaustion. The doctor recommended psychological counseling for Hernandez and up to six weeks of rest. The defense attorney had undergone a complete physical examination, including a treadmill test and an electrocardiogram, the physician wrote. The results of the tests were normal, although Hernandez showed an elevated sugar level.

The news was stunning. If Hernandez was unable to continue, the chances for a mistrial appeared great. If a mistrial was declared, the past seven months, including the six months spent selecting a jury, would be a complete washout. The county had already spent $1.3 million trying the case. There were more than 17,000 pages of testimony.

Halpin proved stoical in his reaction. "This is not a surprise to us," he told reporters. The prosecution had been concerned about Hernandez's health since October 1985, when the defense lawyer entered the Stalker case, he explained. Municipal Court Judge Elva Soper had questioned Hernandez about his health at the time of his appointment as Ramirez's defense counsel, referring to the two instances in Santa Clara County when he had failed to make court appearances for health reasons.

"We always knew his health could be a risk factor in the case. It was a concern we had, but there was nothing we could do about it," Halpin said.

Reporters tried to reach Hernandez at his San Jose office, but were told he was out ill. His wife, who was also an attorney, did not return their telephone messages. They did manage to reach Arturo Hernandez, who had been missing without explanation since the beginning of jury selection on July 21, 1988. He refused comment on his co-counsel's health problems.

Attempting to hide his disappointment, the prosecutor said the chances for a mistrial were good. And "if we are going to mistry it, I'd just as soon mistry it now," he added. It would be unreasonable to keep the present jury around indefinitely, he explained.

Halpin told reporters that even though Arturo Hernandez had not been in court since the start of the trial, he was still a counsel of record in the case. But, he added, it was unlikely he would take the case over.

But Tynan was not so ready to declare a mistrial—or to rule out the possibility that Arturo Hernandez would take over the case. On March 1, he said he would allow Arturo Hernandez some time to familiarize himself with the current details of the case. Even if Daniel Hernandez could not function effectively as a trial lawyer, his nervous exhaustion should not prevent him from supplying his co-counsel with all the details he needed, Tynan said.

The following day, however, Tynan shocked the press and the public with the announcement that he was denying Daniel Hernandez's request for time off. He said Hernandez had not even come close to establishing the need for a long break, adding that stress is "part and parcel of a death-penalty case. . . ."

"Some of us have chest pains. Some of us have bellyaches. One of my friends lost part of his vision. Some of us deal with it better than others," he sternly lectured the defense lawyer. "I do not feel that your health justifies any further continuances in this case."

The judge noted that Hernandez had a history of illnesses and of attempting to terminate proceedings early in the day because he was tired. Hernandez's San Jose doctor had admitted that he was not an expert in stress disorders and nervous exhaustion, the judge added. The physician had failed to convince him it was necessary for Hernandez to take time off.

More than anything else, he needed more help with the workload, Hernandez told the judge. The workload was to have been shared with Arturo Hernandez. Tynan ordered the long-absent Arturo Hernandez to resume attending the daily court proceedings.

Daniel Hernandez told reporters that he, too, would return to court, as the judge had ordered. But he was still miffed. "I'm exhausted. I'm tired. Obviously, the court doesn't consider this sufficient reason to take time off. I'm not going to kill myself, and I'm surprised the court is not allowing me—on a two-year schedule—to take two or three weeks off," he complained.

Halpin was no more sympathetic than Tynan, and responded with classic sarcasm. "I'd like a month on the Riviera myself," he quipped. As far as he was concerned, Hernandez already had help to take the workload off him —from the district attorney's staff, Halpin said.

The prosecutor pointed out that he had made available many records and transcripts to Hernandez, and had even cross-indexed files so it would be easier for the defense lawyer to use them.

"We've prepared the case, not just for us, but for the defense in the hopes they would be prepared to carry this burden. They've had adequate help. They should have been prepared by now," he told reporters.

The irony of the situation was that while the prosecution was doing its best to get Ramirez into the gas chamber, it also had to take every precaution against the possibility that an appeals court might overturn a conviction on the grounds that Ramirez had not been competently represented. To guard against a possible reversal, it seemed at times that they were helping to defend him as well as to prosecute him.

Although the immediate crisis appeared to have passed, Halpin warned that the danger wasn't over. "I think the potential of mistrial will be with us until we complete this case," he said. The problem with Mr. [Daniel] Hernandez is that he has a history of this [complaining of illness]."

When Arturo Hernandez at last spoke out to clear up the mounting speculation over his mysterious absence from the trial, he claimed in an interview carried by United Press International that he had an arrangement with Judge Tynan. He said the judge had agreed to excuse him from attending the trial so that he could work on other cases undertaken by his firm. "Somebody has to pay the bills," he said.

The unspecified fees the Hernandezes were believed to have agreed to apparently referred to some money from the Ramirez family. But the Hernandezes had complained a year earlier that they weren't being paid, and requested to be formally appointed by the court as Ramirez's defenders. The total burden of financing the accused serial murderer's defense would then be passed on to the taxpayers. The request was denied.

Consequently, a serious question of the ability of the Hernandezes to provide a competent defense for Ramirez continued to linger. Halpin therefore had to assume the added burden of ensuring that the case would not have to be re-tried. As a result of the defense's delays in moving to suppress incriminating statements Ramirez made after his arrest, Halpin had to take the unusual step of seeking a court ruling on the admissibility of his own evidence.

Halpin was asked by the judge to research the defense side of the issue of whether the trial had to be moved. And, afraid that the defense's arguments for their motion for separate trials were inadequate, Halpin made both sides' arguments in his response.

The Hernandez team, especially Daniel, frequently appeared to be only a breath away from being charged with contempt of court—both during the preliminary proceedings and later, during the trial. They came close in January 1987, when Judge Dion Morrow was still presiding and the defense lawyers said they couldn't subpoena witnesses because they were out of paper. They also claimed that Morrow had prohibited additional witnesses in support of the defense motion to move the trial out of Los Angeles.

"That's a lie," Morrow replied. A burly, no-nonsense judge, he was furious. "Don't say that again," he ordered. Morrow then threatened to hold Daniel Hernandez in contempt because the lawyer was continuing to press on with yet more arguments after the judge had already stated, firmly, that he had heard enough.

Morrow also delivered a mini-lecture in legal procedure when Hernandez had trouble placing newspaper articles and television reports of the case into evidence.

"The way you practice law, sir, is when you present an exhibit to the court you are supposed to be ready at that time to move it into evidence," the judge grumped.

The pair's miscues included:

- Reportedly failing to list five slayings in their motion for separate trials, always a crucial issue in a multiple-murder case.
- Giving Ramirez the grisly photos of Maxine Zazzara's nude, mutilated body.
- A move by Daniel Hernandez for permission to allow Ramirez to read for the court a fifty-two-page document. Co-prosecutor Yochelson objected: "I think we should have the lawyers represent the clients and not vice versa." The judge apparently agreed. The request was denied.

Judge Tynan was in no mood to take chances on a mistrial if one or both of the Hernandezes was unable to see the case to a conclusion. A week after denying Daniel Hernandez's effort to obtain a holiday from the trial to recuperate and recharge his batteries, the judge appointed fifty-eight-year-old Ray Clark as Ramirez's co-counsel—at taxpayers' expense.

The law was not Clark's first profession. The Florida native had been an electronics engineer for fourteen years after graduating from Howard University, and had worked in California's aerospace industry until it hit a slump in the late 1960s. Concerned by the on-again, off-again state of the business he was in, Clark decided to return to school. He entered the Southwestern School of

Law in Los Angeles. In 1973, the same year he graduated from law school, he was admitted to the California Bar.

Clark had been in private practice ever since then, concerning himself primarily with criminal law. He told news reporters that, while he devoted himself to the Ramirez case, his two partners would continue handling the business of his law firm.

The newly appointed defense attorney had a ready sense of humor that was refreshing after all the rancor during the past months of proceedings. "You know, when I was working at TRW in 1970, I decided there were too many engineers, so I decided to do something else," he told reporters who had surrounded him. "Now, I hear there are too many lawyers."

Although Clark didn't mind sharing a chuckle about his profession, he was dead serious about the awesome responsibilities he had just assumed. The trial was bitter, convoluted—and very, very public.

During an impromptu chat with reporters outside the courtroom, about three hours after his appointment, Clark revealed a peek at his planned strategy. He said he hadn't yet decided if Ramirez would testify, but remarked that he liked to put his clients on the witness stand so that a jury could hear their side of the story.

Then, in a statement that perhaps only a mother or a defense attorney would venture under those particular circumstances about a client who had flashed a pentagram on his palm and proclaimed fealty to Satan during a pre-trial appearance, he added, "Even if he's as innocent as the driven snow, there's a lot to this case. I know the jury would like to hear from him." Whether or not he was guilty or innocent of the awful crimes he was accused of committing, Richard Ramirez hardly provoked images of purity or of cleanly driven snow.

Clark's talk of the possibility of allowing his client to testify in his own defense was a departure from the attitude of many, probably most, defense attorneys. There is no question that a defendant who has been properly prepared, and who behaves properly on the witness stand, can sometimes help his own case greatly by testifying.

The danger lies in the prosecution's opportunity to cross-examine. No matter how anxious a prosecutor may be to question a defendant in front of the judge or jury, he cannot be made to take the stand and testify against himself. But, once a defendant has been called by the defense, the prosecutor has the right to cross-examine. And not only can cross-examinations be brutal, grueling ordeals for a defendant, they can move as well into potentially dangerous areas that would otherwise have been left closed to the prosecutor by restrictions against forced self-incrimination.

If Richard Ramirez did indeed take the stand to testify in his own defense, it would be showtime. It would mark the resumption of the trial as a major media event.

But there was plenty of time—months, in fact—before a decision had to be made on the possibility of Ramirez's testifying. In the meantime, the defendant would continue to sit at the defense table, immaculately dressed in suit, tie, and chains, scribbling occasionally on a legal pad or shifting uncomfortably as other people testified.

When testimony resumed the day after Clark's appointment as a co-defense counsel, it was he, not Daniel or Arturo Hernandez, who cross-examined the first prosecution witness. The witness was a senior deputy coroner who testified about two of the slayings Ramirez was charged with committing in March 1985. Clark's manner was quietly efficient, neither cloyingly courteous nor needlessly antagonistic. He was prepared for the witness, and his questions were crisp, intelligent, and to the point.

The newly appointed defense attorney's refreshingly competent manner seemed immediately to spill over into the entire procedure. The case began moving more smoothly, and the prosecution was benefiting as well as the defense. Halpin actually began to draw ahead of his anticipated schedule for presenting the case. The deputy DA had predicted that it would take him four months. It took him approximately two.

On April 12, the prosecutor called a data-processing manager for Avia Footwear and a Los Angeles County sheriff's deputy to testify. The footwear expert testified that the size eleven-and-a-half aerobic shoe manufactured by his company was an uncommon commodity in Southern California in 1985 when most of the series of slayings had occurred. Prints from that size and make of shoe had first turned up at the Whittier ranch-style home of Vincent and Maxine Zazzara, and later at four other murder sites.

David Laws, who had guarded Ramirez in his high-security area of the county jail for a year and a half, said the defendant once called him to his cell and showed him two grisly pictures of Maxine Zazzara's naked, mutilated body. "People come up here and call me a punk, and I show them the pictures and say, 'There's blood behind the Night Stalker,' and they go away pale," Laws quoted Ramirez as bragging to him.

Deputy Laws and the footwear expert were the last prosecution witnesses to testify. The prosecution had concluded its case.

Halpin said the prosecution case went quicker than anticipated because he presented less actual evidence during the trial than he had at the preliminary hearing. He said he dropped some witnesses in order to present all the evidence in the thirty-one days of testimony spread over two months.

The prosecution's case had been impressive. It had been so impressive, in fact, that the defendant had decided to forgo presentation of a defense. Five days before the defense was to have opened its case, Clark announced to a stunned press that Ramirez had decided not to offer any defense at all. There would not even be an opening statement.

Clark described his client as gloomy and emotionally distraught. "I think he thinks that it won't do any good," he said of Ramirez's decision not to follow through with a defense.

Earlier, Ramirez had been ready and eager to go along with his attorneys' plans to present a defense, including calling about a dozen witnesses on his behalf. But the accused Night Stalker began "wobbling and sliding" back and forth, Clark explained.

"He has a tendency to cut things short. He says he's tired of being in jail, the food is bad, and so forth."

Ramirez had become so upset and depressed that he staged a shouting match while meeting with his attorneys in a holding cell during a trial recess earlier in the week.

Clark said that he personally had hoped to present a vigorous defense, based on the contention that Ramirez was a victim of mistaken identity. "My position is: Hey, let's try to win this—go for the victory on as many counts as possible, or on all of them," the lawyer declared.

Although rare, decisions to forgo a defense are not unprecedented, especially when the prosecution's case is particularly strong. In such cases, the defense simply attempts to convince the jury in closing statements that the state has failed to prove the defendant's guilt beyond a reasonable doubt.

Clark explained that in those circumstances the defense sometimes reserved their arguments until the sentencing portion of the trial in order to try for a more lenient sentence than the maximum allowed. The maximum sentence for the more serious charges against Ramirez was the death penalty.

There was another option available. The defense could argue the case over the defendant's objections. California case law, however, was not entirely clear on whether defense lawyers could go ahead with a defense despite the client's objections in death-penalty cases. Clark said he was consulting with the California State Bar's Ethics

Committee and the California Appellate Project on the question.

The crisis was averted, however. The former aerospace engineer who had impressed almost everyone with his startling ability to master the complicated details of the complex case and to take charge within only days after appointment to the defense team pulled another surprise. He convinced Ramirez to change his mind and to mount a defense, after all.

The thrust of the defense case, as Clark had intimated earlier, would focus on the contention that Ramirez was a victim of mistaken identity. Clark said he hoped to raise a reasonable doubt in the minds of jurors by pointing out weaknesses in the prosecution's case. He had an acronym he used to describe the defense's strategy for saving Ramirez from the gas chamber: SODDI—"Some Other Dude Did It." The attorney told reporters, "We're going to hammer hard on the fact that there is no consistent identification of Ramirez here."

When the defense case was opened at last, Clark argued that release of Ramirez's photo and his constant appearance on television before he was placed in a police lineup tainted the often dramatic courtroom identifications by women who survived the attacks. The constant display of his photo tended to plant the concrete image of Richard Ramirez as being that of the Night Stalker when, in reality, their true recollection of their attacker was vague and indistinct.

Elizabeth Loftus, an expert on eyewitness identification, was called to the stand to help back up the defense's case for SODDI. She testified that when a victim sees a gun, he or she tends to concentrate on the gun and not on the assailant's appearance. She added that research also showed that people often have a difficult time identifying a person of another race.

Among the thirty-five witnesses called by the defense were Ramirez's father and sister.

Surprise testimony by Julian Ramirez, Sr., as a defense witness clearly appeared to catch the prosecution off guard. Speaking through a Spanish interpreter, the accused Night Stalker's father said his son was in El Paso for about eight days starting May 22 or May 23, 1985, for the communion of a niece. He said his son stayed in a hotel the first night, and thereafter slept at the family home.

Despite searing cross-examination by the prosecution, the elder Ramirez refused to change his story. He insisted that his son was in El Paso on the critical days and nights he had listed.

If Richard Ramirez was in El Paso from May 22 until May 31, as his father had testified, he could not have killed *Malvia Keller,* viciously beaten her sister, *Blanche Wolfe,* or sexually assaulted *Ruth Wilson,* Clark pointed out.

Another of the defense witnesses was a professional burglar, who cited the very amateurism of the Night Stalker break-ins to cast suspicion on the identification of Ramirez as the intruder. The witness pointed out that anyone like Ramirez who had begun burglarizing homes as a teen-ager would have acquired more professional skills by the time he was twenty-five. Speaking with a certain amount of pride in his own criminal expertise, the witness scoffed at the burglaries attributed to the Night Stalker as shamefully unprofessional.

Despite the earlier speculation sparked by Clark's statements immediately following his appointment to the defense team, Ramirez didn't testify in his own defense. The disappointed media and other court watchers would not be treated to the spectacle of the cadaverous, unpredictable defendant undergoing scathing cross-examination by the peppery Halpin. Clark explained that the decision about testifying had been left up to Ramirez. And the defendant had decided against it.

If there was any doubt left among court watchers that

Clark was now the driving force on the defense team, it was permanently removed in closing arguments. Behaving as if he had been on the case for months, rather than a few weeks, Clark delivered a finely crafted, spirited statement that poked and prodded at the prosecution's evidence. If even the tiniest bit of doubt could be planted in the mind of a single juror, it might mean the difference between life and death for his client.

Clark hit hard at the prosecution's efforts to link the defendant to the sneaker prints found at some of the crime scenes. He pointed out that although Halpin went to great pains to show that a size eleven-and-a-half Avia sneaker was rare in Southern California during the period the Night Stalker was on his rampage, the prosecution had failed to prove that Ramirez actually owned a pair of the shoes.

And the defense attorney glibly wrote off the outrageous incidents involving the boastful display of the photos of Maxine Zazzara's mutilated corpse and Ramirez's proud claims that he was the Night Stalker as nothing more than acts of immature bravado to impress other prisoners at the county jail.

"Mr. Ramirez was taking on the reputation of the Night Stalker" in order to enhance his social standing in the eyes of other inmates, Clark explained. "Jail is a dangerous place to be, and, in the pecking order, the murderers get the most respect."

Halpin's lengthy and detailed closing argument was interrupted during the afternoon session when it was suddenly discovered that Daniel Hernandez was missing from the courtroom following a recess. Legal assistant Richard Salinas was also missing, although his briefcase had been left on the defense counsels' table. Clark told the court that he didn't know what had happened to his co-counsel or to the paralegal. And he said he was concerned for their safety.

Judge Tynan didn't share Clark's fears for the safety of

the missing lawyers, however. He angrily threatened to issue an arrest warrant for Hernandez. Clark's professed concern for his co-counsel was misplaced. Hernandez had been safe—and would remain safe from everyone but the furious judge.

The lawyer showed up in court the next day to explain his confounding absence during a face-off with Tynan in the judge's chambers. Hernandez said the whole incident was a misunderstanding. He insisted that both Clark and the defendant had known he planned to spend the afternoon out of the courtroom working on other aspects of the case.

"I had lunch, went to the bank, and made some phone calls, and went back to my office," Hernandez explained.

Apparently unimpressed, Tynan demanded, "Was Mr. Salinas in this plan, as well?"

Hernandez said Salinas was to have worked with him.

"Is that why he left his briefcase in court yesterday afternoon?" the judge asked.

Hernandez replied that he knew nothing about the briefcase.

Tynan sternly advised Hernandez that his behavior the previous day appeared to be a "deliberate calculated act of rudeness and contempt," both for the court and for the proceedings. The angry jurist branded Hernandez's conduct as "inexcusable," but stopped short of citing him for contempt. The judge said the only reason he didn't cite Hernandez was because prosecution for contempt would require a hearing, which would delay the case even more.

With the judge's decision, the jury was at last ready to move into the batter's box; their half of the inning was coming up. Witnesses for both the prosecution and defense had testified, and final arguments were concluded.

After more than two years of exhausting courtroom maneuvering, the man accused of being one of the most fiendish killers in California history was ready to have his fate determined by twelve ordinary men and women.

From the time of his formal arrest, Ramirez had given no indication that he expected, or wanted, mercy. Minutes after his arrest, he begged detectives to shoot him or to allow him to kill himself. He whined that he would rather be dead than spend his life in prison.

In court and in his jail cell, his behavior had been so outrageous that it appeared he was deliberately attempting to turn the jury against him. The death penalty could provide another avenue to avoid spending the rest of his normal life in prison.

Throughout the trial, Ramirez had taunted everyone—from judge, jury, and witnesses to spectators and the press. He had shown absolute contempt for the legal system. And he had shown contempt for the society he existed in, by flashing the Satanic symbols he had tattooed on the palm of his hand, and by howling his eerie salute to Satan.

When the judge once ordered him to remove a hat he wore to court one day, he screamed "No!" like a petulant child throwing a tantrum. He called the press a bunch of grubby parasites. He quarreled with other prisoners in the lockup, fought with bailiffs, and picked on his own attorneys. If it was possible to antagonize someone, he did.

Richard Ramirez was a difficult defendant for whom to work up much sympathy. The crimes he was accused of committing were atrocious; his behavior was outrageous. When he talked or screamed or ranted, his words were shocking and sordid. He didn't speak, he spewed, forcing every word out like an evil curse.

He seemed intent on convincing everyone that he had all the demons of Hell in him, from Abraxas and Asmodeus to Belial and Belphegor. If ever there was a criminal who seemed to have little chance of escaping firm, fatal retribution, it was Richard Ramirez.

For that retribution to come in the form of the death penalty, it was necessary for the jury to declare Ramirez to be guilty of only one of thirteen counts of first-degree murder if the slaying was accompanied by one or more of thirty-one special conditions.

In a nutshell, California law provided for the death penalty if a murder occurred during the commission of certain other serious crimes such as burglary, robbery, or sexual attacks. These were "special conditions." And the Night Stalker had compiled an encyclopedia-sized file of special-condition crimes to qualify himself for the gas chamber.

When the jurors filed into their chambers to begin deliberations after conclusion of the judge's instructions, it was doubtful that even the most naïve or reckless gambler among the courtroom spectators would be willing to bet that Ramirez would somehow manage to avoid California's death row.

CHAPTER 15

Curse of the Night Stalker

"Who So Sheddeth Man's Blood, by Man Shall His
Blood Be Shed: for in the Image of God Made He Man."
—Genesis 9:6

THERE IS AN OLD SAW THAT SUGGESTS THE
course of true love never runs smooth. While the same
might be said of high-profile capital-murder trials, it was
certainly true of the Night Stalker trial—even though the
prevailing emotions were anger and hate. The trial
seemed ill-fated from the beginning. It was almost as
though some malevolent spirit loomed over the proceedings. If something could go wrong, it did.

While more pragmatic minds pointed accusing fingers
for much of the trouble to the dillydallying of the defense
attorneys, there were many others of a more superstitious
bent who laid the blame directly at the feet of Richard
Ramirez—and the evil that had driven him to commit his
unspeakable crimes.

It seemed almost as though he were personally orches-
trating the turmoil from his jail cell. After all, it was he
who had insisted on hiring Daniel and Arturo Hernandez, despite the availability of more experienced defense

lawyers who had more time and resources. In fact, there were times, considering their continuous miscues and rancorous relationship with the bench, when it seemed he could hardly have made a worse choice. But was the choice inadvertent, the result of ignorance and arrogance, or was it intentional?

There were other things, too. Members of his family, who seemed genuinely concerned for his welfare, repeatedly made inappropriate statements to the press—statements that, on the surface, appeared as though they could only be damaging to whatever slim chances of acquittal he might have had.

Some observers close to the case said he never believed he could get a fair trial and, consequently, deliberately set out to make a mockery of the entire proceedings.

There were others who believed he was insane and that his attorneys should have pleaded from the beginning for a not-guilty verdict for him by reason of insanity. They thought it was curious that despite the bizarre horrors of the Night Stalker's crimes, and Ramirez's eccentric behavior in the courtroom, no one formally challenged his sanity. Melvin Belli appeared to have suggested that if he were defending the Night Stalker, he might have pursued the insanity angle, when he said Ramirez's medical and psychiatric bills would have been "at least $300,000."

There was also a third group that contended Ramirez was neither pessimistic about his chances, nor was he mad or ignorant. In criminal cases in which the evidence is overwhelming against defendants, accepted defense procedure calls for delaying a trial as long as possible while the memories of witnesses grow dimmer, they die, or evidence is lost, tainted, or damaged. Setting the stage for post-trial appeals and forcing mistrials and, consequently, even greater delays, are part and parcel of the strategy.

Far from being stupid, Ramirez, either on his own or with the help of someone else, may have seen this approach as his only chance and pursued it from the beginning, this group contended. If he was crazy, he was as crazy as a fox.

But, if this was his intent, he failed. The strategy—if indeed that is what it was—failed primarily because Judge Tynan and Prosecutor Halpin and his team were wary of appeals and a possible mistrial. It might have worked with less-vigilant or less-professional opposition.

When the jury left the courtroom to begin deliberations, the seven women and five men carried with them a heavy load—and not just the figurative burden of dealing out justice. There was also a literal burden. They would have to deal with the testimony of 165 witnesses, a trial transcript of some 8,000 pages, and 654 exhibits. They would also have to fill out 106 verdict forms.

But there was yet another burden—one of which they were not aware. That was the bad luck—the curse, if you prefer—that had dogged the Night Stalker case. It had touched other people; soon it would touch them.

Juror Robert Lee was dismissed for sleeping during deliberations thirteen days after the case was turned over to the panel. Jury foreman Felipe Rodriguez reported that Lee had been inattentive, and said he had personally seen Lee asleep on two occasions. Noting that there had been complaints of Lee's sleeping during the trial itself, Judge Tynan replaced him with an alternate.

Although alternate jurors had heard all the testimony during the trial, they had not been present during jury deliberations. California state law requires a jury to begin deliberations anew when a juror is replaced. Consequently, the first thirteen days were wasted.

Only eight of the twelve original alternates remained. One alternate had replaced the man accused of saying he would not vote for the death penalty for a non-white, another replaced a juror who was discovered to be acquainted with one of the witnesses, and a third alternate was dismissed for undisclosed reasons.

Jurors in the case were not sequestered. They went home at night and on weekends. Sequestering of jurors, once quite common in serious felony trials, has become more rare over the past few years because of the high cost to taxpayers for lodging and meals, and because of the enforced isolation from family and friends. Non-sequestered jurors are ordered not to discuss the case outside the deliberation room, and are forbidden from reading or watching news accounts about it. The Night Stalker jury was composed largely of state and county employees.

When interviewed by the press, Wendy Saxon, a criminal justice consultant and an expert in jury behavior, explained that substituting a juror has a great impact on the panel's deliberations. As in any small group, the expert said, jurors assume certain roles: dominant, submissive, helpful, or uncooperative. Some unite in groups of two or three, while others stubbornly cling to their opinions no matter what others in the group may say.

"When you pick a jury you are looking at a sociogram —how they will interact as a group. When you dismiss a juror and replace him with another juror, the entire sociogram changes," she declared.

If the substituted juror was not actively contributing to the deliberations, his loss does not have much of an impact. But if he was a dominant figure in the deliberations or, more likely, the new juror is a dominant personality, the entire trend of deliberations could change.

The consultant recalled working with one jury in which a juror, replaced for allegedly sleeping, later claimed other members of the panel merely wanted to get rid of him because he was the lone holdout for acquittal.

It is difficult to predict whether juries are more likely to convict or acquit a defendant when a juror is replaced because no studies have been done on that aspect, she added.

Deputy District Attorney Philip Halpin took the news matter-of-factly. "It wasn't as though we had not expected it," he explained. He said he had complained of Lee's falling asleep during the trial. "You can't really blame the guy for snoozing through this thing when it has taken us so long to do it," he added with surprising candor. "Hopefully, this will be the last of the delays."

By this time, the spunky deputy DA should have known better than to make optimistic predictions about the pace of anything related to the trial.

Two days later, the jury was stunned by the murder of one of its members. Thirty-year-old Phyllis Singletary of suburban Carson was found inside her apartment, dead of multiple gunshot wounds. "Apparently, she suffered a physical beating before being shot," reported Los Angeles County Deputy Sheriff Bill Wehner. Ironically, the murdered juror was born and raised in El Paso, the defendant's hometown. She had moved to Los Angeles in 1977.

Sheriff's patrols immediately began a search for fifty-one-year-old James Cecil Melton, the dead woman's live-in boyfriend.

Neighbors and friends of the couple said they were not surprised. A violent end for the star-crossed lovers seemed inevitable, many of them told police.

They described Melton as a chain-smoking, short-tempered, heavy drinker who enjoyed showing off his gun collection, and at the same time boasting that he was ready to blow anyone away who tried to break into his white Cadillac Coupe de Ville.

His girlfriend was a petite divorcée with a schoolgirl smile, who so badly wanted to remarry again that she put up with his drinking and beatings. Friends said she seemed proud to be serving as a juror in the celebrated Night Stalker case.

Although twenty-one years separated the couple, the difference in age was less of a problem in their stormy relationship than the difference in their temperament. Those who knew them said they were an unlikely pair.

Melton had a violent temper. He drank so heavily that, a few months before the slaying, he was briefly hospitalized to dry out. He was a natty dresser, and strutted around the fashionable complex where he and Singletary shared an apartment in expensive suits and spit-shined shoes.

Neighbors said the dead woman had also dressed well, but kept to herself. Some recalled that she looked like a schoolgirl as she headed for her gold Nissan 280 Z, at first to drive to her job as a service representative with Pacific Bell, and, later, for her seat in the jury box during the lengthy Night Stalker trial.

The day after the murder, sheriff's deputies caught up with her suspected killer at the Comfort Inn in Carson. As deputies poured into the parking lot, Melton emerged from a second-floor room. The lawmen watched helplessly as he stood on the balcony, pressed the gun to his head, and pulled the trigger. Investigators found a note inside the room, which he had written admitting he killed his lover during a domestic quarrel.

News that Melton had committed suicide didn't surprise many of his former neighbors. "They won't take him alive," one neighbor had already predicted. "He'll probably kill himself because he's feeling so guilty."

News of the young woman's tragic death hit her fellow jurors hard. She was popular and had become close friends with many of the jurors and alternates during the six months they had listened to other accounts of senseless violence and premature death. But this was not merely a name, a face on a photograph, but someone they had come to know firsthand. This was one of their own, and they were devastated by the sudden, savage act that had snuffed out her life. Judge Tynan sent the teary-eyed jurors home early on Monday to mourn her death.

With the threat of another mistrial looming, Judge Tynan named a weeping and distraught female alternate to replace Singletary. He asked the jury to put aside its grief to begin its deliberations anew.

Tynan also denied a request by the defense for a week off to allow the jury to go through "four stages of grief" that had been identified and outlined by a defense psychologist. The judge also refused to allow the attorneys to question jurors about their state of mind—to inquire whether they could overcome the "terrible tragedy" and continue to decide the fate of Ramirez without bias.

The judge conferred with jury foreman Felipe Rodriguez, who told him, "I think we can probably continue. Everyone seems to have put it behind them."

Tynan then firmly announced, "I don't mean to be callous, but we have business to do. We must set aside our grief and get on with our task."

When Tynan asked if the defense had any objections, Ramirez responded in a loud voice. "I have an objection," he croaked. "I think that's fucked up." The judge ignored the rude comment but fixed the defendant with a long, icy stare.

When Hernandez then asked to discuss the decision in the judge's chambers, Tynan's reply was instant and unyielding. "Not a chance," he told the defense lawyer. Hernandez later confided to reporters that he might ask for a mistrial. He claimed that he was afraid jurors might unwittingly "turn their frustration and their anxiety on the defendant."

A week later, Ramirez threw another of his now familiar and periodic temper tantrums during a hearing on a defense motion for mistrial. Hernandez was telling the judge that his client was unhappy about the requirement that he continue to be present in court for hearings, when Ramirez suddenly interrupted. Lashing out in a sudden burst of anger, he shouted to the judge, "I don't want to be here, man! Don't you understand?" When Tynan ignored him, he began again: "Well, what's the problem, then? I won't come back in here. This trial is a joke."

When Ramirez launched into a barrage of obscenities aimed at Tynan, bailiffs grabbed him and led him from the courtroom.

Defense Attorney Clark explained that Ramirez didn't want to come to court because he disliked changing out of his jail clothing into street clothes, sitting around for a few hours, and eating "a flat hamburger" for lunch.

"I think he has good days and bad days," Clark observed. The judge was unsympathetic with the defendant's complaints about the inconvenience the court appearances were causing him. And he was in no mood to indulge Ramirez.

"I really don't want to play these games," Tynan told the attorneys. "If he wants to act like a jerk, we can deal with it—restrain him."

At the judge's direction, bailiffs led Ramirez back into the courtroom wearing a blue jump suit and leg shackles. Tynan coldly advised him that if he didn't want to attend the hearings, he would have to sign a waiver. When Ramirez responded by launching into another tirade of filth, Tynan motioned for the bailiffs to take him out again.

A few minutes later, Ramirez was brought back into the courtroom. This time, he was more subdued and quietly signed the waiver form. Tynan said that during future hearings Ramirez would be kept in the lockup outside the courtroom where he could listen to what was being said in the courtroom through a speaker system.

The hearing had been originally scheduled so Ramirez's attorneys could argue a motion for a mistrial on the grounds that Phyllis Singletary's death had put the jurors in a frame of mind injurious to their client. Tynan refused to allow the lawyers to argue the motion at that time, explaining that the prosecution was entitled to ten days to respond. He scheduled the hearing for the following week.

If the jury reached a verdict in the meantime, however,

the argument would no longer be an issue, and Tynan would not have to rule on it. Hernandez knew exactly what the judge was doing. "It's a dirty little trick they use all the time," he complained. "Halpin is always trying to move things up, but on this issue he's all hot and bothered." There was no verdict the following week, and Tynan rejected the motion for mistrial.

As the jury's deliberations entered their twentieth day, Judge Tynan jailed Arturo Hernandez for one day for not paying a $100 fine for contempt of court. At the same time, he warned Hernandez that he would be jailed for twenty-four days if he didn't pay another $2,400 fine by September 29. Tynan's action was the culmination of a bitter and protracted battle with Hernandez over the lawyer's continued absence from court.

Hernandez was absent from the trial for seven months prior to the request by his co-counsel, Daniel Hernandez, for a six-week leave to recover from "nervous exhaustion." Although the judge had ordered Arturo Hernandez back to court at that time, Tynan later relented. The judge agreed to allow Arturo Hernandez to remain in San Jose, where he had his law practice, provided he telephone the court every day to see if he was needed. After the lawyer failed to keep the promise, he was fined $100. The fine was due September 1, but was not received, so Hernandez was jailed. The protesting attorney claimed that he had mailed the $100 about two weeks earlier.

Tynan imposed the $2,400 fine based on a scale of penalties for each day Arturo Hernandez had failed to telephone the court. The lawyer broke down in tears as he was led away from the courtroom. He was held overnight in the hospital section of Los Angeles County's central jail and released in the morning.

Then at last, mercifully, the jury's wearying ordeal paid dividends. On September 20, 1989, after twenty-two days of arduous deliberation, jury foreman Felipe Rodriguez informed Judge Tynan that he and his eleven fellow jurors had reached their verdicts. It had been four years and twenty days since Richard Ramirez was run down by furious residents of the East Los Angeles barrio—then reluctantly handed over to police.

But before the verdicts could be read in court, the defendant resorted to yet one more of his repeated acts of defiance. He refused to remain in the courtroom, where relatives of several of the victims were already waiting to witness the long-awaited reckoning. Ramirez was led to the holding cell to listen to the verdicts through the speaker system.

Judge Tynan and court clerk Josephine Williams spent more than thirty minutes reading the sixty-three verdict forms. It was virtually a clean sweep for the prosecution. The jury found Ramirez guilty on all thirteen counts of murder, ruling that twelve were murder in the first degree. They decided that the spur-of-the-moment street-corner slaying of Tsai-Lian Yu was murder in the second degree, committed without the premeditation of the other killings.

Ramirez was also found to be guilty of thirty other felonies, including robbery, burglary, rape, sodomy, oral copulation, and attempted murder. In addition, they found that eighteen special circumstances existed, opening the door for the jury to recommend he receive the death penalty.

The victims and convictions included:

- June 28, 1984—Jennie Vincow, 79, Glassell Park. Stabbed to death, her throat slashed. Guilty of one count of first degree murder, one count of burglary.
- March 17—Dayle Okazaki, 34, Rosemead. Shot to death. Her roommate, *Angela Barrios,* shot and wounded. Guilty of one count of first degree murder; one count of attempted murder, one count of burglary.
- March 17—Tsai-Lian Yu, 30, Monterey Park.

Dragged from her car and shot to death. Guilty of one count of second degree murder.

- March 27—Vincent, 64, and his wife, Maxine Zazzara, 44, Whittier. Both stabbed to death and their bodies mutilated. Guilty of two counts of first degree murder, one count of burglary.

- May 14—*Harold Wu,* 66, Monterey Park. Shot to death in his home. His sixty-three-year-old wife was brutally beaten and raped. Guilty of one count of first degree murder, one count of burglary.

- May 30—*Ruth Wilson,* 41, Burbank. Rape, sodomy, oral copulation, burglary. Guilty of one count of rape, one count of oral copulation, one count of sodomy, one count of burglary.

- June 1—*Malvia Keller,* 83, and her sister, *Blanche Wolfe,* 80, Monrovia. *Keller* bludgeoned to death. *Wolfe* beaten but survived. Satanic symbols marked on *Keller* and on walls with lipstick. Guilty of one count of first degree murder, one count of attempted murder, one count of burglary.

- July 2—Mary Louise Cannon, 75, Arcadia. Found dead in her home, beatén, with throat slashed. Guilty of one count of first degree murder, one count of burglary.

- July 5—*Deidre Palmer,* 16, Arcadia. Survived beating with tire iron in her home. Guilty of one count of attempted murder, one count of burglary.

- July 7—Joyce Lucille Nelson, 61, Monterey Park. Beaten to death. House ransacked. Guilty of one count of first degree murder, one count of burglary.

- July 7—*Linda Fortuna,* 63, Monterey Park. Raped and sodomized in her home. Guilty of one count of rape, one count of burglary, one count of sodomy.

- July 20—Maxson Kneiding, 66, and his wife Lela, 66, Glendale. Both shot to death. Home burglarized. Guilty of two counts of first degree murder, one count of burglary.

- July 20—*Chitat Assawahem,* 32, Sun Valley. Shot to death while sleeping. His wife, 29, was raped and forced to perform oral copulation. Their eight-year-old son was sodomized. Approximately $30,000 in money and jewelry was taken. Guilty of one count of first degree murder, one count of burglary, one count of rape, one count of sodomy, one count of oral copulation.

- August 6—Christopher Petersen, 38, and his wife Virginia, 27, Northridge. Both survived bullet wounds in the head. Although seriously wounded, Christopher Petersen chased the Night Stalker from the house. Guilty of two counts of attempted murder, one count of burglary.

- August 8—*Ahmed Zia,* 35, Diamond Bar. He was shot to death while asleep. His wife, 28, was raped, sodomized and forced to perform fellatio. Guilty of one count of first degree murder, one count of rape, one count of oral copulation, one count of sodomy.

Sitting in the holding cell, Ramirez listened to the jury's verdicts without displaying visible emotion. "He was kind of stoic," Ray Clark said. Not so the relatives of victims in the courtroom. Several of the men and women bowed their heads and wept gratefully. At last, their loved ones were about to be avenged. Only one more step remained: the penalty portion of the trial. Tynan set September 27 as the date for opposing attorneys to begin arguing the penalty before the jury.

Halpin had learned the hard way not to take anything for granted in the Stalker trial, and he told reporters, "I'm not going to be satisfied until it's over, and it's not over yet."

Deputy District Attorney Alan Yochelson said the prosecution would present no evidence in the penalty phase of the trial. "The defendant has been convicted of

13 murders, and nothing more can be said beyond that," he declared. "13 murders speak for themselves."

Clark said he was disappointed by the verdicts. "I thought we had raised a reasonable doubt in the minds of the jurors," he told the press. He added that he and Daniel Hernandez would address the jury. "We're going to try to save his [Ramirez's] life. We will try to convince the jury he should not be executed."

After Hernandez confided to reporters that Ramirez had shown no emotion while listening to the verdicts, he added, "He was not surprised about the outcome at all. He was expecting this to be handed down." The defense lawyer added that he personally believed the jury was no longer able to be objective after the death of their fellow juror. "And the media was so overwhelmingly convinced of his guilt that no one gave him a fair trial."

When reporters shouted to Ramirez as he was being led away, asking for his reaction to the verdicts, he glared at them for a moment, then muttered a single word: "Evil!" As he was taken from the courthouse, the convicted Night Stalker defiantly flashed the "Devil's sign" to the crush of delighted photographers by extending his index and little fingers like an insolent demon's talons, keeping the two middle fingers folded into the palm of his hand.

At that time, Richard Ramirez may have been one of the most hated and reviled men in the world, certainly in the United States. But to his family he was still their son and brother, and they remained unwilling to believe that he was the monster he had been painted to be in courtroom testimony and accounts in the news media.

Julian Ramirez, Sr., the Night Stalker's father, sorrowfully told a reporter for the *El Paso Herald Post* the following day that he agreed his son deserved punishment if he did kill 13 people. He added, however, that he was not convinced his son was guilty of the crimes, particularly the gruesome murders and the vile sexual assaults.

"I don't know if he did it or not. But if he did, he didn't do it by himself. Why don't the police investigate to see who else was involved?" the elder Ramirez demanded. "I've accepted he was a thief, but I've never accepted that he did the things they say he did. The media turned him into a monster. He's really just a poor boy who was raised to believe in God," he said.

Mercedes Ramirez, Richard's mother, who spoke for the first time to reporters, insisted that her son was not a Satanist. "We've always been Catholic and raised him to believe in God," she declared. The heartbroken woman theorized that her son probably drew the pentagram on his hand with a ball-point pen, and showed it in court just to make the jury, the judge, and the prosecution angrier.

Both Ramirezes agreed that drugs led their son astray. Surprisingly, they said they received their most loyal support from the citizens of Los Angeles, the city their son terrorized for almost two years. The Night Stalker horror was a calamity for the Ramirez family, too.

Back in Los Angeles, Daniel Hernandez informed Judge Tynan that Richard Ramirez was adamant about refusing to appear in court for his sentencing. But the prosecutor was equally adamant. He was determined to force the convicted serial killer who had terrorized Southern California with his vile crimes to face the judge when sentence was pronounced. And Halpin threatened to fight it out in a major bare-knuckles legal fracas, if necessary.

Yochelson pointed out that state law specified that a defendant in a felony case "must be present when evidence is taken and at sentencing." We want to forgo any possibility of this being an issue on appeal," the assistant DA explained. The problem wasn't a matter of conflicting egos, but a deadly serious issue of criminal law.

"He just doesn't want to be in there," said Clark. "He has sort of lost heart. I don't know when it happened."

Clark said he was aware the law required Ramirez to be in court, but added that he was researching legal case law and believed an exception might exist.

Whether Ramirez appeared for his sentencing was not the defense's most pressing problem at that moment, however. They had to convince the jury not to send their client to the gas chamber, but to select the only alternate course open to them: life in prison without parole.

Over the years, California lawyers have tried various strategies to save their clients from the gas chamber:

- The jury voted for life imprisonment for one killer who was convicted of a particularly vicious murder, following testimony that his alcoholic mother had molested him as a child.
- Brandon Tholmer also avoided the gas chamber following his conviction for killing and raping four elderly women. The defense had sought mercy because he was borderline retarded and had spent almost his entire life institutionalized.
- Another jury voted against death for Joe Hunt, the spoiled and privileged leader of the Billionaire Boys' Club, who was convicted of murder and robbery. The defense argued that historically capital punishment had never been imposed in California in cases in which the victim's body was not found. Ironically, jurors later said the sparing of Hunt's life was predicated neither on mercy nor the inability of investigators to produce the victim's body, but in the belief that execution would be too easy a punishment for Hunt.
- Just a week before Ramirez's conviction, a California jury had recommended life in prison for a man convicted of beating a sixty-five-year-old woman to death and shooting her son. The defense said he was under the influence of cocaine when he committed the crimes. Presumably, this made the killer less responsible for his act. Ramirez was a heavy cocaine user while

he was raging through the quiet valleys around Los Angeles, stealing, raping, and killing.

As a last resort, attorneys will remind jurors that they will have to answer to God if they take the defendant's life.

Ray Clark took a two-pronged approach as he asked the jury to spare Ramirez's life. He offered two possible explanations—the Devil or hormones—as reasons prompting his client to commit the 13 murders.

"What possessed Mr. Ramirez to do these things? We will not know soon," he told the jury, posing a question, then answering it himself. "I think it's inescapable that something was wrong. Let's say he was possessed. The extension of mercy goes to the Devil because he is considered more in need of mercy than anyone else." In other words, even if he were possessed by the Devil, Ramirez deserved mercy. Even Satan himself was not totally undeserving of sympathy, it seemed, according to the reasoning of "The Devil Made Me Do It" defense theory.

Clark also suggested the possibility that Ramirez was so controlled by his sexual hormones that he was helplessly driven to rape. Ramirez may have been no more able to make a rational choice than was an alcoholic or drug addict. The defense attorney cited studies on male and female hormones and their effects.

"[Ramirez] has no claim to your kindness, but if you give him kindness, that is called mercy," said Clark. "Life imprisonment without parole means he will never see Disneyland again. Mr. Ramirez will die in prison."

Halpin was more direct. He urged jurors to confront head-on the evil that was the Night Stalker. Ramirez had, through his actions, earned the death penalty, he said. It was the only answer to evil, he added.

Two of the Night Stalker's surviving victims agreed. *Renata Gunther* was one of them. She was savagely attacked by Ramirez just five days before his capture. "There is no adequate punishment," she told reporters.

Her fiancé, William Carns, the bright young computer expert, shot in the head while he slept beside her, lived, but suffered severe brain damage. His memory, personality, and ability to function were all affected by the horrendous injury, and he would never be the same.

"Nothing can bring Bill's life back to what it was, and nothing can bring my life back to what it was," the young woman observed bitterly.

Miss *Gunther* remained in touch with Carns, the man she had expected to marry. But she broke off the engagement, reportedly due to the personality and behavior changes caused by the brain injuries.

Carns, who was a patient at an Oakdale, Minnesota, home-care facility specializing in head-wound patients, told the *Orange County Register* in a telephone interview that the only justice for him would come when Ramirez died in the gas chamber.

Ramirez still faced trial in Orange County on attempted murder and sexual assault charges for the attack on the couple in their Mission Viejo home. Orange County District Attorney James Enright said he would talk to Carns and *Gunther* before pursuing the case. Ramirez was arraigned and bound over for trial on the Orange County charges in 1987.

The jury had authority only to make a recommendation of death in the gas chamber, or life in prison without parole. The recommendation was not necessarily binding on the judge. According to California law, Tynan could disregard the recommendation from the jury for the death penalty and sentence Ramirez to life in prison. He could not, however, sentence Ramirez to death if the jury recommended life in prison.

At the time the jury was deliberating the Night Stalker's sentence, there were already 265 men awaiting execution on California's death row. Although an average of three California murderers a month were receiving death sentences, no one had actually been executed in California for almost twenty-five years. What's more, lengthy appeals are automatic when the death penalty is imposed. They are part and parcel of the system and the law. Death-penalty appeals were averaging about ten years for each defendant at the time Ramirez was convicted.

The jury's choice, after five days of deliberation, was the gas chamber. No one was surprised, least of all Ramirez. There were nineteen instances of special circumstances, ranging from burglary and sex crimes to multiple murder. On each of the nineteen instances, the jury recommended death.

The recommendations did not come easily, though. At one point, the jury was deadlocked at 6–6; then it squared off at 10–2, favoring the death penalty. As brutal as Ramirez's crimes were, some jurors said they could not help feeling sorry for him and sad that they were impelled to recommend that he be put to death.

"I think you have to consider that he is a human being and has feelings, too," said Samantha Haden, a thirty-six-year-old administrative assistant.

Some jurors said they were unsure about the propriety of the death penalty as a punishment, even for such terrible crimes as those committed by the Night Stalker.

"It was difficult at first because I've never seen anything like that before," said Martha Salcido, a thirty-eight-year-old postal worker. "Sending someone to death is a hard choice."

But thirty-eight-year-old jury foreman Felipe Rodriguez had the answer to that. He pointed out that when other jurors brought up the sympathy factor, he brought up the question of sympathy for the victims.

Alfredo Carrillo described Ramirez simply as "pretty crazy to commit the crimes he did. I think he's evil," the juror observed.

Some jurors revealed that they believed Ramirez had attempted to intimidate them with his stares and smirks.

There were no tears shed for the Night Stalker by Ellen Francis and Judith Arnold, however. The two women, daughters of Night Stalker victims Maxson and Lela Kneiding of Glendale, wept openly with relief and sadness as the jury's recommendations were read.

"It's really been a long, long road," said Arnold. "I have to live the rest of my life seeing my parents and what Ramirez did to them. I can never be the same."

"I don't think we'll find any peace until he's brought out of the gas chamber, dead," her sister, Ellen Francis, added. "How can any human being do anything like that? There is no punishment that will fit the crime."

Colleen Nelson, the eighteen-year-old granddaughter of murder victim Joyce Lucille Nelson, told reporters that her life and the lives of her family would never be the same again, either.

"For every person that he has killed, he has put so many others through a lifetime of pain," she pointed out. "I think Richard Ramirez forfeited his right to life when he killed my grandmother and all those other innocent people."

Don Nelson recalled how Ramirez had beaten and strangled his mother, and the way he felt while he and his brother cleaned up the gory mess Ramirez had left. "Once he's executed," Nelson said of the convicted killer, "he can never again terrorize an entire state."

Two other victims, Virginia and Christopher Petersen, revealed that they lived in constant pain from the injuries they sustained when Ramirez shot each of them in the head. Christopher Petersen still carried a bullet lodged at the base of his brain.

"The nights are the worst," said Virginia. She said she suffered from a sleep disorder and attacks of panic that caused her to scream out uncontrollably in the middle of the night.

Other family members of victims recalled how they had suffered, and wiped tears from their eyes during impromptu interviews.

As for Ramirez, whose request to remain in the holding cell was denied by Judge Tynan, there was little show of emotion as he listened in the courtroom. His only visible response was to rock back and forth occasionally in his chair.

Later, in the underground garage, as he was being returned to the county jail, he sneered to reporters, "Big deal. Death always went with the territory. I'll see you in Disneyland." The "Disneyland" remark was presumed to refer to Clark's earlier remarks to the jury while pleading for his client's life, in which he said of Ramirez that "he will never see Disneyland again."

Daniel Hernandez refused to comment as to whether he believed his client felt any remorse for his crimes. But it was clear that he and co-counsel Clark did feel badly about the outcome. Clark told the media, "Death saddens me." Then in a remark that could leave no doubt in anyone's mind exactly how strong his feelings were about the death penalty, he added, "I would not take Hitler's life."

Hernandez said he thought that all of California should be saddened by the sentence. "We feel sympathy for any person who is sentenced to die," he said.

Julian Ramirez, Sr., who had traveled to Los Angeles for the sentencing, said sadly, "Let us hope that those who have passed judgment on my son will not have others pass sentence on their children, or themselves."

Deputy District Attorney Halpin, however, was delighted with the jury's decision. He had worked long, hard hours, exhibiting a grim, single-minded determination as he painstakingly pieced together the building blocks of his case for the jury. He had convinced them not only that Ramirez was guilty of the crimes he was charged with, but also of the defendant's absolute evil and depravity. The only rational penalty for creating such horror was death.

"He got what he deserved," Halpin responded when asked about his reaction to the jury recommendation. The deputy DA described Ramirez as a miserable human being who killed for self-gratification. Halpin added that he believed Ramirez was a twisted person who seemed intelligent and cared very much about his future, despite his attempts to appear cavalier during the trial.

Once the jury's recommendation was reported, Tynan wasted little time before passing formal sentence. He had lived with the case for many months, and the time for study and contemplation was past. Two days after the jury recommended death for Ramirez, he appeared in court and stood before the judge.

Following the usual procedure, Tynan peered down at the shackled defendant from the bench and asked if he had anything to say before the sentence was announced.

If the high-calorie jail diet and sedentary life-style forced on Ramirez since his arrest had done anything to fatten him up, it didn't show. His bony shoulder blades still stuck out under his suit, and the flat planes of his cheekbones now highlighted by a pasty prison pallor made his face look even more gaunt and wasted than when he was on the street living on drugs and junk food. Stubbornly maintaining the same demonic facade he had so carefully constructed for himself, he was still the same sullen, hateful Night Stalker.

Ramirez responded to Tynan's invitation to speak up before sentencing by fixing his dark eyes on the judge in a cold stare. Then he launched into a disjointed tirade about the injustices of the legal system, the hypocrisy of society—and Satan. As he spoke, it seemed that *he* was the victim, not the innocent men, women, and children whose bodies and psyches he had so casually ravaged.

"It's nothing you'd understand, but I do have something to say," he declared. "In fact, I have a lot to say, but now is not the time or place. I don't know why I'm wasting my breath. But what the hell?"

The Night Stalker spoke in a raspy smoker's voice that was almost a grumble, but it was audible.

"As for what was said of my life, there have been lies in the past and there will be lies in the future. I don't believe in the hypocritical, moralistic dogma of this so-called civilized society," he said.

"I need not look beyond this room to see all the liars, haters, the killers, the crooks, the paranoid cowards— truly *trematodes* of the Earth, each one in his own legal profession." By this time the anger was clearly showing on Ramirez's face. It was twisted with hate and he was spitting out his words in ugly snarls.

"You maggots make me sick—hypocrites one and all," he snapped.

Ramirez told the court that everyone was expendable for a cause.

"And no one knows that better than those who kill for policy, clandestinely or openly, as do the governments of the world, which kill in the name of God and country or for whatever reason they deem appropriate," he said.

The Night Stalker was surprisingly articulate, despite the obvious flaws in his logic. But his words, no matter how well articulated, had the unmistakable mark of the jailhouse sociologist. Blame drugs, blame poverty, blame Mom, blame police, blame the courts, blame society, blame the Devil—blame everyone but yourself. Law enforcement professionals in the courtroom recognized Ramirez's statement for exactly what it was: the classic psycho-babble of the long-term institutionalized, mixed in with a touch of the Devil.

Observers in the back of the courtroom, nevertheless, leaned forward in their seats so they could hear better. They didn't want to miss a word of the one-way dialogue.

"I don't need to hear all of society's rationalizations," he said. "I've heard them all before and the fact remains that what is, is. You don't understand me. You are not expected to. You are not capable of it."

If anyone still harbored any doubt that Ramirez reveled in his reputation for evil and cruelty, he was ready then to tear down their faith in his ultimate goodness—indeed, in the ultimate goodness in all men. He was coldly deliberate about inviting the fear and hate of others. Richard Ramirez, the one-time petty thief from El Paso, had evolved into a bloodthirsty vampire, a werewolf, one of Satan's most rapacious demons. He was the consummate predator, the Night Stalker, and he wanted the world to know.

"I am beyond your experience. I am beyond good and evil, legions of the night—night breed—repeat not the errors of the Night Prowler and show no mercy," he warned.

"I will be avenged. Lucifer dwells within us all. That's it."

Judge Tynan sat patiently, calmly returning Ramirez's stare as the prisoner growled his way through the lengthy statement.

Then the judge pronounced sentence. "It is the judgment of this court that Richard Ramirez should suffer the death penalty," he said. The judge pronounced the dreadful penalty 12 times, once for each conviction for first-degree murder.

Tynan also ordered a long prison sentence on the second-degree murder charge in the death of Tsai-Lian Yu. And he sentenced Ramirez to fifty-nine years and four months in prison for a witch's brew of other charges: the burglaries, rapes, sodomies, and attempted murders.

Ramirez was right about one thing he said in his lengthy statement. No one could understand the psychopathic cruelty that had characterized his evil crimes.

His conduct—including the obscene removal of the eyes of one victim and the leaving of a pentagram, a Satanic symbol, at the scene of another crime—displayed a high degree of cruel viciousness beyond human understanding, Judge Tynan said from the bench.

Halpin dismissed Ramirez's psychopathic mishmash of bits and pieces lifted helter-skelter from Nietzschean philosophy, LaVey's Satanic Bible, and some of the darker heavy-metal songs as "more baloney." He added, "I wouldn't want anyone to listen to what he has to say because he is a pathetic human being who is grasping for some structure in his life."

Aside from the fact that the trial was at last brought to a successful conclusion—at least from the standpoint of the prosecution and the Night Stalker's victims—many nagging questions remain.

For instance, what caused a petty thief to evolve into one of the most fearsome serial killers in American history? Why did he prefer light-colored houses, and why were such a disproportionate number of his victims Asian or Asian-American? What fueled his insatiable sexual appetite? According to witnesses, he engaged in multiple sex acts, sometimes as many as five in the span of an hour or so.

Why didn't the defense pursue an insanity plea? Why didn't Ramirez hire attorneys with more experience in capital murder cases, and more resources to pour into his defense?

What drove Richard Ramirez to a rampage of murder, rape, and robbery remains as much a mystery today as it did in 1985, when his luck ran out in an East Los Angeles neighborhood. Psychiatrists, psychologists, and criminologists may all pontificate about child abuse, impoverished childhoods, the evils of drug usage, and typical serial killer profiles, but the bottom line is that they don't seem to know any more than most of us and possibly far less than many of us why some people become multiple murderers.

Los Angeles County Sheriff's Sergeant Frank Salerno, the lead investigator on the Night Stalker Los Angeles

County task force, has a somewhat jaundiced view of such experts. Most law enforcement officers do. Several months after Ramirez was sent to death row, Salerno offered an opinion on the part the "experts" had played in bringing the Night Stalker to bay. "They would sometimes come up with answers that made sense," he said. "But, by that time, we already figured it out ourselves."

On November 16, 1989, Ramirez was flown, heavily shackled, in an LA county sheriff's helicopter from the Men's Central Jail in downtown Los Angeles to San Quentin Prison. There, he became the two hundred sixty-sixth inmate on the prison's death row. But, although the California justice system appeared to have worked, the sentence was still less than a total victory for survivors and law enforcement officers who wanted him to pay for his crimes with his life. It will be years before the Night Stalker's life ends in the gas chamber—if, indeed, he is ever executed.

According to California law, the death sentences handed down to Ramirez should mean that one day, long before the end of the next decade, he will be led into the execution chamber and strapped into a heavy metal chair. There, a hood will be placed over his eyes, and prison employees will move safely away. Then, at a signal from the warden, a corrections officer will press down on a lever.

The lever is rigged to release cyanide pellets into shallow bowls of acid, creating a deadly gas known as hydrogen cyanide. Of the thirty-six states that enforce the death penalty, five—including Arizona, Maryland, Mississippi, and North Carolina, in addition to California—provide for execution in the gas chamber. Mississippi and North Carolina also offer the condemned the option of either gas or lethal injection. The poison gas used in all five states is always hydrogen cyanide.

Cyanide is one of the fastest-acting fatal poisons known, and death is almost instantaneous. The poison acts by interfering with the ability of the blood to carry oxygen and paralyzing the respiratory center of the brain. The pulse slows quickly and there is a loss of consciousness. There can be convulsions and frothing at the mouth.

The poison is derived from natural acids in several fruits and leaves, including the almond. Hydrogen cyanide is a deadly, efficient killer. It was the gas used in Germany's human extermination camps during World War II.

But regardless of if or when, Ramirez is executed in California's gas chamber, his existence at San Quentin promises not to be a pleasant one. A grim, stone fortress, San Quentin Prison is located at the end of a quiet street in San Quentin Village in Marin County, about fifteen miles north of San Francisco. The pretty, middle-class Bay-area village is the kind of small, serene community that the Night Stalker selected for his nocturnal wanderings and violence.

The beauty of the village is all outside the walls of the prison, however. Inside, some 5,000 burglars, thieves, rapists, and murderers are jammed together in maximum custody. And despite the best efforts of Warden Dan Vasquez and an experienced staff of corrections officers, convicts extort money and favors from one another, they gang-rape and they kill one another with clubs, their own hands, or tiny shaved pieces of metal fashioned into razor-sharp prison "shivs."

They bully and quarrel and fight. Ramirez is among his own kind there. He may remain among them confined in a Spartan five-foot-by-ten-foot cell for a long time. If he is like most of his fellow condemned prisoners, he will spend his time sleeping, reading law books, watching television, or exercising.

The last execution in California occurred on April 12, 1967, when Aaron Mitchell, who killed a Sacramento policeman, became the five hundred first person to be executed by the state.

The next person most likely to die, if the state resumes executions again, is Robert Alton Harris, who arrived on death row on March 14, 1979. He was convicted of the 1978 unprovoked execution murders of two teen-agers he kidnapped at gunpoint from a hamburger stand in San Diego. One of the sixteen-year-olds was a policeman's son.

Slightly more than half of the condemned have been on death row five years or longer. The inmate with the longest stay has been there eleven years. And fifteen have been there since 1979. An average of three new prisoners a month are added to the death-row population at San Quentin.

As Daniel Hernandez predicted, if Ramirez is ever executed, he is unlikely to be strapped into the gas-chamber chair before the year 2000. In addition to the attempted-murder and sexual-assault charges he still faces in Orange County, at this writing, Ramirez is expected to be tried sometime in 1991 for the murder and attempted murder, respectively, of Peter Pan and his wife in San Francisco.

A series of automatic appeals on the murder convictions and death sentences returned against him in Los Angeles have already begun working their way slowly through the court system. Ramirez may appeal to a number of California and federal courts, all the way up to the U.S. Supreme Court.

In the meantime, just about the time that Ramirez was transported to San Quentin, Los Angeles County supervisors finally handed out reward money to citizens who had helped in his trackdown and capture. Twenty-one people eventually shared in the $36,777 bounty.

One of the largest checks, for $10,388, went to Jessie

Perez for providing police with information that helped develop a profile of the man he knew as "Rick" and suspected might be the Night Stalker. Another $3,250 check went to his daughter, Pauline Perez, for persuading her father to go to police with his information.

After The Trial

LIFE ON DEATH ROW HAS BEEN GOOD TO THE Night Stalker!

He found adulation and true love there; not from among his fellow inmates, but from dozens of breathlessly admiring females who besieged him with personal visits, mash notes, love letters, sexy photographs of themselves and marriage proposals.

Former photographers, models, college coeds, a fellow Satan worshiper, a fundamentalist preacher who hoped to convert him to Christianity, one of the jurors who voted for his conviction, and others have emerged at various times as his outside advocates, courted him or fought over him. Some members of the killer's volunteer harem were more faithful to Ramirez than others.

At one time so many death row groupies were fighting among themselves for audiences with the celebrity cutthroat that Ramirez had to ration their meetings so he could set aside valuable fifteen-minute blocks of time in the crowded San Quentin visiting room for loyal family members.

Kelly Marquez, a former nude model who said she began visiting Ramirez because of her opposition to the death penalty, was pregnant and contemplating a quieter life with a more promising mate when, she says, another admirer of the notorious serial killer and baby raper tracked her down. The other woman knocked on her door and tried to kick her in the stomach, Kelly alleges. That was after Kelly received a series of threatening notes and telephone calls, and after someone left a dead cat in front of her mobile home.

But it was another woman who, for a while at least, seemed had the inside track on the Night Stalker's affections. That woman, a blonde beauty named Christine Lee, even moved from her home in New Jersey to the San Francisco Bay Area to be closer to the man of her dreams.

Christine appeared on television's "Donahue" show with Cindy Haden, the former Night Stalker juror who reincarnated after the trial as one of his most outspoken advocates. Cindy also appeared on "Geraldo," where she modestly described herself as the condemned serial killer's "best friend," but not as a girlfriend or would-be lover.

But Christine also claimed to be much more than a friend, and boasted to the supermarket tabloid *Globe* that she had accepted a proposal of marriage from Ramirez. Furthermore, she said, corrections authorities at the prison would provide the happy couple with a trailer to use as a love nest for conjugal visits two weekends a month. In torrid love letters quoted by the *Globe*, the condemned man talked about his desire to suck on her toes.

Although the love letters were the real thing, the young woman's hopes for a future with Ramirez as man and wife and the talk about conjugal visits were wishful thinking. The marriage wasn't to be, and corrections authorities had no plans to provide the couple with a honeymoon trailer, regardless of whether or not they were married.

The relationship had already begun to come apart, Christine conceded to the talk show host, and during his introduction at the beginning of the program Donahue disclosed that Cindy had come between Christine and her one-time sweetheart. Christine complained that the former juror, and other women, were visiting Ramirez at the prison, and said he told several of them that he was in love with them. That was all part of a lowlife scheme to sweet-talk older women out of their money, the talk show guest—who was in her mid-twenties—explained.

Christine said Ramirez telephoned her at home as she was preparing to leave for the show and cursed her for ruining his business and costing him money. She claimed he was after Cindy's money when he told her that he was in love with her. The former juror denied he ever asked her for money, and said she never gave him any. The nasty bickering continued throughout the show.

Christine was furious at Cindy for describing her during another television program as "delusional." When Cindy agreed that she had used the term, Christine angrily accused her of being "the one that's delusional." The fireworks exploded again when Donahue referred to Cindy as a "young woman."

"Young?" Christine snickered in feigned disbelief. Ramirez referred to Cindy behind her back as "Grandma," the leggy blonde confided to the talk show host and his audience.

The struggle for the Night Stalker's affections was deadly serious business on the part of the death row groupies attracted by his brooding menace and dark celebrity. Love letters to the imprisoned killer were filled with proposals for marriage, promises of lovemaking and of having his babies.

Ramirez responded with romantic letters of his own. Among his other perversions, he was a foot fetishist, and wrote about his desire to lick and suck the toes of some of his prettier correspondents, begged for money and at times included crude drawings of bare feet, hearts, huge smacking lips or of knives dripping with blood.

But most of his frenzied female admirers dropped out of the competition for his attentions or transferred their affections to other more current killers after the condemned man ended the bizarre love lottery by selecting a forty-one-year-old freelance magazine editor to be his bride.

A native of Burbank who moved to the Bay Area city of San Rafael a few minutes' drive from the prison, Doreen

Lioy was smitten with the serial killer in 1985. A picture taken after his arrest showed him wearing a bandage, and she felt sorry for him. Since falling in love with the sinister executioner, she has been quoted in the media as saying she believed he was an innocent man. For Doreen Lioy to be right about that, a virtual army of police, prosecutors, jurors and innocent survivors of the Night Stalker's rampage had to be dead wrong.

Doreen was never previously married and claimed to be a virgin. Her professed virginity was reportedly part of her appeal to the Satanist, who was known for kidnapping and raping little girls. But there would be no opportunity for the beaming bride and groom to alter her status as a virgin because, although California permits conjugal visits for many inmates, the privilege isn't extended to occupants of death row. The union would produce no little Night Stalkers!

At San Quentin, weddings were performed on the first Thursday of the month, and on October 3, 1996, Richard Ramirez and Doreen Lioy were united in marriage in the main visiting room at the prison by a corrections employee functioning as a justice of the peace. The ceremony began at 11:10 a.m., and was concluded six minutes later.

The visiting room was crowded with about sixty prisoners and visitors. Nine other inmates, including seven from the prison's general population, were also married that day. The Ramirez ceremony was the first of three for death row inmates, and it drew most of the attention. Even in a prison visiting room filled with some of the Golden State's most vile killers and other vicious criminals, and their families or friends, the crimes of Richard Ramirez were so frightening and grossly depraved that he stood out from all the rest. For a time, he was an American Jack the Ripper, casting an evil mantle of fear over one of the world's greatest cities.

Visitors chatting with other prisoners cast furtive glances across the room at the bony Satanist, carefully avoiding his eyes. Although he was surrounded by vigilant guards, the Night Stalker still had the ability to instill fear by nothing more than his chilling presence. He was the monster under the bed, the living nightmare of every child and of every adult.

Wearing a white wedding dress with chiffon sleeves that extended just below her knees, the beaming bride appeared at the gates of the fortress-like prison at about 7:50 a.m. She was accompanied by the groom's sister Ruth, brother Joseph, the brother's seventeen-year-old daughter and two lawyers. None of the bride's family was present, not even her twin sister.

Doreen's married sister, Denise, was a member of the Burbank school board, and told a reporter that her twin's behavior had caused them to sever their ties. The sister described the marriage as "a family tragedy." Ramirez was not a person who could be accepted as part of their family, she said. The estrangement began when family members learned that Doreen was using assumed names to write letters to newspapers supporting the Night Stalker during his trial, the sister said. Efforts by family members to stop the letter writing failed.

When Doreen wasn't writing to newspapers, she was often busy writing to Ramirez. According to the *San Francisco Chronicle*, she directed an avalanche of seventy-five letters to him shortly after his arrest. When she was finally allowed to visit him for the first time, they had to talk through phones while separated by a heavy glass partition.

Despite the awkward conditions and difficulties courting Ramirez, the future bride was already competing with the other frenzied groupies for visiting time; first at the Men's Central Jail in Los Angeles, then at the city lockup in San Francisco where he was held briefly to await trial for the slaying of Peter Pan and the shooting of the accountant's wife. When the nasty cat-fighting and feverish squabbling among Ramirez's romance-hungry groupies began seriously interfering with normal jail operations in San Francisco, he was transferred to San Quentin. Doreen later claimed that Ramirez proposed on their third visit, and she immediately accepted.

On the wedding day the thirty-six-year-old groom wore a pair of freshly starched prison blues. The ominous dark shades he wore at his trial had long ago been replaced by round prescription glasses. Although he was carefully searched before being led inside, he was not handcuffed or fitted with any other restraints during the ceremony. Before the nuptials got underway, the Night Stalker solicitously advised his niece to pull her skirt down to cover her knees. Joseph's pretty teenage daughter was attracting too many hungry looks from sex-starved inmates.

In place of a wedding cake, a row of vending machines along one wall was available for snacks. Joseph stood up as best man for his brother. There was no maid or matron of honor. The groom appeared nervous as he placed a gold ring on the finger of his bride, and she gave him a wedding band described in some reports as platinum and in others as silver. It definitely wasn't gold. Satanists, Ramirez had explained to his bride, did not wear gold.

Consistent with prison regulations, the couple was permitted to exchange three kisses: once before the ceremony, once during the ceremony, and once after its conclusion. A few minutes later, the bride and the rest of the wedding party, except for the curly-haired groom, left the prison. He was shackled and led back to his cell on death row.

Incredibly, another of the Golden State's most notorious killers not only was allowed conjugal visits after marrying a prison groupie, but fathered four children and set up a money-making ministry even though he was once condemned to death.

Charles Denton "Tex" Watson was hippie cult leader Charles Manson's personal hitman and launched the murderous assault on pregnant actress Sharon Tate's mansion that led to her death, and those of four other people in 1969. A wealthy supermarket owner and his wife were also slaughtered by Watson and a hippie murder squad two days later.

The Texas native was awaiting execution in 1972 when a

disastrous 5-4 U.S. Supreme Court decision in a case known as Furman *vs.* Georgia invalidated capital punishment laws, and freed thousands of America's most savage killers from death rows around the country. Watson and his gnomish leader, Manson, were two of the killers freed from death row at San Quentin by the ruling, and their sentences were automatically commuted to life behind bars.

Watson was moved to the California Men's Colony at San Luis Obispo, where he was wooed by a bevy of young female admirers, including a stunning German girl who moved to the Golden State to be nearer to the object of her desire before losing interest when he professed to have become a born-again Christian.

Kristin Joan Svege quickly took her place and began mending the killer cultist's broken heart. After a wedding in the prison chapel, the couple took advantage of forty-eight-hour conjugal visits, permitted every two months for well-behaved prisoners. Watson was no longer on death row, and he was well-behaved.

Watson and the Night Stalker were far from the first ruthless killers to attract breathless prison groupies lured by their malevolent celebrity. Wild West gunslinger Buckskin Frank Leslie was doing time for shooting his wife to death when Belle Stowell began writing to him. Leslie was notorious for abusing the women in his life and one of his former wives was known as "the Silhouette Girl" because he made her stand in front of a wall while he traced her outline with pistol shots as a prelude to love making. Buckskin Frank and Belle married after his pardon in 1896, but once he was free, his old bad habits returned and they soon were divorced. The divorce may have saved Belle's life.

Other groupies have died violently after their jailbird boyfriends and husbands were released from custody and freed from the enforced discipline of prisons. But barring another Supreme Court decision like the 1972 debacle, the Night Stalker's bride shouldn't have to worry about being sodomized, mutilated and murdered by her sweet-talking husband the way his victims were. It seems highly unlikely that even the most optimistic card reader would predict a pardon or parole in his future.

Early in 2004 Ramirez was still locked behind bars at San Quentin, awaiting eventual conclusion of the long, drawn-out appeals slowly meandering through the higher courts. He was one of more than 620 men on death row waiting execution. Fourteen women in California were locked up on their own death row.

Since California resumed executions in 1978, ten inmates had been led into the gas chamber or strapped onto a gurney to die by lethal injection. But the process of actually getting California's nastiest killers into the death chamber for their date with the Grim Reaper is frustrating and time-consuming.

As anticipated, Robert Alton Harris was the first to die after California restored capital punishment. Advocates for the remorseless killer fought up to the last minute to keep him alive. Before the cheesecloth-wrapped pellets of sodium cyanide were at last dropped into a vat of sulphuric acid a few minutes after 6 a.m., on April 21, 1992, four stays of execution were granted by federal judges. All were overturned within nine hours. The U.S. Supreme Court finally stepped in and brought the macabre game to an end. As part of its order vacating the fourth stay, the court declared, "No further stays of Robert Alton Harris's execution shall be entered by the federal courts except upon order of this court."

Harris's execution in the green octagonal gas chamber marked the first time capital punishment had been exercised in California in twenty-five years. He spent thirteen years and one month on death row before justice was finally meted out. Compared to the other nine men who have been executed since his death, he was one of the short-timers.

When armed robber Robert Lee Massie was finally executed on March 27, 2001, he had spent twenty-one years and ten months on death row. And that was just for his most recent killing. He was awaiting execution for the 1965 robbery slaying of a San Gabriel housewife when he was freed from death row by the 1972 Supreme Court decision. Then he was released from prison and claimed a new victim in another armed robbery. Darrel Keith Rich, executed just before Massie, waited on death row for nineteen years. Stephen Wayne Anderson, who was executed a few months after Massie, spent more than twenty years awaiting his appointment with death.

By early 2004, Ramirez had already outlived the hard-nosed prosecutor who won guilty verdicts on all forty-three charges of murder, burglary, rape, robbery, sodomy and other offenses against him in the Los Angeles trial. Phil Halpin, who retired in 2001 after thirty-six years as a deputy DA, died of cancer in Bend, Oregon on July 25, 2003—his sixty-fifth birthday. When the dedicated career prosecutor died, Ramirez, like hundreds of other condemned men and women, didn't even have a date set for his execution. And he still hadn't been put on trial in the Peter Pan case. In 1995 the trial was postponed indefinitely, pending the resolution of appeals on the Los Angeles convictions.

In the meantime, Ramirez, like his fellow condemned at San Quentin, spend their days holed up in one-man cells in three two-story buildings in the most secure area of California's oldest, and one of its most decrepit, state prisons. The prison opened in July 1852 at Point Quentin in Marin County, and early in 2004 still lacked many of the high-tech security features of more modern lockups.

Despite the presence of bloodthirsty Satanists, mutilation murderers, serial slayers, hit men and cop killers, and frequent showers of urine, feces or makeshift darts tossed at them, wary guards deliver meals, collect dirty laundry and escort the dangerous inmates to showers and to the exercise area. Every day Ramirez and his neighbors are fed two hot meals and a sack lunch in their forty-square-foot cells, and are regularly escorted to showers in a room fashioned from a couple of converted cells.

The best behaved of the condemned prisoners, about a

hundred men, live in the oldest wing, constructed in 1934 specifically for death row inmates. It is known as North Segregation, and guards can carry out their functions with minimum contact with the prisoners. Most death row inmates today are waiting out their appeals on East Block, a shabbier five-tier unit built in 1927 for general population prisoners and later remodeled to accommodate the rapidly expanding number of men on death row.

If the Night Stalker had enjoyed even an outside chance of qualifying for North Segregation, he blew it when guards conducted a body cavity search as he was being processed into the prison after his transfer from the San Francisco lockup. Officers reportedly discovered a metal canister containing a key, a needle and a syringe hidden in his rectum. The rectum is a favorite hiding place used by convicts to conceal potential escape equipment and other contraband.

Ramirez not only wound up on the less desirable East Block, but he was assigned to the Adjustment Center—which was reserved for the baddest of the bad. He was an escape risk, a known troublemaker and exactly the kind of dangerously violent inmate the Adjustment Center was set aside for. Guards there wear full riot gear, including bulletproof vests and helmets, and carry shields and pepper spray. On one side of the unit, solid doors have replaced the bars and metal screens that made it possible for inmates to splatter guards with body waste as part of a ritual insiders refer to as "gassings." On the other side of the cells, guards are shielded by a floor-to-ceiling Plexiglas shield. The solid doors and the Plexiglas help, but some of the most persistently nasty inmates still manage to get at the guards when they are delivering meals or carrying out other duties that require close contact. The threat of exposure to AIDS or hepatitis C are serious concerns.

Most Adjustment Center inmates exercise alone in one of thirty-four wire cages referred to as "walk-alone yards," doing push-ups and sit-ups, shooting baskets, tossing a ball, or merely walking around. Despite the security efforts and precautions, a few years after Ramirez's arrival at the Adjustment Center, four of his fellow inmates managed to pry loose a rusty link of chain fencing and break through, threatening corrections officers. A guard ended the menacing shenanigans by shooting one of the troublemakers. Armed guards patrol the exercise yard from an elevated platform.

Ramirez and his ominous companions are expected to stay right where they're at until the time finally comes when they are led into the death chamber through a door in the North Segregation area and at last pay the ultimate penalty for their crimes.

If the Night Stalker's appeals are exhausted during the term of current California Governor Arnold Schwarzenegger, it appears highly unlikely that he can expect any last-minute reprieves from the movie star-turned-politician. Schwarzenegger demonstrated his firm commitment to protecting the public and maintaining social order early in 2004 when he refused entreaties for mercy from Hollywood activists and other anti-death-penalty forces by turning down the clemency bid of mass killer Kevin Cooper. A savage rapist and lifetime criminal, Cooper hacked two children and two adults to death with a hatchet and slashed the throat of an eight-year-old, more than twenty years earlier. The Ninth U.S. Circuit Court of Appeals was more pliable than the governor. Cooper was temporarily spared when the court ordered a last-minute stay after failure of the clemency bid.

California now allows the condemned a choice of execution methods: the gas chamber, or lethal injection. So the monster who bludgeoned, stomped, stabbed, slashed, strangled and shot his screaming victims to death can choose the method of dying that he considers the least frightening or potentially painful. There will be no one carving bloody pentagrams into his chest, digging out his eyes with a knife or sodomizing him—only lethal chemicals coursing through his gaunt frame while feather-headed apologists and naïve admirers demonstrate outside the prison gates with pleas to spare his life.

Ramirez's wife has vowed to take her own life when that long-overdue day of reckoning finally arrives, according to a newspaper report. If Doreen Lioy Ramirez does indeed make good on her vow, her death will mark up one more victim for the Night Stalker.